CROWDED CANVAS

CROWDED CANVAS

some experiences of a life-time

by

Max Warren

Honorary Fellow

of

Jesus College, Cambridge

HODDER AND STOUGHTON

LONDON SYDNEY AUCKLAND TORONTO

To

MARY

who

while doubling for

MARTHA

is still always

MARY

Preface

MY AMBITION FOR THE EARLY MONTHS OF RETIREMENT HAD BEEN TO BEGIN
the writing of a book about the decline and fall of the British colonial
empire, viewed from the standpoint of the Christian missionary movement, which had been one of that empire's principal beneficiaries and
also one of its chief victims. This book still needs to be written.

But, with gentle persuasiveness, Mr. Edward England, for the pub-
lishers, prevailed on me to attempt some more personal reflections over
a different field. This I have tried to do, though what I have written is
not strictly an autobiography. There are far too many gaps in what is
hardly even a narrative but rather a selection out of a variety of
experiences. 'I am a part of all that I have met', and, indeed, my main
embarrassment over my selection is that so many that I have met and
who have profoundly influenced me find no mention in these pages.
I hope, however, that it will be realised that they are here none the less.

A bare minimum of acknowledgements must be gratefully recorded.
In the summer of 1972 some C.M.S. friends arranged for me to have
my portrait painted. A fine photograph of this by my friend, Mr. Alfred
Hepworth, one of the Abbey lay vicars, forms the cover of the book.
The ordeal of sitting for a portrait proved in this case a pleasure, thanks
to the charm and skill of the artist, Brenda Bury. Easy to look at,
gracious to command, entertaining to listen to, she made the sessions a
delight.

I owe a debt of peculiar gratitude to Susan Harverson, once my
private secretary at C.M.S., who undertook the typing of an often
barely legible manuscript. Bernard and Doris Nicholls, Greta Preston,
Ena Price, and Douglas Webster, were invaluable critics. The dedication
is a salute to the patience of a life-time, and in particular to what was
involved in abiding three months of uncommunicative broodiness while
I was conjuring up the past.

'Waymarks'
East Dean
near Eastbourne   MAX WARREN

December 1973

Contents

Illustrations

[1] By permission of the Church Missionary Society
[2] *The Times*

Surely there are in every man's life
certain rubs, doublings and wrenches
which pass awhile under the effects
of chance, but at the last, well
examined, prove the mere hand of God.

SIR THOMAS BROWNE

Religio Medici

I

1904 - 1912

Childhood in India

Neither Youth nor Childhood is Folly or Incapacity.
Some Children are fools and so are some Old Men.
But There is a vast Majority on the side of
Imagination or Spiritual sensation.

WILLIAM BLAKE

in a letter

MY earliest memory is of dancing fire-light, and of my mother reading to me. I am looking into the flames and listening. I must have been three or four years old.

It can be cold on winter evenings in the plains of Northern India, so we had a fire. Fire-light is one of the oldest ministers of magic. Looking into a fire is a spell for the imagination. And listening introduced me to the magic of words. Long before I could read I was learning to listen, perhaps the most valuable lesson I ever learnt. Those two earliest memories set the pattern for much that was to follow.

But, as I hold it true with him who said that 'a child cannot be too careful in choosing his grandfather', I must dip a little further into the past. For I was singularly fortunate in the choice of both my grandfathers.

On my mother's side he was a naval officer, James Wylie East, who retired with the rank of rear-admiral. His father had been Rector of St. Michael's, Bath, for many years, a legendary figure in the family, and as an evangelist something of a fire-eater. James East's mother, Ann, was a daughter of the Rev. William Day, Vicar of St. Philip and St. Jacob, Bristol, who went up to St. Edmund's Hall, Oxford, soon after the end of the American War of Independence. Some few years earlier a number of undergraduates of that College had been 'sent down' for being enthusiastic Evangelicals. Things were easier by his time, but he was of the same persuasion. That piece of heredity has remained unbroken for two centuries.

Grandfather East will appear in unexpected fashion very much later in this record, but at this point I like to remember that in 1869 he led a British treaty-making naval expedition up the Niger river. With him, as a passenger, he had Dr. Samuel Adjai Crowther, the first African Bishop of the Anglican Church. In his diary of that trip grandfather mentions quite casually that he had installed the Bishop in his own cabin. It never occurred to him that any lesser courtesy was called for. This grandson was to be much involved in the race issue a hundred years later, so the choice of a grandfather who was 'colour-blind' was important.

Grandfather Warren was a bank manager at a time when banking in Ireland was still an activity carried on in the main by a large number of small banks with very limited resources. Bank failures were frequent, and grandfather's bank failed in some measure with a lot of others in some financial scare. I remember well my mother telling me of the tightly-restricted economic circumstances of my father's youth, because grandfather felt under a moral obligation to repay as many as possible of his bank's creditors. That, at least, is the family tradition. I am disposed to believe it because punctiliousness over money matters has been family practice. Certainly stringency in that home continued for many years. Father was only able to go to Trinity College, Dublin, as a 'sizar', that is a student who, in those days, was expected to some extent to 'work his passage'. Money was always tight and luxuries were unknown.

I am proud to think of that grandfather who for so many years took the burdens of others on his own shoulders. He had, so I have been told, a glorious sense of humour. My father certainly inherited this as well as the disciplined sense of duty. Plain living can sometimes provide a useful elevation from which to explore high thinking, and high merriment.

Yes, I am well satisfied that I chose my grandfathers with such care. And my grandmothers matched the qualities of their mates.

Where I was careless in a way which I have regretted all my life was in failing completely to acquire my grandfathers' respective skills. Both, for instance, had a good head for figures. Two of my uncles were outstandingly able as mathematicians. Grandfather East was an artist of exquisite touch, as his naval sketchbooks and logs bear testimony. All my mother's family were musical. But painting, sketching, music and mathematics completely passed me by. In addition grandfather Warren had enormous skill with his fingers, rejoicing the young with the things he could make. My two hands consist exclusively of thumbs!

No, I was inexcusably careless about my heritage. My fortune lay in the fact that on both sides of the family I drew on a rich stock of 'Irishness' which is always a reliable source for the unaccountable! From it I derived some capacity to dream dreams and see visions. Imagination can be a painful gift but the pain is worth it.

What, then, was I doing in India looking into the dancing flames and listening to my mother reading?

My father, after graduating, served a curacy in Dublin and then offered to the Church Missionary Society. He went out to India in 1892, to Jubulpore. My mother followed a year later and they were married in Bombay. Two brothers, Lionel and Jack, and a sister Theo, preceded my belated arrival in August 1904. Born, as my passport records, in Dun Laoghaire, Eire (so much more interesting and confusing than Kingstown Co. Dublin!), I was taken out to India when I was three months old and was there until 1912.

We went first to Benares (now Varanasi), thus anticipating by sixty-seven years the arrival of a third and fourth generation of residents in the persons of our daughter Pat, her husband Roger, and their children Richard and Mary. But this will be properly recorded at a later stage. Early in 1906 we moved to Sikandra, near Agra. But I must make mention of the courage of my mother in taking her new baby straight

to Benares where, only sixteen months before, her little daughter of
five years old had died of bubonic plague. In those days there was no
inoculation against that perilous disease. Courage was typical of my
mother. She was born in the Service tradition and her sense of duty
never failed. My two brothers remained at home in Ireland, nine and
eight years respectively older than myself.

What did India mean to me? There is first a confused kaleidoscope of
memories. I can see myself sleeping out under the stars in the hot
weather. I remember well being rolled up in the bedding and rushed
indoors when some storm of dust or rain threatened. And there was the
thrill of night journeys by railway, the long climb up into the hills by
'dandi', and a dim memory of precipitous hillsides and far-stretching
distances. Back in Meerut my most vivid memories are of the bugles
sounding from the lines of an Indian Regiment not far from our
bungalow, and the wonderful thrill of the King's Birthday Parade, for
Meerut was one of the main garrison towns in India. Tin soldiers were,
inevitably, my favourite toys.

It was, I suppose, a lonely childhood, though I was never conscious
of loneliness. However, being forced to be somewhat self-contained I
developed a shyness which has, in curious ways, inhibited me ever since.
Yet, at the same time, it stimulated my imagination, almost too much
so, for I lived largely with my own thoughts. I remember I told myself
stories which, as reading increased, drew on the world of other men's
imaginings. Here I am sure was born that insatiable taste for reading,
and with it the ability to read very quickly which has been so great an
asset ever since. What is more, reading has always been for me a form
of listening. Books have always been 'persons' to me, not just the person
of the author so much as the book itself talking, while I listened. Even
biographies have meant for me attention to three people not one, to the
author, to the subject, and to the much more expansive conversation of
the book itself. Good writing has an independent life of its own. And
always there is the magic of words, sometimes almost intoxicating in
the visions they evoke and the explorations to which they beckon.

India meant all this to me, but much more besides. The scene of a
secure and happy childhood, it never felt strange and alien. Like other
children similarly situated I became bi-lingual. One result of this feeling
that I was at home in India has meant that in all the travelling which the
future held, in all the meeting with strangers of many races in many
lands, I have never felt myself to be alien. Everywhere I felt at home.
I owe this facility above all to my brown playmates who shared my
Indian childhood, and to those devoted Indian members of our household who were, in such a deep sense, the utterly reliable friends upon
whose goodness and patience I made such continuous demands. Like my

naval grandfather I grew up 'colour-blind'. It was no curiosity of memory when fifty years later I visited India again that I felt I was coming home. Nor was it strange that one of the first to greet me in Meerut was one of those childhood friends. It was his father, my especial guardian, who travelled with us for the first part of our journey to Bombay in 1912. When at some station he got up to leave us he took my two hands in his and asked me to be sure to come back to India. I promised I would. I took a very long time to redeem that promise but I kept it in the end in more ways than one.

At the end of 1911 my father was appointed acting Mission Secretary for the United Provinces Mission of C.M.S. and we moved from Meerut to Allahabad. I can still remember that railway journey and how, as we passed through Delhi, I had pointed out to me some of the stands and pavilions which shortly would be the scene of the Delhi Durbar. There India would salute the King Emperor and his Empress, the last proud assertion in pomp and circumstance of an age that was about to end. When I was next in Delhi India had become an independent nation. If Edwardian England enjoyed, beneath its surface turbulence, a deep inner security, as nationwise it did, so Edwardian India was a golden sunset for those too young or, being older, too stupid, to read the storm signals for what they were.

One other vivid picture is of the journey to England. Etched unforgettably on my mind is of being taken up on deck early one morning to look away to starboard to where the volcanic island, Stromboli, was a-smoke. I can still see the surge of the sea and the dark grey-green of the water not yet lit by the sun. It has still the sharp lines of a photograph. I can feel the rush of the sea and the chill of the wind. Why this particular memory is still so fresh I have never been able to understand.

10/15/77

I am going to like this!

2

1913 - 1923

Schooldays

Rarely can one say with precision which spark lighted
the train or where and when it fell. One remembers the
man—that he gave out heat and light; one remembers
a sense of communication with him and through him;
one remembers above all having been emancipated by
him from the terrible anonymity of a boy lost in a
crowd.

CHARLES MORGAN

in Liberties of the Mind

M Y father followed us back from India in the spring of 1913. Of that year much my most vivid recollection is of the Leicestershire village of Galby where my father did a *locum tenens* in return for the use of the rectory. There was a good tennis court and my memory recalls endless summer afternoons of tennis parties to which school friends of my brothers came over. I was the ballboy on these occasions and enjoyed myself hugely. It was a halcyon summer.

Of those five schoolboys four were killed in action within the next three years, my eldest brother Lionel among them. The fifth, my brother Jack, was fortunate in proving himself a skilled trench mortar officer, and was picked on to lead training courses in England. Then, when the U.S.A. joined the Allies, he was sent over to train members of their first expeditionary force. Jack missed the worst of the fighting in 1916, 1917 and early 1918 but was back in action in time to get gassed, wounded and win the M.C. The gassing almost certainly made him the more susceptible to T.B. and led to his early death after five years as a missionary in Uganda.

I have mentioned that summer holiday of 1913 and those tennis parties because for me they speak poignantly of the lost generation, whose absence explains why those who, like myself, were half a generation younger, later found ourselves called to positions of great responsibility long before our time.

In September 1913 I started my English schooling at Heddon Court, a preparatory school at Cockfosters, long since defunct. So far my mother had been my tutor. During the years in India she had followed the syllabus and guidance provided by the Parents' National Education Union to such good effect that, on being tested, I was found to be, in some subjects at least, up to the level of my contemporaries. This was certainly due to my mother and the method used and not to me. I was still a very shy and diffident small boy wholly lacking in self-confidence. But somehow mother had taught me how to learn, which, after all, is far more important than being overloaded with knowledge. Nearly sixty years later when our daughter in India was following the same method with her Richard and Mary we discovered that the office of the P.N.E.U. was just off Victoria Street. We had the pleasure of meeting the ladies running it; and there, sure enough, on the files were my own reports for 1912 and 1913. There was one little spark of hope. For 1912 the records state 'History very good'! But 1913 was more ominous. Against the subject 'Handwriting' the note is 'fair'. Miss Molyneux, the Principal in 1972, explained that that really meant 'very bad'. How right that verdict was, and how vast the company who since then have had cause to echo it!

As a preparatory school Heddon Court was much like any other, with a staff of very mixed quality. The liveliest, Duncan O'Callaghan, fired me with enthusiasm for Geography, for me a new subject. Then the war came. He joined up at once and was killed at Neuve Chapelle. He lit something in my small mind and I look back to him with gratitude.

In some strange way I feel those deaths far more today, sixty years later, than I did at the time. I suppose I know now what the world lost in that blood-letting. As a small boy I couldn't understand. The war was an exciting background. I remember so well being on the pier at Eastbourne one day in that summer of 1914. The Fleet had been mobilised and I had the enormous thrill of seeing, through the telescope at the end of the pier, the great line of battleships, cruisers and destroyers of the Channel Fleet on their way to what we knew later was Scapa Flow. I hardly needed that experience to whet my appetite to learn the details of every ship in the British and Allied Navies and of the enemy. I think that at the time I could have passed an examination in the tonnage, armament, and complement of every ship in the British Navy. A small boy's memory for something that really excites him is formidable!

I also remember seeing the glow in the sky when the Cuffley Zeppelin was shot down to crash only a few miles from the school.

The favourite game at school was '*L'Attaque*'.

Such was the level at which the war touched small boys who were safely sheltered from its horrors. How vastly different it was to be in the Second World War, or must have been in 1914 for the small boys of Belgium and Northern France.

However, even I was dimly aware of the element of tragedy in seeing my mother's grief when her brother was killed soon after her eldest son. And of her I must speak again.

She had suffered a good deal in India from a low fever, and increasingly from severe migraines which became more marked in the war years. We were living in Hampstead at the time and far and away the most vivid memories of war-time holidays was the almost clockwork regularity with which every few weeks mother was prostrated with these agonising headaches, had to lie in complete darkness, unable to take food, and experiencing terrible nausea. One lesson I learnt from her suffering was to move quietly, to shut doors quietly, indeed to be quiet. In the sequel we obviously could not invite other noisy companions to the house, so I learnt more than ever to live with my own thoughts and in my own imaginings, reinforcing the experience of earlier years in India.

Normally my father would have returned to India in 1914. But with the coming of the war and my mother's increasing ill-health he resigned from overseas service. The C.M.S. appointed him as Assistant Home Secretary with a special responsibility for visiting schools. I still have his notebook in which he put down every deputation visit he paid and every school he visited. For his own amusement he recorded the mileage he travelled. In six years he covered over sixty thousand miles, thirty-five thousand of them under war-time conditions. It is an impressive achievement. He must have been a good speaker to schoolboys. When later I was an undergraduate at Cambridge I was several times asked if a certain visiting preacher was any relation. Each time it was to say how deeply he had impressed the school. This would be at least four years later. Being myself quite unable to remember any sermon I ever heard at school I judge that father must have been a preacher well above the average. Schoolboys attending compulsory chapel must be about the most critical audience in the world.

I mention my father's time in England because it meant that from the ages of nine to sixteen I was frequently in my father's company. They were, for him, years of acute anxiety for my mother's health, and all a father's wonderings about his sons on active service, and all these while carrying on a tremendous programme of travelling and preaching. What profoundly impressed me was that nothing ever rattled him. Full of humour, he was always gentle and wonderfully thoughtful. His caring for my mother and his insistence on my sharing in that concern was a spiritual education in itself. It could have been a grim experience for a schoolboy. Yet my memory is always of his gay spirit and his tremendous sense of fun, and, with this, a quiet self-discipline upon which I look back with wonder. He belonged to a generation which could combine gaiety and humour with a steel-like capacity for self-sacrifice and the splendour of never thinking of himself at all, let alone that he was making sacrifices. One illustration may serve. He had a strong puritan streak which, among other things, took the form of refusing ever to use public transport on a Sunday. When he had to preach somewhere in London he would always walk to the church and walk back. Sometimes the church would be in South London and it might be a ten-mile walk each way. I never knew him to break his rule or to think it in any way remarkable to have kept it.

Small boys easily become hero-worshippers. I will always be grateful that for me the hero was my own father, and that he never had a competitor. I imagine that unconsciously, during those years, I patterned myself upon him, finding in him an ideal and, with it, the germ of a hope that I might become something like him when I grew up. That was not to be, but my father's example and my memories of India were always there. And they must have contributed decisively to my later decision for missionary service and ordination. But no kind of pressure was ever put on me to shape my future. My boyhood was no forcing house. Yet I was over-serious for my years. I suspect that I only very narrowly escaped, if I did, from being a prig.

At my preparatory school I only made one friend, a curious friendship, the bond between us being two-fold. I had an in-built facility for spinning tales and he appeared to have an in-built capacity for listening to them. The tales developed into a serial which went on term after term when we two always paired for those interminable 'crocodile' walks which in retrospect, though not in fact, occurred daily. Our other bond was the fact that we were both always in trouble, though it appears to have been mostly for carelessness in work. Anyway it was a neck-and-neck race between us throughout our time at that school as to which of us was the most frequently invited into the headmaster's study, made to bend over and be given six of the best with a fives-bat. It was a curious form of punishment, in my case, for errors in Latin prose. But the good man who wielded the fives-bat had a very sick wife and was burdened with all the war-time responsibilities of sixty boys, and how many other anxieties and sorrows we could not know. I rather think he felt that carelessness in work was especially wicked in war-time. Further to this, in my case, was the fact that I had been given a very generous scholarship solely on the ground that I was the son of a missionary. Wickedness, which in another might have been held venial, assumed criminal proportions in one with such a background!

The only distress I suffered from this flagellation, which was so stupid as to be incapable of creating psychological disturbance, was that it seemed to cause wholly disproportionate sorrow to my parents, who viewed my record of punishments with some alarm.

But this is to look only at the more negative aspect of this part of my schooling. I owe two great debts of gratitude to Heddon Court. The school had a very good library and we were made free of it, being expected to read as much and as widely as we liked. Then, for good measure, we were taught to learn quantities of dates and poetry and whole chapters of the Bible by heart. I do entirely endorse the wise words of G. M. Trevelyan who, in his 'Autobiography of an Historian', has recorded

I was made to learn dates and poetry by heart, as all children ought to be while their memory is still good and retentive, instead of being stuffed with generalizations about history and criticisms of literature which mean nothing to their empty young minds.*

*G. M. Trevelyan, *An Autobiography and Other Essays*, (Longmans 1949) p. 7.

So those early school years passed, and passed uneventfully. The headmaster was a good man and the sting caused by the fives-bats was after all transient. He gave me a very generous scholarship when I passed the common entrance into Marlborough to which I went in 1918.

Among my active dislikes, and I have a few mostly of a gastronomic kind, is a dislike bordering on contempt for the ex-public school boy who affects to despise his school, and deploys his ingenuity in sneering at it in prose or verse, well aware that the school can make no riposte. I am the last person to romanticise schooldays. I might have entitled this chapter 'The Open Prison'. Of course, in comparison to the freedom of the University that followed, school was a prison. Conformity was a way of life, to rebel against which was a waste of nervous energy. But Marlborough was an 'open' prison. Within the conformity there was ample scope to pursue the adventures of the mind, which, after all, is the primary object of a school. It is at least possible that between the ages of fourteen and eighteen the alternative to conformity would be anarchy, which offers a precarious form of freedom.

I owe to Marlborough a varied debt to which I would pay my tribute. In those days the school was a spartan one—cold baths every morning, however bitterly cold the weather, early school before breakfast in freezing classrooms, long 'sweats' across the Marlborough Downs with the wind whistling through one like a knife, not too much food and what there was unattractive. Things are very different now. But in those days between lunch one day and breakfast the next there was some bread and scrape and a cup of cocoa, nothing more. You kept alive by cooking gargantuan and indigestible meals on the communal gas-rings. And then there were, of course, compulsory games. These did no harm even if you did not become very proficient. You learnt the meaning of team work, and that does no harm in later life.

After a first year in a junior house I went up to my senior house, B3, with a gentle courteous man as house-master. I gathered the impression that we were considered a rather slack house. But after a year a new house-master was appointed, an ex-Guards officer who later became the headmaster of another public school. Almost at once the tone of the house changed. Over the next three years we became 'cock house' in rugger, cricket and hockey. I found a place in each of these teams and, with the head of house, was in the Fives pair which, and if memory serves, also won the inter-house championship. I remember that I played without gloves, finding I could get a far stronger strike on the ball with my bare hands. It stung somewhat but the sting was compensated for by greater accuracy. I had another facility and that was being able to kick equally well with either foot, an advantage which got me into the house rugger XV as full-back.

Physically small-boned, I lacked, and still lack, any natural physical courage. Perhaps for this reason I still hold in mind one creative moment when, playing in a house match, I made my first flying-tackle at a hulk of a fellow twice my size and brought him down, thereby saving a try. There was nothing remarkable about this. No one could guess what it meant to me at the time. I can see the place now and re-live that moment, for it assured me that with a little effort I might some day develop guts. There and then I acquired a measure of self-respect and self-confidence which had eluded me so far.

But my gratitude to Marlborough will always be deepest for the fact that I was privileged to enjoy such magnificent teaching. After the inescapable hurdle of the School Certificate, as it then was, one specialised. Everything pointed to my going on to the 'history' side. My love of reading, an already developing historical sense nourished by my childhood in India, and an active imagination were the pointers. And here came my luckiest break of all.

For some reason which I cannot recollect I received an invitation to tea from the Master of the History sixth, Mr. J. R. H. O'Regan — 'Pat' as he was known to everyone at Marlborough. An Irishman, with a brogue you really could cut slices off, with a lovely wife as Irish as himself but very much younger, he captured my adolescent enthusiasm not by the initial invitation but by his urgent insistence that I come again. His adorable wife was unquestionably an additional persuasive. What capped it all was that his house had been built by himself on the pattern of a Roman villa. Here was ancient history become contemporary before my eyes.

I think that, with the penetrating intuition of a great teacher, he saw in that first meeting that here was a mind in a chrysalis stage which he could help to nurture, not necessarily to become a 'Red Admiral' or some gorgeous fritillary, but at least a passable 'Cabbage White'. So he set to work to educate my imagination, guiding my reading, lending me books, making his house a place to which I could come at any time to browse, giving me an adult's friendship just when I needed it most, my father having recently died. The following year I moved up to the History Sixth and had him directly as my form-master.

Pat O'Regan was that rare kind of teacher who could by his eagerness, his sheer enthusiasm for the subject, and his intellectual grasp, make the past come alive. You were 'there'. You weren't hearing about it. You weren't reading about it. You were there, part of the past itself. You were remembering where, in and through your ancestors, you had been. This was great magic. It was heady, intoxicating stuff. But it

was also down-to-earth. For Pat O'Regan the past was a clue to the
present, with signals pointing to the future. A medievalist himself, he
insisted on us understanding the forces making the world into which
we ourselves were to go to play our part. All his teaching endorsed the
challenge of the Marlburian poet, Charles Hamilton Sorley,

> We do not see the vital point
> That 'tis the eighth, most deadly, sin
> To wail, 'The world is out of joint' —
> And not attempt to put it in.*

To Pat O'Regan, with the exception of my father, I owe more than to
any other man I have ever known, though as this record will show that
is not lightly said.

Pat always used to run down at a jog-trot from his house to school.
One morning, at the end of my first year in the History Sixth, he was
running as usual when he collapsed and died instantly. It was a terrible
shock to us all. But if ever a man was fulfilled, through filling others
full of his own spirit, that man was Pat O'Regan. His beloved wife,
who has continued one of our dearest friends, knows well that to me,
as to how many others, he had given all he had, his best.

For me, thanks to Pat O'Regan, I was out of the chrysalis stage and
was about to try my wings. I wish he could have known the fullness of
his reward in this pupil he had taken such pains to train. Academically
speaking anything I later achieved must be credited to Pat O'Regan's
account. But there are more enduring things than can be achieved in
examination halls. Pat gave his friendship, the self-giving kind. To have
known that was to become every man's debtor in the days ahead.

For the last two years at school I shared a study, each year curiously
enough, with a boy studying science and preparing to read medicine. For
some reason the first steps in dissection always involved experimenting
with dog-fish, and the study smelt revolting until my companions were
promoted to frogs or other less odoriferous creatures. I am sure I owe
a debt to those two very good companions, G. Nesbitt Wood and C. H.
Forsyth. Deeply committed as I was to the world Pat O'Regan had
opened up for me, it was all the more important to recognise this other
world of science to which I was never to hold a key. But at least I was
aware of its existence and could respect those who understood its
mysteries.

In 1921 I made an unsuccessful attempt at a scholarship at St. John's
College, Cambridge, where my eldest brother had enjoyed his Fresh-

*Charles Hamilton Sorley, *Marlborough and Other Poems*, (C.U.P. 1922), Poem XV—
'A Call to Action'.

man's year before the war. My failure was a blessing in diguise. It gave
me an extra year at school. On my next attempt in 1922 I got a sixty-
pound 'Rustat' scholarship at Jesus College, Cambridge. With that
behind me I had two full terms, nine whole months for uninhibited
reading in which I was able to cover a very great deal of the ground for
the first year's work at the University. This was to prove no small
advantage.

Through the effluxion of time and not through any demonstrable
capacity for leadership I had become a house prefect and now, in my
nineteenth year, a school prefect also. There were few duties involved,
and none calculated to make me a leader of men. When, in quite other
fields, leadership was thrust upon me it assumed a very different form
from that empire-ruling quality which, so it is commonly assumed,
public schools were exclusively designed to produce. Some of my
contemporaries qualified later on as 'blues ruling blacks'. I met some of
them and greatly admired both the rulers and even more the ruled!
But that was not to be my destiny. Fortunately Marlborough could
train for other kinds of leadership as well. Through the alchemy of Pat
O'Regan's friendship and that of another I must shortly mention I
learnt the first steps of another kind of leadership.

Meanwhile that last year at school was a very relaxed one, and in a
particular field stimulating. The Rev. C. B. Canning, later to be headmaster of Canford School, took a weekly class for boys who had their
university exams behind them, his subject being English literature.
Through him I discovered Meredith and Hardy. I will always be grateful for those weekly reflections of his on those two giants.

Imagination-wise I may have been slowly emerging from my
chrysalis, but as for religion I was still not awake. Confirmation meant
nothing to me for it was a routine operation so taken for granted as
being appropriate at the age of sixteen that only a boy with profound
spiritual convictions of an agnostic sort could have resisted the summons to conform. Chapel services, likewise, made no conscious impact
on my life. From childhood I had been taught to read a passage of the
Bible every day and to say my prayers. These I did with regularity but
lacking 'the warmth of desire'.

Spiritually speaking the most important influence on my last years at
school was a science master, the Rev. W. B. Smith, irreverently and
familiarly, but for no obvious reason, known as 'Honk'. He kept open
house on Sunday afternoons. I went frequently, for tea and cake were
provided. Quite often I was the only one present. He was, if my
memory serves me right, a quite definite High Churchman, and not
very much at home in the Broad Churchmanship which prevailed at
Marlborough. In a very natural way the subject of our talk would turn

to the Christian Faith. He would patiently answer my questions, always with meticulous courtesy respecting my very adolescent, self-confident, and dogmatic evangelicalism. He was a great gentleman. I think I must have learnt far more from him unconsciously than I was aware of at the time. Something must surely rub off when a man old enough to be one's father takes one's spiritual fumblings seriously, never exploits one's ignorance, never forces his own opinions, but always treats one with respect, however little deserving of it one might be. What is more, he never tried to give easy answers to difficult questions, and so I began to learn that in the life of the spirit there are no easy answers. I sometimes forgot this later on, but the basic lesson stuck. It was worth learning if one was ever to be a leader in helping others to discover truth.

3

1923 - 1927

Cambridge

I praise God for his space of Cambridge air.

CHARLES WILLIAMS

Collected Plays

THE quotation from Charles Williams is from words put by him into the mouth of Archbishop Cranmer in his play *Thomas Cranmer of Canterbury*. They appropriately head this chapter, for Cranmer also was of Jesus College, Cambridge. But first I must recount some of the experiences which made it possible for me to enjoy so greatly and profit so abundantly from four blissful years of 'Cambridge air'.

My father had died in 1920. Already I have mentioned how Pat O'Regan's friendship at Marlborough had begun at that crucial moment. Immediately after the war there was a grave shortage of missionaries. Father responded at once to a request from the C.M.S. to go out to the Central Provinces (now the Madhya Pradesh) to Jubulpore, the place where he had first started his missionary service in 1892. Exhausted as he was by six years of incessant travelling to schools all over England, he was far from physically strong enough to undertake fresh work at the age of fifty-three. When illness struck within six months of his return he was too weak to rally and he died on 13th September.

His death crystallised for me the impact of his life which I have described. I never had the least doubt from then on that somehow or other I was going to be a missionary. However, I did not spend time dreaming about the future. I had an immediate concern, my mother. Father's unfailing thoughtfulness and care for her had set a standard. I could not, of course, come up to it. A son, after all, cannot take the place of a husband. Yet I knew I had a peculiar responsibility greater, even than my older brother's, for I had lived with my mother through the years of war, its sorrows, and her own terrible attacks of migraine. At least I knew what to do when she was stricken. For many years the migraines continued. Father's death was for her a devastating experience to which, with her natural reserve of temperament, she could never give expression. Not for her the solace of tears. I never saw her cry.

Very slowly she picked up the threads of life again and, I imagine, she understandably built up her life around myself. My older brother Jack was up at Queens' College, Cambridge, taking the shortened degree course for ex-soldiers. He was looking towards Ordination and had recently committed himself to missionary service, the result, in part, of a very deep spiritual experience which had come to him at the Keswick Convention in 1919.

That experience was in turn to have far-reaching repercussions for myself. For one result was that he became much more aware of this hitherto little-known brother eight years younger than himself. Jack was an out-going person like Father, and he was also a born leader. I think he was very dismayed by my intense shyness and general spiritual inertia. And I suspect he felt, and rightly so, that I could very easily become mother-fixated out of loyalty to father. Anyway, whether that was so or not, he set to work to pull me out of myself, and insisted on my going to parties and learning to be sociable. It was fairly drastic treatment, which perhaps explains why I have detested parties ever since! But the treatment began to work. I actually found to my great surprise that I could make friends with girls. This was an experience with only one precedent. At the age of five I had a five-year-old girl playmate up in the hill-station of Mussoorie. Later she was to become the wife of Lucien Usher-Wilson who sailed for East Africa in the same year in which I sailed for West Africa, and who was to become Bishop of the diocese of the Upper Nile. But that friendship was a remote memory.

One of the girls I got to know under Jack's educational programme was a little older than myself. She, being romantically inclined, came almost to the point of proposing marriage, a very *avant-garde* performance in 1920; or was it 1921? I was considerably alarmed. Only my brother's determination prevented me from retiring once and for all into my shell.

During the month of August each year from 1919 to 1925 Jack led a children's Mission at Eastbourne, under the auspices of the Children's Special Service Mission, and there, from 1920 onwards, I joined him and slowly learnt to come to terms with other people, and religion came alive for me for the first time. And it was a religion of enthusiasm. Young men and women from the universities and medical schools gave up the month of August to running these seaside Missions at many places, doing so with a *joie de vivre* which was infectious.

As important as anything was the fact that I found in my brother not only a friend but a leader who taught me what Christian leadership is — the acceptance of responsibilities on the one hand, and on the other a complete trust in the capacity of others in the same team to be responsible, to be ready to let others, in their several fields of activity, be themselves leaders. In a word, Christian leadership is not being a 'one-man band'. That was a priceless lesson to learn, to watch it being demonstrated before my eyes, to recognise it as the only kind of leadership to which to aspire.

To that joyful comradeship of young men and women, overflowing with enthusiasm for Jesus Christ, I owe my life-long conviction that true religion is essentially joyful, precisely because it has for its basis the unwavering assurance of the utter trustworthiness of Jesus. That indeed was the heart of the message, communicated day after day from the beach pulpit at Eastbourne, as at many another seaside resort, a message directed to the children and to their parents. The message was given with great simplicity. No doubt the simplicity was often very naïve, yet it was completely sincere, and behind its delivery lay a great deal of private and corporate prayer. On the basis of such a very simple evangelical religion my Bible reading acquired what it had so far lacked, 'the warmth of desire', a warmth and an enthusiasm which have grown down the years. I wish I could say the sameabout my prayer life. In this I have made very heavy weather, but more of that later.

The C.S.S.M. did another thing for me: it broke my tongue-tied shyness. Much against my will Jack insisted on my getting up on the beach pulpit and giving an 'object' talk at one service. I have forgotten what it was I talked about and it only took about two minutes. What I do remember is my knees knocking against each other, unnoticed by the audience because a high wind was flapping my flannel trousers. That was the first time I had ever spoken in public. I was to do so many more times on that beach in the coming years. I can think of no better preparation for a preacher than for him to learn to throw his voice towards two or three hundred people, while there is a high cross-wind blowing and the surf is dashing down on the pebbles twenty yards behind him. Once you have mastered that trick no public platform will ever frighten you.

All this may seem a strange introduction to Cambridge and the years at the University. But without that experience of the C.S.S.M. at Eastbourne, and several similar Missions at West Kirby on the Wirral, I would never have been set free to enjoy Cambridge; to make a large number of life-long friendships; to lose myself and find myself in other people; to begin to see how the relatedness of things and people and events is the key to knowledge, the key to people, and the key to a living religion. All this I began to learn before I went up to Cambridge, and my most patient and persevering teacher was my brother Jack.

One thing more must be recorded of August 1923. Then three of us covenanted together to offer for missionary service with a view to building up what would today be called a team ministry somewhere overseas. We agreed to wait for guidance. It came far more suddenly than any of us expected.

I had only been at Jesus College for a few weeks when Earnshaw-Smith, a former C.M.S. missionary in Northern Nigeria and at that time Chaplain of Caius College, invited me to his rooms for tea with four or five other men to meet the Rev. G. T. Manley, the C.M.S. Secretary for Africa. At that party an appeal was made for a team of men to offer for service in Northern Nigeria. At once I wrote off to the other 'covenanters', both medical students at Bart's, to ask if they thought this might be the pointer for which we were waiting. Things began to move quickly. The next term, to my great surprise, two men both far senior to me called to say they had heard about our plan, and could they join? Soon there were six of us, and very much to Mr. Manley's surprise and, I suspect, some embarrassment, he found he was presented with six men prepared to go to Northern Nigeria directly they had qualified in their several professions.

To get so clear a directive about the future within a few weeks of going up to the University for one's first term was breathtaking. Some might well argue that it was bound to narrow one's horizons and to do that far too soon. I have, in retrospect, sometimes thought so myself. At the same time it did provide a base of stability from which to explore what College and University had to offer. That stable base I needed, for I was still extremely young for my age and somewhat volatile.

Having gained a scholarship in history I found myself quite extraordinarily fortunate in the three tutors who, in successive years, gave to me most generously of their learning and encouraged me in every possible way. Claude Elliott, later to be knighted and to become Head Master of Eton, was my first supervisor of studies. He was an astringent critic and would never allow a purple passage in an essay to escape a caustic question as to what it really meant. He was one of those rare teachers who could make medieval constitutional history intelligible, and Stubbs' Charters almost enjoyable reading. In this respect he was unique in the Cambridge of his day. It used to be said of him that a man could get a good 'class' in the Tripos on Elliott's notes alone. That I did get a good 'class' in the first year's exams and had my scholarship increased to eighty pounds I certainly owed in large measure to my tutor.

My second year brought me the further good fortune of having as my supervisor of studies one of the most remarkable men in Cambridge at that time, Bernard Lord Manning. A quiet scholarly man, richly endowed in mind, a deeply convinced Christian, a Congregationalist of most vigorous independency and infinitely catholic sympathies, he was physically delicate, having only one functioning lung. This quiet scholar could hold the Jesus College Boat Club in the hollow of his hand — the only man living who could! He possessed for me something of the spiritual and intellectual dynamism of Pat O'Regan of Marlborough. He too could make the past be present. It was a most exhilarating year.

To my infinite regret I never got very close to Bernard Manning. He was unfailingly kind, lent me books, was a magnificent supervisor. Looking back, I think he had a slightly quizzical attitude towards me. A devout and committed Dissenter, he was more at home with Anglo-Catholics and Roman Catholics than with the somewhat one-eyed, over-energetic Evangelical Anglican such as he found me to be. He wasn't too sure what made me 'tick'. I wasn't sure myself. I may be mis-reading the past. But through being over-busy here and there the opportunity of cultivating a rich friendship was forfeited, to my very great loss.

However, with Elliott and Manning behind me the first part of the Historical Tripos was negotiated successfully. I forget who it was who, early in my time at Cambridge, gave me most sage advice. He insisted that if I had worked hard during the year and knew my subject then for a full week before the examination I should shut every book and spend the time on the Cam, punting along the 'Backs' or up to Grantchester. His theory was that with the brain completely rested, with the examination paper in front of you, if there was anything in your head it would come out. I followed his advice in all the examinations for which I sat and it worked infallibly. I commend this piece of elementary physiological common sense to all examinees.

With Part I behind me there now arose the question of what to read for Part II. Somewhere in the distance ahead was the prospect of Ordination. This argued for some part of the Theological Tripos. In those days it was possible to opt for the section dealing with Ecclesiastical History. This I chose to do for it belonged to the same discipline in which I was being trained. All I had to do in addition was to attend several courses of lectures in theological subjects one of which, to my endless gain, was to listen to Sir Edwyn Hoskyns expounding the Second Epistle to the Corinthians.

For this final year at Jesus College my supervisor of studies was Percy Gardner-Smith, himself an ecclesiastical historian of distinction, who combined a dry and slightly cynical humour with immense kindliness and a very deep interest in the men he had to supervise. His somewhat coldly analytic mind and innate suspicion of euphoria in religion was a very healthy and valuable check on my immature certainties. In his essay 'Master and Pupil' Charles Morgan writes of the 'faculty of looking always "inside the pupil himself", of drawing him out, of enabling his particular talent and so, in the true sense, of educating him', and calls it 'an admitted virtue in tutors; indeed, all that is best in the system of our great universities springs from it.'* This was a virtue all my Cambridge tutors possessed, and none more so than Gardner-Smith.

Mercifully he released me from having to attend any lectures, satisfied that I knew how to dig meat out of books more rapidly than most lecturers could feed it to me. And he was always there for guidance and correction. During the year he suggested that I might try for the Lightfoot Scholarship in Ecclesiastical History, the University 'blue

*Charles Morgan, *Liberties of the Mind* (Macmillan, London, 1951), pp. 129–30.

ribbon' in this field. For this purpose he thought I ought to go at least once or twice to listen to the then Dixie Professor of Ecclesiastical History, a man of phenomenal learning. Obediently I went. But when at the end of the third lecture we were still being entertained with details about the flora and fauna of Upper Bithynia in the time of the younger Pliny, a subject that was absorbingly interesting but totally unrelated to my subject of study, I decided I must forego the entertainment. The Dean was not altogether surprised.

My most formidable hurdle was the special period set for the Lightfoot that year which involved reading large numbers of books in French. While at Marlborough a young master had put me on to read some of the French political and economic thinkers of the nineteenth century, so reading French was not too difficult. Fortune further favoured me in a less happy way. In the semi-finals for the inter-college hockey competition we had just scored our eleventh goal against St. John's to their two when, as I was charging down to help get another, one of their exasperated full-backs in clearing the ball drove it straight on to my knee-cap, putting me completely out of action. This, on top of a good deal of overwork, sent me to bed with shingles. Bed-bound for six weeks, I was able, with the aid of a French dictionary, to absorb enough knowledge about the Merovingian Franks in Gaul, my special period, to satisfy the examiners and I was awarded the Lightfoot. This was worth eighty pounds a year, was held for three years and was another welcome relief to the family finances. The College was pleased and I was told later that my health had been drunk in the Senior Combination Room.

Nevertheless it was a disappointing end to my hockey career. I was playing centre-forward and my accident upset the closely co-ordinated team work which had so far been so successful. In the finals we were beaten by Emmanuel. I was told at the time that had I been playing, and had we won, I would have been considered for election to the 'Wanderers', which would have meant I would in this respect only have caught up with my brother Jack. But the 'rubs' in life pay off, as I have indicated.

Early in that summer term of 1926 the General Strike took place. We were a politically ignorant generation. So when volunteers were called for to drive tubes and buses and trains the University rapidly emptied. We didn't think of ourselves as strike-breakers though in fact that was what our activities represented. We volunteered for the sheer fun of it, which I suspect remains a considerable part of the motive behind a later generation's enthusiasm for demonstrations, though undoubtedly there is today a hard core of political serious-mindedness in the young which was not there in Cambridge in 1926. Those of us

who were in our final degree year were at first forbidden to volunteer.
The rule, however, was relaxed a few days later though, alas, we found
there was no more scope for driving anything! Instead we were enrolled
as special constables, driven down to Whitechapel in a convoy of cars,
issued with tin helmets and truncheons and told to stand by for riots.
None occurred. In three days we were back in Cambridge with a few
weeks left for reading before following earlier practice and spending a
week on the river in preparation for Part II of the Tripos. The prescription worked as satisfactorily as on previous occasions and, so far as work
for my degree was concerned, academic activities were over.

But Cambridge was not all reading books, attending lectures, being
inspired by great teachers, working for examinations. The liberal
quality of the education it gave lay as much in its non-academic
activities as in any conscious pursuit of learning. What was absorbed
unconsciously was every whit as important as formal instruction.
Indeed, the greater part of my reading was done in vacations when I
averaged six to eight hours a day, with not much more than four hours a
day at the University. It was rubbing minds with other men that
rescued book-learning from becoming something unrelated to life. One
indirect result of reserving vacations for reading was that I was able to
be at home with my mother which did something to reduce the burden
of her loneliness.

Rubbing minds with other men, making friendships which were to
be life-long, these were a vital part of the creative experience which was
Cambridge. And my generation had one signal advantage. There were
still in residence in my first year a considerable number of men who
had been on active service during the war, had either been demobilised
late, wanted to do a full degree course, or were at a theological college.
Knowing such men gave a sharp corrective to facile thinking.

One such was the man who was to give me the deepest friendship
of all for the few short years before he was killed in an air-crash in the
Sudan in 1937. This was Guy Bullen, one of my brother's generation
who, after war service and graduating from Queens' College, was now
at Ridley Hall. It was he who, with his friend Willie Oswald, had come
round to my rooms in Jesus College and had asked if they might join
what was already spoken of as the Hausa Band, the group of men
preparing for service in Northern Nigeria. After ordination Guy was
a curate at Holy Trinity, Marylebone. In 1926 he sailed for Northern
Nigeria where I joined him a year later.

Guy was another of those characters, of whom I have been privileged
to know many, for whom the horrors and terrors of war, far from
brutalising them, had made them the more gentle, the more sensitive,

the more humble, and yet all this with characters of tempered steel. Gentle and strong, patient and courageous, always with a superb sense of humour, laughter never far away — that was Guy Bullen.

To be welcomed as a friend by a man so much older and more experienced than myself was a tonic form of self-discovery for one who was only very slowly growing up. I am sure that his friendship and the quality of his life and Christian devotion did something for me the depth of which I cannot estimate. For, odd though it may appear, being taken seriously by a man whom I so greatly respected taught me not to take myself too seriously. Guy's lively sense of humour, a humour wholly without malice, his chuckling sense of the ludicrous, taught me to recognise the absurdities in myself, and assuredly prepared me for some of the buffetings that lay ahead.

Most of my friends, however, were, naturally enough, my own contemporaries, though, as it happened with a few exceptions, for the most part members of other Colleges. This was in part the result of friendships begun in the C.S.S.M. circles in which I had been moving. In part it was due to my following a particular piece of advice from my brother, for which I shall always be grateful. While at Cambridge he had been on the executive committee of the Cambridge Inter-Collegiate Christian Union, a strongly evangelical and evangelistically-minded group, which in my time numbered about two hundred men. Jack strongly advised me to join the C.I.C.C.U. directly I went up in my first term. Equally strongly he urged me not to limit myself to the C.I.C.C.U. but, as I had already committed myself to the vocation of missionary service, also to join the Student Volunteer Missionary Union, which was the missionary arm of the Student Christian Movement. I followed his advice in both respects.

In joining the S.V.M.U. I found myself caught up with a no less devoted but rather less inhibited group of Christians. Among these the President, when I joined, was James Welch, a man who was to play a considerable part in my life in years to come and to be a much-valued friend. A brilliant mind, a penetrating thinker, James was a man with a rare empathy with all kinds of people. After giving fine service as a C.M.S. missionary in Nigeria he was appointed Principal of St. John's College, York. From there he moved, largely at William Temple's instigation, to the B.B.C. as Director of Religious Broadcasting in the war years. This was followed by a time as Chief Education and Social Science Officer of the Overseas Food Corporation in connection with the Ground Nut Scheme in Tanganyika. From there he went over to the new University at Ibadan, Nigeria, as Vice-Principal and the first Professor of Religious Studies. On his return to England in the fifties he was put in charge of Management Training and Education for the steel firm of Richard Thomas and Baldwin. Later he taught philosophy at the Battersea Polytechnic, which later became the University of Surrey. I list that record to illustrate the versatility of the man. To have had the stimulating friendship of such a man and of his wife Mary, with her no less lively mind, has been one of life's good things.

James Welch was a towering personality even as an undergraduate, worthy to be in the same bracket as another contemporary, Michael Ramsey of Magdalene, later to be Archbishop of Canterbury. James was beyond question the ablest man of that generation recruited for missionary service. He was succeeded as President of S.V.M.U. by Michael Davidson of Christ's, himself later also to be a C.M.S. missionary in Nigeria. He was a man of immense industry, of great business acumen, and a vast capacity for unaffected friendship. Like James Welch, Michael Davidson found Africa wonderfully congenial, and deep friendship with Africans profoundly rewarding.

I mention those two men because it was their width of vision combined with a deeply committed Christian discipleship which helped to save me from ever thinking that there was any one form of Christian experience, least of all my own, which alone was valid.

I was lucky in my undergraduate generation. In matters Christian it was the last in which it was possible to be at one and the same time College representative of the C.I.C.C.U., as I was, and also Secretary of the S.V.M.U., and also on the S.C.M. Executive at the headquarters in London. A greater rigidity on the part of the C.I.C.C.U. set in which was to make such a combination in future impossible.

I cannot easily weigh the relative influence on myself of these two student societies in the years that have followed. With the advantage of hindsight I venture a definition which, of course, I can only refer to myself. S.C.M. taught me to value a man or woman for himself or herself and to enjoy them as people. The C.I.C.C.U. taught me never to forget that being a Christian meant being a disciple and not a fellow-traveller. A disciple has other responsibilities for people in addition to enjoying them. What I can never regret is having learnt both lessons and I have always been grateful for the memory of all those who taught me.

Given my missionary commitment it was inevitable that I should try to persuade others to share it. This meant a huge expenditure of energy in organising meetings at which men would have an opportunity of meeting some of the great missionary personalities who could easily be inveigled into visiting Cambridge, one traditional recruiting ground for missionaries.

I can vividly remember in particular working out a very full programme of tea-parties and coffee-parties at which men could meet Barbrooke Grubb, the missionary pioneer of the Argentinian and

Bolivian Chaco. Another was Archdeacon Owen from the Kavirondo country in Kenya, a mighty warrior, for ever at odds with the colonial government and the White Settler community, and an inveterate correspondent to the *Manchester Guardian*. From him I caught the passionate conviction that the Gospel has to do with politics as well as souls. I learnt about ecology from him long before anyone had thought of inventing the word! And there were many others, not forgetting that unquenchable enthusiast, George Ingram who could get you on your knees within five minutes of meeting him, and would have you lined up for North India within half-an-hour unless you were very strong-minded. They were all great men. A limited horizon was impossible in their company.

A concomitant to this expenditure of energy was an attempt to rationalise the competing programmes of the various societies in the University which sought to interest men in service overseas. With the indispensable help, as Senior Friend, of the Rev. F. Woolnough, Chaplain of Christ's College, we formed the Cambridge University Missionary Council, which secured general advertisement for all such activities. It was a useful preparation for other ecumenical ventures later on.

One's enthusiasm could have its very embarrassing moments. I can still feel my discomfort one morning, while shepherding some thirty undergraduates from my own College to a 'Missionary Breakfast', the timing of which coincided with morning Chapel, when whom should we meet on his way to Chapel but the Dean himself, and incidentally my Supervisor of Studies. The look on his face assured me that at my next tutorial there would be one of those comments to which there can be no possible answer!

My closest friends, out of a galaxy of them, were Raymond Scantlebury of St. John's, Jack Adeney of Clare, Cecil Thorne of St. Catherine's, and Alan Gray who 'kept' on the same staircase as myself. This range of friendships was typical of my Cambridge experience where the wider life of the University meant more to me than life in College. How is one to assess the wisdom or unwisdom of casting one's net wide or concentrating one's energies? On the whole the Jesus men of my years were happiest enjoying the intense intimacy of College life. My interests were almost by accident of circumstances wider. I know I lost much by being a 'bad' member of College. Gain or loss, I do not know what judgment to make. But once again, as all through my life, I was to be rewarded far beyond my deserts when forty years later the College made me an Honorary Fellow. This astonishing award I attribute entirely to the machinations of the only Fellow of the College with whom continuous contact has been maintained down the years,

Dr. L. A. Pars, praelector in my time and a most generous friend ever since.

Alan Gray, whose rooms were opposite mine, had come up from St. Paul's School as a classical scholar. Friendship started and could have been shipwrecked on the first Sunday of our first term. We both decided to attend the Freshmen's Sermon in Holy Trinity Church. We sat together in the front pew of the north transept immediately under the pulpit, which I was to get to know very well some years later. Bishop Taylor-Smith was the preacher, to become in time another friend. Years later when he was staying with us at Holy Trinity Vicarage, I enjoyed telling him how I had never forgotten his sermon that evening though I had no recollection of anything he had said! I explained that my eyes had been rivetted on a girl sitting under the gallery on the other side of the church. He was gracious enough to allow the excuse in the circumstances, his hostess being present.

I remember well, as Alan and I walked back to College, asking him if he had noticed that girl across the church. Bearing in mind that he and I had only met for the first time a few days before, it was wholly understandable that Alan flashed me a suspicious glance, obviously wondering with what kind of character he was beginning to consort. But my indifference to the sermon and my enthusiasm about the girl were prophetic, for she has been my wife for more than forty years.

Alan was kind enough to risk giving me another chance and has been a refreshingly reliable friend ever since, though for many years now he has been in the Antipodes, first in Tasmania, then New Zealand and latterly in South Australia. We share a common enthusiasm for philately.

Raymond Scantlebury was a born conspirator, all his charm and guile being entirely dedicated, with a single-mindedness I have never known equalled, to the one object of introducing other people to Jesus Christ. Ours was to be an exciting partnership in this activity ten years later. The friendship began at Cambridge. Raymond never captured people's attention for himself. He was utterly unselfregarding. He insisted on sharing his own friends with me, and of him much more anon. One illustration may serve. As leader of the C.S.S.M. at Cromer he won the attention of a schoolboy, which attention he at once diverted to his Lord. In so doing he secured the man who was one day to be the leading liturgiologist in the early days of the Church of South India, then Bishop of Uganda, in due course first Archbishop of that Province, and now Bishop of the Diocese of St. Edmundsbury and Ipswich. In the course of all this that schoolboy, Leslie Brown, has given me one of my most cherished friendships. He and I both look back to Raymond with the deepest veneration.

Jack Adeney was a friend in a quite distinctive way. Almost all of my recollections of our Cambridge days are of our arguments. Jack was argumentative by temperament. I was argumentative by birth, being Irish. Somehow we stimulated each other, certainly he stimulated me. It is no bad thing to see a lot of someone who is always asking you questions as to what you mean by what you say. It is an astringen. experience of great value. Jack and I share one handicap in commont Both our handwritings are almost indecipherable. I think that on balance Jack's really is worse than mine. Not the least interesting part of his later career in the Middle East was when he was Archdeacon of Cyprus during one of the stormier periods in the long reign of Archbishop Makarios.

Cecil Thorne of St. Catherine's very early began to be interested in the possibility of missionary service in Nigeria. Another undergraduate of his year in the College was Leslie McKay, son of Archdeacon McKay of Oshogbo in Nigeria. Cecil and I drifted into a friendship which was sealed when he joined the Hausa Band. He served for eight years in Nigeria and then joined the home staff of the Society as an area secretary. Later, after serving several parishes in England, he became an army chaplain, an experience in which I think he found a fulfilment which had in a measure hitherto eluded him. He was my immediate predecessor as a curate at St. John's, Boscombe. As with so many Cambridge friendships, roads have diverged, and yet the ties of the years have not been broken. Cecil was one of those who when we met we found ourselves picking up exactly where we left off, however long the gap between may have been. There is a quality about this kind of friendship which is deeply satisfying. Continuity in life is one of those indispensables for sanity, and a friendship unaffected by separation provides a very special kind of continuity, and with it a deep assurance that the things seen are indeed temporal and the things unseen eternal.

This record of four Cambridge friends demonstrates that whatever our other limitations our lives were to be confined within no narrow horizons.

In the autumn of 1924 my brother Jack sailed for East Africa as a C.M.S. missionary to work at Kigezi in Uganda. For five years I had been a junior member of the party responsible for the C.S.S.M. at Eastbourne. Jack had the complete confidence of the C.S.S.M. authorities and they accepted his extremely rash proposal that I should lead the party in 1925. Leadership was certainly thrust upon me. But as I was to discover dramatically again and again in the years ahead, God tempers the wind to the most closely shorn lamb. Always he has provided me with generous-minded, able and older men who have given me their backing and the support of their mature experience. At Eastbourne there were two such of real spiritual greatness of soul, Admiral Horsley, father of another Cambridge friend, Douglas, and Colonel Winn, a retired officer of the Royal Engineers. Both old enough to be my father with a good few years to spare, they made up in spiritual maturity that which I most obviously lacked. Yet they treated me as the leader, though all that I could bring to that position was a lot of enthusiasm and a readiness to sweat it out over administrative details. Equally indispensable was the devotion the rest of the party had to my brother which they were prepared to extend to me.

That August was a creative experience. I proved then the truth I had begun to learn by watching my brother, that Christian leadership has nothing whatever to do with self-assertion, but everything to do with encouraging other people to assert themselves, while being willing yourself to tackle the chores.

At the end of the Mission, Ruth Sharp, a medical student who had been the leader of the girls' side of the work, told me she would not be available in 1926. I turned for advice to Margaret Gurney, daughter of an Eastbourne doctor who had always been a regular supporter of the C.S.S.M. Margaret had been in charge of the girls' camp that year, and was the obvious person to whom to turn for advice. She mentioned two girls who had just taken their degrees at Girton, Cambridge. Knowing neither of them, I asked Margaret to decide. After weighing the matter carefully she said that she thought the right one for Eastbourne would be Mary Collett. I wrote off at once and heard from her that she was willing to take on this responsibility, and also that of collecting her own team of helpers. I invited her to come over to our home in Norwood to talk over details. When I opened the door to welcome her I found she was the same girl who had held my attention spell-bound all through the Freshmen's sermon on my first Sunday in Cambridge two years before!

A very wise and dear friend of mine of later years, Douglas Webster, once defined a coincidence as 'two happenings which God brings together for a purpose'. Believing as I do that all life has a theological dimension, I am sure he is right. At any rate, the chain of circumstances which brought Mary and me together was the most important coincidence of my life. I have some evidence for believing that she and quite a lot of other people think the same.

From our talk that afternoon I knew that this was the girl for me. What I could not see was how on earth I could expect her to have a parallel reaction. However, the immediate task was to prepare for the Mission in 1926. We found we were entirely at one as to methods of working, and, what was as important, shared a similar spiritual experience and religious background, though she was far more mature than I was, remaining so ever since, as family and friends can testify. All my life I have had people to look up to for the quality of their leadership. What could be more ideal than to carry this experience into marriage. However improbable the prospect, that became my ambition from that afternoon. I do not think that anyone, least of all Mary, suspected my feelings until long after the Mission in 1926 was over. For Christmas that year my mother and I went down to Tunbridge Wells, where we met Mary's mother and her sister Evy.

I was one of a generation in which it was still common practice for a prospective suitor to ask permission to approach a daughter of the family. Mary's father had died when she was still a small girl, so it was to her mother that I spoke. I had no prospects to offer except that of sharing a missionary's life. But this did not seem to be too great an obstacle as Mary had already been in touch with C.M.S. Mary's mother, with graciousness as well as courage, urged me to be sure of my own mind and then to try my luck. About the latter I was very despondent. In the end through sheer cowardice I sent my proposal of marriage by post. A telegram arrived in reply saying 'Yes' and on 14th May, 1927, we became engaged.

There will be much more about Mary from now on, where not explicitly then by implication, for we were both determined that ours was to be a partnership with no reservations. Soon after we had become engaged we read together a book by W. C. Willoughby, *Race Problems and the New Africa*. In it we found the following description of the ideal of Christian marriage as meaning

> the joy of going through life hand in hand with the comrade of one's choice, sharing one another's burdens, stimulating one another's courage, doubling one another's sagacity, buckling on one another's armour, wearing one another's laurels, and easing one another's pain.

I do not know a better definition of what a real marriage can be. We set it before us as the pattern to which to work. We have proved the joy without any reservations.

But Cambridge was not yet a chapter concluded. There was much more Cambridge air still to be breathed. The year 1926 had been enormously stimulating in work and sport and friendship, with love providing its own tension of anxiety and hope. In the realm of friend-ship it yielded a new experience also which was to enrich the whole future. A group of us, mostly in Jesus College, found ourselves united in a common bond of friendship with Algy Robertson, at that time Theological Secretary of the S.C.M., later to go to Poona with the Christa Seva Sangh, and later still to become Father Director of the Anglican Order of St. Francis. Algy was a devout and deeply convinced Anglo-Catholic and at the same time a man compact no less of evangelistic passion in the best evangelical tradition. It was his obvious love for Jesus Christ which won the response of this by no means homogeneous group of undergraduates. It was, I think, Algy himself who first broached the idea of a 'brotherhood of expectancy'. We never did become a brotherhood but I suspect that for all of us, as for so many whose lives Algy touched, there remained a savour of expectancy in all our living. Before one of our later voyages to Africa, that dear friend and most remarkable missionary, Mabel Shaw, sent us a message to say she was praying for us that 'you may meet Christ round every corner'. That was precisely Algy's attitude to life.

Equally important for me, and for all my future ecumenical activities, was that I discovered this quality in an Anglo-Catholic. Anglo-Catholicism, despite all the saints it has nourished, has never found any response in my mind, other than a proper respect, while much of its practice I have found repellent. An inveterate Irish Protestantism in my inheritance may in part explain this religious myopia, if such it be, but I think rather that it stems from a life-long experience of deriving spiritual nourishment through other channels. But that is as may be. Algy showed me how possible it was to be wholly 'one in Christ' with someone, many of whose deepest convictions I could not share. That experience has gone on being enriched down the years by innumerable friendships and meeting with all kinds of discipleship. It was Algy Robertson who taught me to expect to find Christ in everyman and to worship him wherever I found him. That, I judge, is as good a definition of the ecumenical experience as one can discover. 1926 was a turning point in this respect. What a year!

That same autumn held two other stimulating experiences. In 1925 the Missionary Council of the Church Assembly had launched a 'World Call', an attempt to bring the parishes of England more alive to their missionary responsibilities. The Missionary Council enlisted for this purpose groups of undergraduates to take the message to the parishes. In 1926 the experiment was repeated and I was asked to lead a group from Cambridge to the diocese of Salisbury from 7th–13th September. The conductor of a short retreat beforehand, which was held at Marlborough, was Canon E. S. Woods, then Vicar of Holy Trinity Church, Cambridge, and later Bishop of Croydon and then Bishop of Lichfield. All who knew Edward Woods can guess how inspiriting that retreat was in preparation for a considerable ordeal. None of us had preached in parish churches and we had no idea of what kind of reception we could expect. In the event we had a wonderfully kind welcome to which I was able to pay testimony when, later, the Bishop of Salisbury, the Rt. Rev. St. Clair Donaldson, invited me to address the Diocesan Conference and report on our collective experiences.

The other experience was a related one. The Africa Secretary of C.M.S., the Rev. H. D. Hooper, had been asked to provide five stewards for the International Conference to be held at Le Zoute in Belgium from 14th–21st September. He asked me to be one of them and to find the other four. This promised to be a very exciting prospect, and I had no difficulty in persuading Jack Adeney to join me, and Norman Parfit (later to be a missionary in China), and Joe Church, (then at Bart's and later to be for many years a missionary in Rwanda and Uganda). But I lacked the fifth. Then one day during July I learnt that a team from Oxford was coming to Cambridge for the 'World Call' and to one of their meetings in the Market Place I went, by way of backing them up. Much their most attractive and convincing speaker was a girl. She seemed to be a good choice for our fifth steward. So promptly and without more ado, the meeting being over, I went up to her and without further introduction told her of Le Zoute and said 'Will you come with me to Belgium?' Jack would have been well satisfied with the progress being shown by his shy little brother! Ruth Shaw, as promptly, said 'Yes'. Later she was to go to Australia as the wife of the head of one of the Fairbridge Farm Schools. Our team complete, we went over to Belgium on 14th September and had a week of very hard work as stewards, but also of great stimulation. There I heard Sir Frederick Lugard speaking on problems of Government in Africa, and one evening had the privilege of being asked to dine with Dr. J. H. Oldham, the beginning of another inspiring friendship.

Meanwhile early in July I had gone to Ridley Hall for Ordination training. I had, with the full approval of C.M.S., decided that I would go out to Nigeria as a layman, leaving the question of the 'when' of Ordination open. But it was obviously sensible to complete the academic side of my training first. Having taken an honours degree, the practice in those days was for a Cambridge man to read the Cambridge Ordination Course, rather than the General Ordination examination. For this I was exempt from the Church History papers. I was able to concentrate on the Bible and Christian doctrine.

But a theological college is not an academic factory. We had to learn to see what applied theology meant, and this Ridley Hall began to teach me. The Principal at the time was Dr. A. J. Tait, a generous-hearted and most lovable man with fire in his theological belly. He made one feel the thrill of Christian doctrine not as a set of formulae but as an attempt to describe truth, yet always as an open-ended attempt to which there could be no finality this side of seeing the truth face to face. Always in his teaching there was deep Christian devotion. There was nothing dry-as-dust about his lectures. Most revealing of all were his Greek Testament Bible-readings once a week during evensong in Chapel. Here we had a brilliant exemplar of how to take the text of Scripture and uncover its meaning by the use of the original language and the revealing of the historical context. Sitting under Dr. Tait for four terms shaped my devotional life ever after. From him I learnt what it means to be a 'servant of the Word' — the written Word as our immediate introduction to the Living Word.

But I must record a complementary experience. Throughout my time at Ridley I got up every morning at 6.0 a.m. to spend an hour with my Bible. As the guide to its study I took three commentaries of Bishop Handley Moule, those of the Ephesians, Philippians and Colossians.

I owe to that good Bishop, himself a one-time Principal of Ridley Hall, a particular debt of gratitude. It was he who taught me in the quiet of those early mornings to listen for the personal voice of God speaking to me as a person and asking for a personal response. To use Martin Buber's great phrase, I listened to the God 'who called me by my name'.

Others like Hoskyns, and as I have stated particularly Dr. Tait himself, were teaching me to read the Bible as a scholar, though always as a scholar on his knees. George Adam Smith, whose commentaries on the Prophets I read avidly, taught me to read the Bible as an historian and a moralist should read it, finding it as contemporary as the daily newspaper. Still others were to show me its corporate significance in the life of the Body of Christ. All these were quite indispensable. But I believe there is no substitute for a grounding in the conviction that here is a book out of which at any time and in any circumstance I meet the God who speaks to me and who demands my attention and response. That grounding, apart from what I had learnt at home, I received in those early morning hours. And the instrument used by the Holy Spirit was those commentaries by Bishop Moule.

The radio programme 'Desert Island Discs' assumes that one will have with one on the desert island a copy of the Bible and Shakespeare, and then one can make a further choice. Pressed to the limit of spiritual and physical endurance, and I have been so pressed, I know I could manage with the Bible alone. All I would want besides would be a large supply of paper to make notes.

Ridley gave me many more new friends, but the two who shared 'A' staircase with me must find special notice here. Immediately above me lived Hugh Herklots from Trinity Hall. He filled me initially with some awe, having been President of the Union and having had a book of poems printed while still an undergraduate. But he carried his laurels lightly with a disarming charm. For some years a Professor of Theology in Canada, he later made no small contribution to the Ecumenical Movement through his work with the Youth Department of the British Council of Churches. His prolific output of books on one aspect or another of the ecumenical enterprise represented an heroic effort at Christian education. Very properly he became in due course the Moderator of the Church Training Colleges and a Canon of Peterborough Cathedral.

Immediately above him resided Leonard Hickin from Magdalene. Nothing jeopardised our friendship, not even my assiduously prosecuted self-appointed task of waking him up at what seemed to him an unreasonable early hour but to me a prerequisite of real Christian *askesis*. One of life's wonders is that I have retained so many friends. That Leonard is one of them is not the least of the wonders. For thirteen years he was a C.M.S. missionary first in Cairo and then in Northern Nigeria, another member of the Hausa Band. Ridley Hall can claim some real pre-eminence in having made sure that the Ordained Ministry was always a Ministry of the Church Universal.

Among many memories of that happy four terms was the privilege I had of entertaining Temple Gairdner of Cairo, already a hero for me long before Constance Padwick's magnificent biography which appeared in 1929. It was as stimulating as it was humbling to have this experienced veteran of work in the Muslim world listening to my ambitions for literature work in the Western Sudan, this being my private dream, and kindly encouraging me to follow the dream as a not impossible one.

Here I would add a reflection. The extraordinary kindness and trust I had already received from men and women older and more experienced than myself early determined me that I would always support youthful enthusiasms and try to share the dreams of the young. It was to be one of the great joys of being General Secretary of the C.M.S. that I was able to give free rein to this determination, a small repayment of the debt I myself owed to so many.

A postscript to this period of Cambridge life may be added, if only for its link with experiences many years ahead. My diary for the 29th and 30th March, 1927, shows that part of those days was spent in the Jerusalem Chamber at Westminster Abbey. The Bishop of Salisbury and the Rev. F. Underhill were the two seniors who played a leading part. Most of the company were undergraduates or had recently taken their degrees. The purpose of the gathering was to consider the pos-

sibility of forming a 'Brotherhood of Expectancy', a loosely-knit
fellowship of those who were looking for a revival of the spiritual life
within our own Church, and who desired to be ready for any call to
service which might come to them. Algy Robertson was present. I
think he was the energising mind behind the gathering. I have in my
possession a printed report of the proceedings. On the second day the
chair was taken by A. M. Ramsey, and five short introductory speeches
were made. The report reads:

> M. A. C. Warren made a plea for unity among us: this however
> must be no mere haze of good fellowship but the true unity in
> diversity, wherein differences are fearlessly recognised but not
> allowed to sunder. With an allusion to *The Christ of the Indian Road*
> he begged us to emphasise not the 'whats' that divide but the 'Whom'
> that unites; that which we have in common — our common love for
> Jesus Christ, our common expectation of the moving of the Spirit,
> and our common desire to be used.

That emphasis I have never found any reason to change. The day
ended with a period of silence and commitment in Westminster Abbey.

Later that summer, on 12th July, I went to Lambeth Palace for the
Reception for Missionaries presided over by Archbishop Randall
Davidson. This was followed by an inspiring service of dedication in
Westminster Abbey.

10/10/77
Rich!

4

1927 - 1931

Nigeria and Illness

. . . when you are really alone, lying at the bottom of
a pit on the mud, stripped of everything— there is
nothing left but yourself, and a bit of sky overhead;
and then you do learn what you are and what is of
value— or you have a chance to— and begin to live
as a whole person . . .

ANN BRIDGE

Four Part Setting

MARY and I both knew that according to C.M.S. 'regulations' my first tour in Nigeria must be as a single man. Our hope was that after eighteen months I would come home, that we would be married, and then go out to Nigeria together.

I had no plans for a curacy and, indeed, Ordination remained a possibility on the horizon, the occasion to be determined by the demands of the work. My vocation was that of a missionary. If priesthood would serve that vocation then if a Bishop was good enough to accept me for Ordination, I would be ready when the time came. It was against that possibility that I had taken the qualifying examinations.

This will appear a somewhat cavalier approach to the ordained ministry, but only so if missionary service is estimated as being less important in the service of the Kingdom. That is something I have never accepted. Furthermore, in the missionary vocation there is no distinction of value between layman and priest, between man and woman—diversities of operations, yes, but the one Spirit dividing to each one severally as he will. I began with these guide lines and have held to them ever since.

The autumn of 1927 was spent by Mary and me in shopping expeditions, acquiring all kinds of curious clothes worn in those days by Europeans in the tropics—sun-helmets, spine pads, cholera belts—as well as other forms of equipment for camping, including a hip-bath which was useful for service as a trunk! On any reckoning I was not going to a centre of Western civilisation. Even so, I took with me only a fraction of the outfit which Geoffrey Moorhouse has so engagingly described in his book *The Missionaries*.

Meanwhile we speculated happily about the future we were to spend together in Northern Nigeria, little realising that for Mary her first visit there would be exactly thirty years later. Even less, as we dreamt our dreams, did we expect our engagement to last for five years, short of one week, before we could be married.

Looking back, I must have been a very disconcerting fiancé. I was certainly a thoughtless one. Mary must often have wondered who or what she was intending to marry. Was it Max? Or was it really Northern Nigeria, or at least the Hausa Band? Indeed, it must sometimes have appeared as if I was already married to both and that she would be joining a polygamous household as the junior wife, not absolutely secure that she was even the favourite one. Yes, I was the limit, and I sadly admit it. That very last evening before I sailed Mary and I spent our time making a large-scale map of Nigeria on cloth, a visual aid for her to take round with her on the programme of speaking about Nigeria which I hoped she would undertake. There were to be other times when she would have been fully justified in breaking off our engagement. That she did not do so that evening was a miracle.

Next day, 23rd November, we started for Liverpool, but not before a cable had arrived from Uganda to say that Sheelagh had been born to Jack and Kathleen in Kabale. My brother Jack had married Kathleen Ardill on 1st January, 1927. Kathleen, a doctor, was the daughter of C.M.S. missionaries in South India, so Sheelagh had a formidable inheritance. Many years later she was to follow in the footsteps of her father and mother and herself serve in Uganda and, in a crisis in that country's affairs, demonstrate that she had all her father's qualities of leadership and courage.

November 23rd was a cold, wet day. I do not recommend anyone going to a seaport, or airport for that matter, to see off some they love. Certainly neither mother nor Mary enjoyed the experience that damp depressing day. Mary and I learnt our lesson. It was hard enough going to Euston in 1965 to wave off Pat and Roger to India. Far better it was to wave them off from outside the Porter's Lodge of Westminster Abbey when they returned to India in 1971.

Dr. Walter Miller, the veteran and only survivor of Bishop Tugwell's party which had walked up from the coast in 1899, was my travelling companion, and I was eagerly looking forward to learning all I could from a man who was already something of a legend. Now we were off at last. For four years Northern Nigeria had been at most only just below the surface of my thinking. Often I was quite definitely airborne in my dreams. Every book about Northern Nigeria upon which I could lay my hands I had read. I had been editor of a small magazine designed to seek further support for the Hausa Band, and had even launched into authorship with a pamphlet with the title *Seeing Visions in Mud*. Recruiting other members for the Hausa Band and seeking to honour our commitment to C.M.S. to raise extra money for our support meant developing the nucleus of a miniature 'home' organisation. This had taken up a tremendous amount of time and energy during undergraduate days not otherwise unoccupied. Not unnaturally I was altogether keyed up on that voyage on the *Apapa*, too much so indeed.

I suspect that Dr. Miller viewed the Hausa Band with very considerable misgivings, for which he could hardly be blamed. He must have been informed that the C.M.S. was anxious to break out into much more extensive work in Northern Nigeria than was represented, as far as the Hausa country was concerned, by the small compound in the centre of Zaria City. He knew that the Hausa Band was intended to be the spear-head of change. Already Guy Bullen had arrived in

Zaria and Willie Oswald was on the Bauchi Plateau. And here was a third representative of a very disturbing prospect.

The voyage out proved curiously disappointing. I could get very little out of Dr. Miller about the real situation. I think he guessed that I was living in a dream world. He knew the real one by a lot of hard-won and bitter experience. He was too great a gentleman to wish to disillusion me too soon. Time would do that, and time might be on his side also with regard to the Society's plans. I see nothing discreditable to him in attributing that thought as having been in his mind. After all he was the real fount of knowledge about the Muslim Emirates of Nigeria, and he knew the Government's attitude. 'Wait and see' was a good motto in the old Africa, a great deal less sound today!

Symbol of my dreams and a measure of their optimism and unreality was that I had with me a large-scale map of the Sahara. It was there to beckon me on to the day when, at last, fluent in Hausa and Fulani, I would go off on literature-distributing expeditions. I had been enthralled with a book entitled *The Veiled Tuareg* and was quite prepared to add their language to the other two. Unwittingly two very great men, Temple Gairdner of Cairo and A. T. Upson of the Nile Mission Press, both pioneers in the use of literature in presenting the Gospel to Muslims, had encouraged my dreaming, no doubt reckoning that my feet would make contact with the earth again before too much damage was done!

My first glimpse of Africa was the low and very uninspiring skyline of the colony of the Gambia, where we anchored a long way out from its capital, Bathurst. Then came Freetown, Sierra Leone. Here we were able to go ashore. Fourah Bay College was our objective and we were taken round by its recently appointed Principal, Cecil Horstead, later to be the second Archbishop of the Province of West Africa. Something of the romance of the past still lingered in that gravely neglected part of our former colonial empire. The very beams which supported the roof of Fourah Bay College came from the spars of the captured slave ships brought into Freetown Bay by the British Navy to be sold or broken up. More searchingly one remembered that missionaries, men and women, Methodists, Baptists, Roman Catholics and Anglicans came to this corner of Africa, sometimes to die within a few weeks of arriving, rarely to live more than a few years. There can hardly be a few square miles of land anywhere else on earth which contain the bones of so many missionaries. They came and died with the twin objects of bringing the Gospel to Africa and making some small atonement for the Slave Trade. And they were not pioneers of the colonial empire, a fact which is sometimes obscured in contemporary writing.

That visit to Sierra Leone was a moving experience. Yet how utterly unlike my dreams the future was to be. Not the wildest flight of imagination could have pictured the scene in St. Catherine's Chapel at Westminster Abbey when, forty-two years later, in the presence of the Dean and others of the Abbey Clergy, the Vice-Chancellor of the University of Sierra Leone, Dr. Harry Sawyerr, was to invest me with an Honorary Doctorate of that University, not a recognition of my services but a tribute to the contribution C.M.S. had made to Sierra Leone.

What fun it is not to know the future! What a blessing not to know it when it is not funny!

Our next stop was at Takoradi in the Gold Coast. There was no Tema harbour then and once more we lay well off shore, and watched the surf-boats rising and falling with the great Atlantic swell, while passengers were lowered in 'Mammy-chairs' for their precarious journey to the land.

At last, twelve days out of Liverpool, we arrived at Lagos, were most kindly welcomed by Bishop and Mrs. Melville Jones and by Mr. Wakeman of the C.M.S. Bookshops, and then caught the night train to Zaria.

The next ten crowded months are a confused bundle of memories, a few outstanding, and most of these associated with Guy Bullen whom it was such a joy to meet again and with whom the deepening of the friendship begun at Cambridge was to be for me God's light in the gathering darkness. Guy was obviously hungry for someone to talk to and with whom to share his growing perplexity. Already he had discovered, as I was quickly to discover, that any prospect of our fulfilling the C.M.S. policy of expansion was likely to be shipwrecked on Dr. Miller's deep-rooted conviction that the site of the Mission *inside* the Muslim city of Zaria must be held at all costs.

Here some history is necessary. As yet my understanding of history was largely academic. It was only through my experiences in Nigeria that I became fully aware of how living a reality history is, how the past is vividly alive in the present, how we can't escape it, least of all when we imagine we are repudiating it.

The British Protectorate was established in Northern Nigeria only in 1902. Bishop Tugwell's depleted party, which included Dr. Miller, had arrived in 1899. The Niger Company was still maintaining a very haphazard authority along the river. The French had their own ambitions as to who was to control that river basin. The Muslim Emirates, their power still unbroken, maintained the traditions of the Middle Ages. With foresight and imagination Dr. Miller had spent some time living in a Hausa community in North Africa and was already proficient in Hausa, one result of which was that he secured the right to live in the heart of Zaria City before this became a privilege forbidden by the British Administration.

This also explains the great influence Dr. Miller had in the early days of Sir Frederick Lugard's pro-consulship. Dr. Miller already knew far more intimately what were the realities in some of the Emirates than did any British official. Indeed for a time his knowledge was indispensable. For Lugard's resources of political officers and soldiers and police were grotesquely inadequate for the control of an area 760 miles from east to west and over 300 miles from north to south, comprising the Northern Provinces alone.

I well remember Dr. Miller's vivid description of one incident when the Emir of Kontagora was besieging Zaria in some feudal dispute. A message was sent to the nearest British post of which Captain Abadie was in command. He with a handful of men galloped up to the murra-murra ridge which today looks down on the village of Wusasa. The Emir of Kontagora's camp lay stretched out away ahead. Putting spurs to his horse Captain Abadie charged straight up to the Emir's tent and proceeded to handcuff the Emir and stop the siege!

That was the epic background of Dr. Miller's earlier years. And something of the flavour of those years still lingered in 1927. Lugard was not just a memory. He had trained the administrators with whom Guy Bullen and I were to do much business.

It can be readily understood that government officers tended to look askance at a Christian missionary who had sufficient knowledge of local politics and sufficient prestige to be instrumental in getting a corrupt emir deposed. It was even more embarrassing to have him living in a Christian enclave in the very heart of a Muslim city. For the cause of this anxiety one must look to the death of General Gordon in the Sudan. That death, and the perennial threat of a 'Mahdi', haunted British administrators wherever they ruled over resentful Muslim populations. The possibility of a Nigerian 'Mahdi' was not so fanciful after all: one had already made an unsuccessful bid to repeat the story of the Sudan. I remember well when Guy Bullen and I were staying with the Lieutenant Governor in Government House, Kaduna, hearing him say, as he pointed to a wall-map of Northern Nigeria, his finger on the easternmost province of Bornu—'the pulse of Bornu beats in time with the Nile valley'. It was his way of intimating why Christian missionaries were not welcome in the Muslim areas of Northern Nigeria. After all, thousands of Hausas made the pilgrimage to Mecca every year, and there was a substantial Hausa community settled in Omdurman and Khartoum. A descendant of the Madhi also lived there. 'Ideas have legs', as someone has observed!

But we of the younger generation had one asset—Guy Bullen.*
Guy had a positive genius for getting alongside all kinds of people
and winning their respect, their trust and finally their affection. In his
short time in Nigeria he had already achieved this with not a few
members of the administration. It was at least as much due to their
trust in Guy, as to their desire to get the Mission out of Zaria City,
that the administration offered us a square mile of land only just outside
the city perimeter, provided we vacated the compound inside.

But here the irresistible force of one man's will came up against the
irreducible demand of the British administration. What that administration had no power to do was to evict the Mission which had got
there before the British had established their authority. Could Dr.
Miller be persuaded to see that the small compound in Zaria was a
cul de sac, not an advanced base for expansion? Dr. Miller had not
only vast experience on his side, was incontestably the most knowledg-
able person about the country and its people, and was more than a
little sceptical of the *bona fide* intentions of the administration—he could
not see, nor could any of us, how short-lived that administration was
to prove to be, nor how rapidly in very unexpected ways the closed
areas of the north were to accept a Christian 'presence'.

So it was that many an evening saw Guy and myself sitting out on
the flat roof of the garage next to his house, and there talking, talking,
the stars round the sky. Not once nor twice we watched the Southern
Cross, visible on a clear evening, rise and disappear before we went
to bed. How we wrestled with our commission and its apparently
hopeless prospect of fulfilment!

One thing we could do and that was to insist on continuing negotiations with the Government. For this we had the authority of the Society.
Likewise we claimed the right to explore possible sites, and indeed
to travel into areas where there was no prospect, then, of the Government ever allowing a Christian Mission to operate. We insisted on
hoping against hope. We believed that to allow the past to shape the
future without acting in the present was a sure prescription for the
frustration which can kill.

Just before Guy went on leave we arrived at a provisional agreement
with the Resident of Zaria that if we were able to renounce our
property rights in Zaria City he would be willing to specify the precise
area which the Mission could occupy, the square mile already referred

Guy Bullen, by his friends, was published by the Highway Press in 1938. Within the
inescapable limits of space and the inadequacies of language this small book gives a
faithful picture of the man who was so widely beloved. I had the privilege of writing the
chapter dealing with his time in Nigeria, 1926–1935.

to. This was on the Zaria-Kaduna road. At the centre of the area was a large granite outcrop. Guy and I, going out to prospect the area, climbed the rock. It was an unforgettable moment. All round us was virgin bush with scattered here and there a smallholding. It was to be several years before, with the full support of the Society, Guy overcame Dr. Miller's resistance and the now flourishing village and medical complex of Wusasa began to come into existence, with outreach in all directions such as we had always believed to be possible. I was not to see it until 1957, by which time the square mile had been transformed. But the view from Wusasa rock that day had for both of us a Pisgah-touch.

Meanwhile for me there remained a three-fold task—to learn the Hausa language, to teach six senior boys the rudiments of English history, and to help in the little dispensary.

Learning Hausa I found to be very slow work, despite the valiant efforts of a very patient Mallam who had, however, no idea how to teach a language. My main trouble was that I have no musical sense and found the subtler sounds very hard to master. I had to wait nine months before I got a real chance to grapple with the language properly through going on trek for the best part of a month with one of the schoolboys who had a very limited command of English. So *faute de mieux* I began to speak a kind of Hausa.

One day on this trek, when we were up on the Bauchi Plateau in a predominantly pagan area, we came on a Saturday evening to a village which had a rest house. Unknown to us this village contained a substantial Christian congregation and had a catechist as their minister. He asked me to give the sermon at the Sunday service next morning. He knew no English. The language of the congregation was some tribal tongue unknown to my Hausa companion. So it became obvious that I must do my best in Hausa, the accepted *lingua franca*.

I worked for hours on that sermon, which proved to be the only one I was ever to preach in the Hausa language. I chose as my text 2 Timothy 2:8, 'Remember Jesus Christ, risen from the dead'. In Hausa this is much more vigorously expressed by a negative, 'Never forget that Jesus Christ is alive'. If I had to leave a message with a little isolated Christian community, which I was most unlikely ever to see again, this seemed a good one. If, as most likely, they did not understand a word of my exposition at least the text might help them, and it is after all a very large part of the Gospel.

My task of teaching English history to the senior boys was no easy one. Their own command of English was relatively restricted. What is more, I had no choice of subject but had to follow the curriculum set for the Junior Cambridge examination. The set period was the

sixteenth and seventeenth centuries. I found it hard to spark a light
except over the matrimonial adventures of Henry VIII which had a
fine local flavouring and caught the enraptured attention of the class.
Otherwise it was heavy going, and how could it be anything else?
Not one of the boys had ever been away from Zaria. Common sense
would seem to suggest that the history of Africa was a more suitable
theme.

But before this programme is ridiculed as absurd it is worth remembering one or two things. In 1927 extremely little was known of
the real history of Africa. The enormous range of research which has
since demonstrated the recorded story of much of Africa right back
to pre-history had not then been undertaken. Again, however meaning-
less English history might be, yet in learning it in English meant they
were learning the English language without realising it. And in so
doing were preparing for the independent Nigeria which was far
nearer than any of us dreamed possible. When in due course that
independence came one of those boys became Director of Medical
Services for all Northern Nigeria. One became the Principal of the
School of Pharmacy for Northern Nigeria. One boy was later to
become Pro-Chancellor of Lagos University. The same school a few
years later was to produce the Head of State of a Federal Nigeria, a
Vice-Chancellor of the Ahmadu Bello University of Zaria, a Federal
Commissioner for Mines and Power, and a Chief Agricultural Officer
for the North Central State —all this from that one small Christian
school. And all of these men were, with one exception, convinced
Christians. Here was the true monument to Dr. Miller's devoted
ministry. His insistence, against all Government advice and pressure,
upon providing an education in English, equipped at least a few for
the *real* future.

Missionary education in Africa is open to many criticisms, some of
them just. What is indisputable is that they and they alone prepared
the leadership which was to take over that responsibility for the
independent African nations when in rapid succession, amid fanfares
and rejoicing, the Union Jack was run down and the symbol of the
new nation run up. It is not too much to claim that, in so far as Britain
retains a good and close relationship with these new nations of Africa,
which were once her colonies, it will be owing in some considerable
measure to men like Dr. Miller. My own very small share in preparing
some of the future leadership in Nigeria was a privilege for which
I shall always be grateful. It isn't everyone whose house-boy becomes
a Pro-Chancellor!

Yet in reality my contribution was negligible. I taught that class for
only two terms. But one memory remains from a visit to Wusasa

thirty years later. A public reception was laid on for Mary and myself. At it one of the original six made an extremely witty speech in quite flawless English, speaking without a note. In the course of it he quoted accurately several sentences which he had remembered from my lecture, if you could call it that, on 'The glorious revolution of 1688'! I have never received a prettier compliment.

But real credit must be given where credit is due. Behind the amateur fumblings as teachers of Dr. Miller, Guy Bullen and myself there was, all the time, the highly professionalised skill of Mary Locke, a fully qualified teacher. It was she who saw to it that the whole curriculum was covered and the manifest deficiencies of her colleagues compensated for by her own talent. She was an infectious teacher with a rollicking sense of humour and a lack of reverence for the male half of creation which anticipated 'Women's Lib' by half a century! Withal she was a first-rate missionary.

Our rectangular compound with its high mud-wall, its mud-built houses, three of them two-storied and well-structured, had at one corner a little church and opposite to it a squat little building which comprised a waiting room for out-patients, a small dispensary, and a ward with four beds. To this dispensary there came every morning twenty or twenty-five men and women to whom medical aid of the most elementary kind was purveyed.

When our qualified nursing sister, Dorothy Saunders, went on leave, the responsibility for this work, against all probability, was vested in me. Dr. Miller was a qualified doctor but he had completely abandoned the practice of medicine and was committed whole-time to translation work. I was even left one day to lance a very large and unpleasant abscess which he was unwilling to tackle.

For this unexpected responsibility I had, if possible, fewer technical qualifications than I possessed in the field of education, and they were few enough. But at least I knew my own ignorance and had sufficient knowledge to avoid lethal accidents. While still an undergraduate at Cambridge I had for a number of terms followed a course of weekly lectures on tropical medicine and hygiene. And during holidays a friendly doctor, who had his own dispensary, introduced me to some of the simpler prescriptions. The stock in the Zaria dispensary was small enough to make actual poisoning of patients extremely unlikely.

Today, of course, I would not be allowed to do any of the things I did forty and more years ago. But we were surrounded with folk who were sick, and there was no one else available. A few years later a young district officer wrote a book advocating the training of medical auxiliaries for use in areas where qualified medical help was unobtainable. His views on this and other subjects were too revolutionary for the authorities. He left the colonial service and became a successful novelist. I have always reckoned that in the circumstances of those days he was right. A little knowledge may well be a dangerous thing, but coupled with a lively awareness of the extent of one's own ignorance, it can often relieve a mass of suffering.

At our dispensary the greatest demand was for Epsom salts, the therapeutic value of which as a universal panacea was accepted by all, and was probably successful in most cases! Ulcers due to yaws or syphilis, or simply to dirt getting into cuts, were the most common objects for attention, and one leper came with great regularity to have his sores washed with warm water highly charged with disinfectant. It was the only caring he was likely to receive. For me the advantage was that my store of Hausa gradually increased. And I like to think that my most active assistant, one of the senior boys, did become the Principal of the Pharmacy School of Northern Nigeria many years later. I imagine he got his first inspiration in that little 'first-aid' outpost.

My worst experience was when one of the local policemen brought his wife and asked me to take out one of her teeth. Dentistry was not in the course I had taken at Cambridge! But the dispensary possessed an old-fashioned tool-case of dental instruments. After prolonged scrutiny I chose one which seemed best shaped for its purpose. What that poor woman endured without even a groan I dare not try to imagine. After a lot of hard work the tooth came out. The husband was profusely grateful. I am less sure that he could speak for his wife.

Then one day our Fulani milkman came in to say that about five miles out of Zaria there was a gang of labourers chipping granite for the permanent way of the railway. The European foreman had asked if there was anyone in the city who could come out to do elementary first-aid work. Dr. Miller agreed to my going out to investigate. Soon, with one of the schoolboys, I was going out twice a week. Everything was marvellously primitive. The water supply was a pool covered with green scum. Our basin was filled with this and then heavily dosed with Potassium Permanganate. The resulting colour transformation was viewed by the patients awaiting attention as big magic. The work was simple enough, as almost all the trouble was small sores caused by flying splinters of granite cutting into the men's legs. The application of a little Alum worked wonders. To save further infection I dusted the wound with disinfectant powder and bandaged the limb. This had an unforseen result. Zaria was the nearest town. Over the weeks so many bandaged legs were seen in the Zaria market place that questions were asked and before we knew where we were the numbers attending the dispensary in our compound more than doubled. Upon such a slender foundation can a reputation be built up. I became known as 'Likita', the Hausa for doctor, the first honorary doctorate to come my way.

One improbable request came one day when an angry crowd came to greet me beside our local pool of Bethesda. Their spokesman, in a mixture of Hausa and 'pidgin', asked me to determine the condition of a cow. Unaccountably veterinary science had also been omitted from the course at Cambridge. But they would take no denial. So I told them to fetch the cow. In due course they produced its skin! Apparently the cow had been known to have fits and was taken away secretly into the bush and killed by its owner, who was now trying to sell the meat to the workmen. Not qualified to diagnose bovine epilepsy from contemplation of the cow's skin, I was confronted with a need for Solomonic wisdom. It looked as if a riot might occur in which the cow's owner would be lynched. After a prolonged study of the skin, while thinking furiously and summoning a very limited store of Hausa to my aid, I pronounced judgment. 'If', said I, 'you are so foolish as to eat the meat and become ill, then take the owner to the Alkali's court in Zaria.' The Alkali was the local judge. 'If you eat, and have no ill effects, then there is nothing to worry about.' This portentous display of wisdom appeared to satisfy the crowd. No one died. There was no court case. The number of patients increased.

Those were the days, there is no doubt about it. For myself, apart from the fun I was having, there was the satisfaction of knowing I was doing something useful. But I also know that getting out of the compound was a real 'escape' from what was becoming a claustrophobic atmosphere, in which I felt more and more that all my hopes were doomed to frustration. Guy had gone home on leave and I was very dispirited and lonely. Also, though I did not realise it, I was starving myself. Out of my annual salary of a hundred and eighty pounds I succeeded in saving a hundred as a contribution towards our joint account when Mary and I were married. This was an act of insanity. You cannot do that sort of thing in Africa and get away with it, especially if your spirit is defeated. I had to learn this the hard way.

As recorded already, I had gone up to the Bauchi Plateau for local leave. There I did far too much walking including a day-long walk to the Sudan United Mission station at Langtang, another bit of stupidity. Shortly after getting back to Zaria I was playing hockey with the boys. Dr. Miller had taught them the game magnificently and shortly before this we had taken on a European team, captained by an Irish International, and had easily beaten them. But this particular afternoon I wasn't feeling too good. Back in my room, just before taking my bath I took my temperature and found it was 104°. Dr. Miller came over at once and got me driven over to the European hospital on the other side of the city. There the doctor took a very grim view of the situation and said that both my lungs were seriously affected and that I must go back to England at once.

I was too stunned with the suddenness of events to realise what all this involved. Someone took me down by train to Lagos. Of the steamer journey I remember nothing except that the cabin steward had to change my bedding every morning as it was saturated with perspiration. On arrival at Plymouth I remember sitting in the lounge where a very anxious-looking Mary found me. On her arm, a position much later to be happily reversed, I walked down the gangway to greet mother and then be driven to a nursing home. There a cousin of Mary's, Dr. Soltau, came to see me and tapped a vast quantity of fluid out of my left pleura to my immediate easement.

Before leaving the Nigerian part of this odyssey I must record one piece of experience which was to mean much in the coming years. In those days there were no air-mails. Sea-mails were slow. A letter from England to Zaria, and vice-versa, took a fortnight. This meant that at least a month and sometimes six weeks would pass before questions could receive answers. Yet some form of empathy was at work between Mary and me and it was quite commonplace for each of us to provide answers to questions we had not yet received. I think this was in a real sense my salvation for already, before I was taken ill, I had lost my dreams. Considering how very short a time Mary and I had had really to get to know each other 'in love', this empathy and telepathy was wonderful. I attribute it to a quality of dynamism in Mary's personality for, as I have indicated earlier, I was a very mixed-up person, quite unprepared for a mature relationship.

The Society's physician, Dr. J. H. Cook, fixed me up to go to a sanatorium at Linford in the New Forest. Of this journey by ambulance I have no recollection, though Mary remembers it well. I think I was still in a somewhat numbed state of shock. The next nine months were not very pleasant. The good doctors at the sanatorium made frequent attempts, always unsuccessful, to get through my thickened pleura to collapse the most seriously affected lung. Their failure was fortunate because in practice the main force of the disease transferred its attention to my small joints. Lumps started to appear on both wrists, both ankles, one foot and one elbow and my right jaw. Then an eye got inflamed. Dr. Cook, an eminent ophthalmologist himself, suspected Tubercular Iritis. A consultant confirmed this. I was warned that it was possible the prognosis was inaccurate and that the eye might recover. But if the trouble was there the other eye was liable to be affected and I might lose both. Knowing it was possible to enter the Kingdom of Heaven with only one eye I opted for the operation and had the affected eye removed. I was greatly cheered when I learnt that my ambition to do Arabic studies would be unaffected because there was much less eye-strain in reading with one eye than with two. This I have proved conclusively to be true. However, it was all a bit of a shock.

Our mother's anxiety for both her sons must have been terrible, for in the spring of the year 1928 Jack had been invalided home from Uganda with T.B. For him it was the last bit of the road and on 20th January, 1929, he died at Walmer in Kent. Jack and I had had very little touch with each other after he left for Uganda, but, as I have tried to indicate earlier, he was responsible for a vital stage in my 'growing up', and was also the preceptor of many lessons still to be worked out in the future. Something of the quality of the man has been well caught in the early pages of Patricia St. John's book *Breath of Life*, the story of the Rwanda Mission of the C.M.S.

Meanwhile, during those long dull days at Linford when the temperature chart obstinately refused to convey any cheerful information, some of the tedium for Mary and me was relieved by my dictating to her my share in an interpretation of the Hausa Mission and the future of the Hausa Band to which we gave the Hausa title *Ina za ka?* — that is, 'where are you going?', or, more colloquially, 'what next?' It was not a significant contribution to literature. It was, I think, an attempt to sort things out: to see where things had gone wrong: to reaffirm God's initial guidance: to point to a possible future. Thanks to Guy Bullen, and to a steadily increasing number of recruits for the Hausa Band, an exciting future, and a constructive one, was assured. God fulfils his plans in many ways, not infrequently by removing one of his 'silly vassals' to another field of service!

Dr. Cook was obviously very worried by the lumps which were appearing at so many points on my anatomy. This, with the Iritis, convinced him that an expert in another field of medicine was called for and Sir Henry Gauvain of the Treloar Homes came to see me. In a matter of seconds he saw what was wrong. The Tubercle bacillus had gone to the bones of my small joints. He offered to take me at once at his own private nursing home at Morland Hall, Alton.

C.M.S., with its characteristic generosity to its missionaries who are taken ill, assured me that I would continue to receive my salary, made an additional grant, and this, with some of my mother's savings, encouraged us to believe we could face the next two years and be financially solvent at the end of it.

The author, aged 1½, 1906

author's father at Galby Rectory, August 1913

The author, aged 5

The author with his parents, 1914

At Cambridge

The author's brother Jack

Convalescence at Morland Hall, 1931

After the wedding, 7th May, 1932

Only much later when I was declared 'symptom free' did I discover just how desperately ill I had been. Soon after my arrival at Morland Hall, Dr. Fairbanks, a consultant from St. Thomas' Hospital, was brought by Sir Henry to see me. On his way back from examining me Dr. Fairbanks, once out of earshot, asked, 'Have you ordered the coffin? I give him six weeks!'

Sir Henry had other ideas. He had just appointed as his assistant a young woman, Dr. Forster. Apparently he told her it was to be her special assignment to pull me through. Anyway I had the rare experience of a very clever young doctor doing my dressings regularly for the best part of a year. At one time I had, if I remember right, ten abscesses open simultaneously. What with both arms and both legs in splints, dressings sometimes took up to two hours. But Dr. Forster's skill and patience were such that apart from some reduction of movement in one elbow and one wrist I emerged from this experience without the loss of any joint. Splints were uncomfortable, though one got used to them. What to me was one very great blessing for which I could not be too grateful was the fact that throughout the illness I suffered no pain.

Unknown to Dr. Fairbanks, the battle for survival was to be fought and won on another dimension also, and hereby hangs a tale.

On the first morning after I arrived at Morland Hall Sir Henry came round to see me. He was a large man with a fine big head which found itself most easily creased into smiles. He sat down at the end of my bed—I was in a chalet in the grounds—he said to me with great seriousness but with a twinkle in his eye, 'I can give you all the food you want. I can let you have all the fresh air available, and all the sunshine. But there is only one thing that will get you well and that is the sunshine inside.' Though somehow I had never doubted that full recovery would come, that was a tonic challenge. Thanks to an innumerable company of friends known and unknown, who held me in their prayers, the sunshine inside prevailed. Those prayers were greatly needed, for I was about to undergo a fairly drastic and dramatic bit of treatment of which Sir Henry knew nothing!

One morning early in my stay at Morland Hall I was lying in my bed, outside the chalet, at peace with the world. One of the patients, George Lyward, came to visit me. After we had introduced ourselves he asked me what I had been doing before being taken ill. I told him that I had been a missionary in Nigeria. 'What made you want to be a missionary?' That kind of question always flummoxes me. There is no simple answer. One cannot embark on a life-story. So normally I make a more or less stupid answer. In this case I said something lame about 'a sense of adventure'. It was a ridiculous answer, yet one of the best things I ever said, for back came the question, 'Do you know the derivation of the word "adventure", the two Latin words *ad* and *venio*, "to come up against".' I confessed to having enough Latin for that. Then came the devastating remark, 'I wonder if you have ever really come up against anything.' Put thus baldly it does not sound much of a remark, though a bit startling after less than five minutes acquaintance. But the conversation was so unexpected, the challenge so sharp, that I was silenced. He talked on for a few minutes and then left me with my 'moment of truth'. How true could Browning be?

> Just when we are safest, there's a sunset touch,
> A fancy from a flower-bell, some one's death,
> A chorus-ending from Euripides,-
> And that's enough for fifty hopes and fears, . . .
> The grand Perhaps!

It was certainly something of a sunset touch, something of a dying within myself that happened that morning, for as by a flash of lightning I had seen something of my inner self exposed. God works in strange ways. That odd, almost inconsequential conversation, as it may have seemed to that stranger, compelled me to begin asking myself some real questions about myself.

Next day George Lyward came back. I told him I thought he had put his finger on the spot and would he please continue probing. Satisfied that I meant it, he began. For week after week (during the period the consultant had cheerfully prognosticated as perhaps six weeks of life!) George proceeded to strip me down to essentials. He had taken some training in psycho-analysis and I had no shadow of doubt that he knew what he was doing with me, and that he had been sent to do something no one else could do.

There were often times when I wondered if there were any more essentials left to be discovered. What was devastating was that everything that came up from 'the depths' was clearly seen to be what the Bible, without mincing matters, calls 'filthy rags'. All my past, all my relationships were under scrutiny. If I was to go through with this dimension of healing then no holds could be barred.

One unforgettable morning he told me that my real trouble was that while I was my age intellectually, emotionally I was at most eight years old. 'That gap has to be bridged,' he said. 'How do I do that?' I asked, and, 'How long will it take?' I had now committed myself to him for healing at another level, the one Sir Henry hinted at with his words 'sunshine inside'. Curiously I remained quite detached from the physical healing that was also in progress. For me it was obvious that the physical healing by itself would be fruitless, unless the other was accomplished as well.

To my query about bridging the gap George replied, 'Oh, it needn't take very long if you are really prepared to be completely honest with yourself, and will trust me.' How difficult and painful it is to be completely honest with myself I was to discover—indeed the discovery has had to be life-long—but already I had learnt enough to know that this was the most important encounter of my life—that I was really face to face with God for the first time. George Lyward was God's instrument—the man in the gap—but the real business had to be done between myself and God. And at one stage, as I went down into the abyss, I lost God altogether. Early on in the 'analysis' to which I was submitting myself I had come to face the fact that for too long I had been living on a 'second-hand' religious experience, something sheltered because inherited. In saying this I am in no way repudiating my religious heritage. To deny one's earlier 'intimations of immortality' is a form of blasphemy. As the earlier pages of this narrative will have made abundantly clear I was already, in a multitude of ways, a debtor to the grace of God through family and teachers and friends. But I could not build on this heritage because I was sheltering behind it.

What my Father had meant by way of inspiration, the window-opening friendship of Pat O'Regan, the leadership of my brother Jack, the sharing in a vision with Guy Bullen, Mother's patient devotion, Mary's persevering love at this time of the apparent failure of all our hopes—all this was real, splendidly real. Nevertheless I knew that I had never been confronted with the totality of the divine demand upon myself. I had never yet 'come up against God'. And that 'adventure' is terrifying. 'How awe-ful is this place'.

I can remember vividly a night some little while later when, in my despair with myself, I thought I was going mad. The phrase from Francis Thompson's *The Hound of Heaven*, a poem greatly beloved by Guy Bullen, haunted me—'the labyrinthine paths of mine own mind'. I could not hear the relentless footsteps 'hurrying after'. All that I seemed conscious of was the labyrinth. The further I wandered the murkier it became, and it appeared to be spiralling downwards. I suppose I did fall asleep at the last. But I was a rag next morning. How this did not become apparent to doctor and nurse I do not know. It was just as well it didn't. Had my para-medical treatment been discovered I suspect that George Lyward would have been packed off by the next train!

When he came round later that morning I told him that I had been in hell, that there seemed to be no bottom to the well I was descending.

'Oh, yes there is,' he said. 'Do you know what you'll find at the bottom?' Wearily I replied 'No, what?' 'You will discover God and his name is Love.'

That reads very prosaically. But to a very sick man, physically, mentally and spiritually sick, to hear that said by the one to whom I had committed myself body and soul, it was a revelation of hope. From that moment I never looked back. Very gently, partly through the therapy of dream interpretation, George drew me up out of the abyss. He taught me then the priceless lesson that having seen myself as I really was I must learn to love that self precisely because it was that self that God loved. There is a whole Gospel in that lesson. That is how I found my way slowly back to Galatians 2:20, or to put it more truly, how the Christ of St. Paul, of my Father, of Pat O'Regan, of Guy Bullen, of Mother and Mary, and of how many other friends, became truly mine.

Was this a conversion experience? In the commonly used sense of the word the answer must surely be 'no'. It was rather a personal encounter of a kind which meant that someone I had always known had revealed himself to me as being of necessity 'the Great Unknown' and *only then* to be for ever afterwards in a quite indefinable way 'well-known'.

George Lyward left soon after. I was not to see him again until forty-two years later, when at my invitation he came, still a layman, to preach a notable sermon in Westminster Abbey. So thoroughly had he done his work that he passed right out of my life and my ken, and yet was always present in the lessons he had taught which, in my turn, I was to be able in some measure to pass on. It was an incredible experience this unknown Man of God coming to me at precisely the moment of my deepest need, a need so deep that I was wholly unconscious of it.

George Lyward was to devote his life to a great enterprise of picking up the broken pieces of innumerable lives of young delinquents. Finchden Manor in Kent became his centre of work, and something of what he has tried to do is well described in *Mr. Lyward's Answer* by Michael Burn.*

George Lyward died on 23rd June, 1973. *The Times* carried a fine tribute to his work at Finchden Manor in its issue of 28th June. The tribute ended with a reference to his having been invited to preach in Westminster Abbey. Having my own grounds for gratitude I at once wrote to *The Times* hoping that a further brief note might be added. But space did not permit. In that note I wrote as follows:

*Published by Hamish Hamilton, 1956.

As the Canon of Westminster who invited George Lyward to preach in the Abbey in 1971 I hope I may add a brief note to Mr. Dunhill's moving tribute in *The Times* for 28th June. In 1929 I was lucky enough not to be a delinquent or particularly disturbed, but I needed George Lyward's help nonetheless. At the time I was physically very ill indeed, having just returned from Nigeria with T.B. George Lyward was for a short time a fellow-patient with me in a nursing home. With penetrating insight he quickly discerned that I was profoundly sick in mind and spirit. He set to work to put things right. It was a purging process, but like the Finchden boy 'he brought me up against barriers and helped me over them—or not so much helped me as helped me to help myself over them.' He gave me an entirely new idea of the love of God, in the strength of which I have lived ever since.

I wish that brief notice could have appeared in *The Times*. I insert it here as a summary of all I have written of George Lyward's personal ministry to me.

So 1929 passed into 1930. It was not an easy year, as may be imagined, but for Mary it was a desperately difficult one. I couldn't explain to her what was happening to me. It was one of those rare experiences when one had to 'wrestle with the angel' by oneself. Often Mary would come down from London and sit by my bed and hardly get a word out of me. These were bitter months for her, made bearable by having a job to do. Elsie Thorpe, holding a unique but indefinable office in C.M.S., decided that Mary should go on the staff of Kennaway Hall, one of the C.M.S. training colleges for women missionaries. This gave Mary something creative to do and helped her over the hurdles of her concern for me. But there were not lacking people who cared for her who urged her to break her engagement. This she refused to consider. To my shame I confess that the thought of releasing her never entered my selfish head. She was my sheet-anchor even when she did not know it.

At last came the day when Sir Henry came to tell me that I was well, that, as the medical profession cautiously puts it, I was 'symptom free'. Once again he was sitting on my bed. 'I have got a very hard thing to suggest to you,' he said. 'You are now well and could go home tomorrow. But your ankle-joints will not be safe to support you for a long time yet. If you are prepared to stay in bed for another year I think I can almost guarantee that you will have no recurrence of this trouble.'

This was quite a poser, financially and otherwise, but we saw the sense of it. Sir Henry was something of a wizard. I remember him telling me one day that this particular form of T.B., 'Bovine' T.B. from infected milk, was on the way out. Many years later, in a London teaching hospital, a specialist brought his class to stand round my bed. He pointed to my jaw, my ankles and wrists, and asked them to guess the origin of the scars. No one got anywhere near the right answer. He then told them, and added, 'Take a good look at them. You are unlikely ever to see anything of the kind again.' I was a very fortunate mortal to have found myself entrusted to Sir Henry Gauvain.

The year 1930–1931 was a very different experience from the year before. Now Mary and I could not only hope but plan. I was due out, all going well, in July 1931. Obviously adjustment to the outside world would take some time—and it proved a much slower business than I expected. However, we decided to aim for May 1932 for our wedding, although at the moment nothing else about the future was clear.

When in years to come the subject has come up in conversation that I once spent three years in bed, the normal reaction is an expression of horror and sympathy. I have always gone on to insist that it was one of the most worthwhile experiences of my life. The fundamental ground of that affirmation I have fully declared. But there was another reason for gratitude. These years had given me an opportunity for almost uninterrupted reading. Hitherto I had been a specialist in history, and a student of books about Nigeria. Now I was able to range widely, to read Tolstoy and Sinclair Lewis; Keyserling's *Travel Diary of a Philosopher* and Tamar Karsavina's *Theatre Street*; Theodore Dreiser and Sheila Kaye-Smith; Arnold Bennett and H. G. Wells; Knut Hamsun and Sigrid Undset's unforgettable *Kristin Lavransdatter* — these in their related unrelatedness were part of the feast I enjoyed. In an old exercise book I listed the volumes read that year. I dated the reading, and recorded what they meant to me. There were fifty-four of them, a very liberal education, with no examinations to cast a shadow over the future!

During two-thirds of my time at Morland Hall I shared a double chalet with a young Jew, Solly Olins. He was a spine case and found life as tough going as I did. We became good friends and each helped the other to cheer up when things were particularly grim. How true it is that 'two are better than one . . . if one falls, the other can help his companion up again, but alas for the man who falls alone with no partner to help him' (Eccl. 4:10, N.E.B.).

It will be obvious that I cannot speak too highly of the professional skill of doctors and nurses which brought me physical healing. But there was more to it than professional skill. The staff at Morland Hall knew that morale was nine parts of the battle. They must often have been tired, not least with the sheer effort of being cheerful in front of patients, but they never let us down. Of Nurse Guest, the one with a chief responsibility for me, this was supremely true.

5

1931 - 1936

Ordination

. . . like the light of morning at sunrise, a morning
that is cloudless after rain . . .

2 Samuel 23:4 (N.E.B.)

THESE five years were to be something of an apprenticeship. I had, at most, only served the first part of my 'Articles'. How this apprenticeship was to take shape was determined by a visitor who came to see me at Morland Hall in the spring of 1931; this was Raymond Scantlebury.

Already recorded as a special friend of the Cambridge days, Raymond was now curate of St. Mary's Church, Southampton, under Canon R. B. Jolly. He was busy building a vigorous work among the young people of the parish, but nothing in this world could make Raymond 'parochially-minded'. Already he had hatched a plan, and it was this which he had come over to discuss with me. 'What are you going to do when you get out?', he asked me. I replied that I did not know, but that we hoped to get married. Ordination was now definitely in my mind but I had no idea where, and I was in touch with no Bishop. Indeed both Mary and I were 'coasting' into the future without any clear plans at all. Raymond then sprang the question, 'Would you like to be Youth Secretary for the Diocese of Winchester?' The fact that there was no such appointment in existence was for Raymond a matter of insignificance provided he could find the man he wanted. *Toujours l'audace* was ever Raymond's principle of action. I drew his attention to a number of practical difficulties which might stand in the way, the immediate and most obvious one being that of selling the idea to the Bishop of Winchester. A minor problem of that sort didn't worry Raymond in the least. His experience was that if you had a good idea you could always sell it. But for the grace of God Raymond would have been a 'con' man at a very high-class level. Having got the assurance from me that, if the improbable happened I would accept, he went on his way.

The sequel is worth recording if only to illustrate Raymond's powers of persuasion and the very remarkable things which can happen when someone like Raymond gets his head. He took an early opportunity to convince his Rector, who was also Rural Dean of Southampton, that youth work ought to be put on a diocesan footing. The Rector agreed to get the idea put on the agenda of the next meeting of the Rural Deans with the Bishop. Some sympathy with the general idea having been expressed at the meeting, Raymond got his amenable Rector to ask the Bishop if Raymond might have an interview to explain what was in view. What Raymond said in that interview with the Bishop, Theodore Woods it was, I have no idea. But the Bishop, like all his family, was a man who kindled to enthusiasm. He accepted the idea in principle but said that the man must be attached to a parish.

In no whit disturbed by this wholly reasonable demand, or even recognising it as a problem, Raymond drove over to Boscombe to see the Vicar of St. John's Church, the Rev. G. Foster Carter, a man who kindled to enthusiasm as generously as did Bishop Woods. The only difficulty was that the parish could not afford two curates. Again, I never discovered what arguments were used but it was agreed that, provided it was clearly understood that the parish would not have to find a full stipend, then a place would be found on the staff of St. John's for a part-time curate who would be the new Youth Secretary. Raymond was nothing if not practical. Realising that Mary and I wanted to get married and would need something to live on, he thereupon called on a prominent Bournemouth business man, Mr. R. Bevington, and persuaded him to make up the balance of what was then reckoned to be a curate's living wage.

The really subtle point of this saga is that the Bishop accepted me for ordination and for this appointment without seeing me, though he must have been aware that I had passed the necessary examinations. The Vicar accepted me on his staff without seeing me. The business man agreed to his part of the bargain without seeing me. Such was the persuasive power of Raymond Scantlebury! I think this whole remarkable episode has something of the unique about it.

In due course I received a most gracious letter from Bishop Woods offering me the appointment and telling me when to present myself for ordination. Perhaps such startling procedures explain why later C.A.C.T.M.* had to be invented and some degree of restraint imposed upon the episcopate.

The whole astonishing business had one immediate by-product. Mary and I having, in this wholly unexpected manner, found our immediate future provisionally settled and marriage now something we could actively plan for, vowed to each other that whatever the future might hold we would never take any steps whatever to seek some new position for ourselves. Whatever might be offered must come 'out of the blue'. To this vow we have remained faithful ever since. Indeed, in the next two appointments that were to come our way, nobody, not even our closest friends, knew that we had come to the point of feeling that if an invitation did come we would at least take it seriously. All through our life together this decision has lifted an enormous weight off our spirits.

Ambition is a curious thing. It has, I suppose, inspired many of the greatest human achievements. It has also ruined countless lives. I am thinking of ambition about promotion and preferment. I claim no merit whatever in having been free of this particular kind of ambition.

*The Church's Advisory Council for Training for the Ministry.

Indeed I have sometimes had an uneasy feeling that, far from being noble, it was a form of cowardice. But nobility simply does not come into the question. The enormous sense of freedom in being certain that the future is out of one's own hands secures at least a touch of the peace that passes understanding. There are many of my friends who would give the same testimony.

This chapter covers the five years from 1931 to 1936 which I described at the start as being in the nature of an apprenticeship. That is a fair description, though it was to prove a multiple apprenticeship—to marriage; to the ordained ministry; to beginning the exploration of that remarkably pluralistic society, the Anglican Communion; and to a new kind of missionary vocation very different from the one we had planned for ourselves.

For the moment, however, I must retrace my steps. Until July of that year, 1931, I was still at Morland Hall, though by now sitting up out of bed quite a lot and greatly enjoying the company of a new fellow-patient, Lakdasa de Mel, someday to be Metropolitan of India and a life-long friend.

The days of duress were shortening fast. One of them stands out unforgettably because of a strange experience. One beautiful sunny afternoon in May or early June I was lying quite relaxed on my bed gazing out at the sun-dappled trees which bordered the grounds. I had nothing on my mind. Then quite suddenly I was in an enormously large room. At the far end of it was a table and lying on the table a huge sword, the kind which would call for two hands to wield it. I moved down the room till I reached the table and there I tried to lift the sword. A voice, as though at my side, said to me, 'Little heart, you cannot lift that sword. Only Great-heart can lift it.' Immediately I found myself looking at the sun-dappled trees. Whatever had happened could only have taken a few seconds. I certainly had not been asleep. Of all my friends I am, I suppose, the least susceptible to anything which might be called mystical. I am painfully prosaic. But that experience was as real and as vivid as anything I have known in my life. What did it signify? I knew at once what that voice wanted me to understand. I had not been through deep analysis without discovering quite a lot about myself. Here I was about to launch out to a new life, a life of genuine 'ad-venture' with God and for God. Yet I was already getting myself out of focus. I was beginning to think I had learnt my lessons and was now ready for anything. The voice jerked me back to reality.

The next ten months of adjusting myself to living with ordinary people again in ordinary circumstances, and doing quite ordinary things, proved to be one of the most difficult ten months of my life.

In some ways I think they may have been the most difficult for Mary. Certainly she carried me through them while I was painfully discovering how little capable I was of lifting a rapier, let alone a huge sword. But that ten months ensured that I did not enter upon matrimony or the ministry 'unadvisedly, lightly or wantonly'. I hope and think there was even something of humility as I went forward into my apprenticeship. The four-fold apprenticeship which I have defined may serve as a pattern of the four years at St. John's, Boscombe, in the diocese of Winchester.

First came marriage.

Prophetic in more ways than one were two messages of unknown origin which appeared on successive days in the personal column of the *Morning Post*. The first read:

MARY—May manage money marry me—MAX

Next morning came the reply:

MAX—with or without money—MARY

Presumably this was someone's crytogram. Entertaining and intriguing as it was, it was superbly appropriate. There was never much risk of Mary having much money to manage, but whatever has come in subsequently she has managed it, and done so infinitely better than I could have done. Had we lived perhaps nineteen hundred years earlier we would have accepted the messages as a propitious omen. As it was we just hoped that whoever that Mary and Max might be they would be as happy as we were going to be.

Our wedding took place on 7th May, 1932, at St. John's Church, Tunbridge Wells, where Mary's uncle, her mother's brother, the Rev. Thomas Bewes, was Vicar, though most unfortunately he was ill at the time and unable to take part. The church was filled with a congregation that was rejoicing with us both, many of them having prayed with and for us all those long five years. Mary was given away by her Uncle Willie, Mr. W. G. Collett, her father's brother. Mary set the tone of the occasion as she came up the aisle on her uncle's arm, leading the congregation in singing 'Praise my soul the King of Heaven' —no nonsense here of a shy retiring bride solemnly veiled! We had one special prayer for that service framed round the words we had made our own five years before (quoted on page 45). Here we were publicly plighting a troth already pledged and proved.

Handley Hooper, Africa Secretary of C.M.S., married us. Raymond Scantlebury read the lesson, 1 Corinthians 13 in Dr. Way's translation; Gordon Guinness, soon to marry Mary's first cousin, Grace Bewes, who was one of her bridesmaids on this occasion, took the prayers. The Rev. Barclay Buxton, the venerable Vicar of Holy Trinity

Church, inaccurately described later in the local press as 'a college friend of the Bride and Bridegroom', gave the blessing. Mary's sister Evy was the chief bridesmaid. The two little bridesmaids were Sheelagh, Jack and Kathleen's daughter, and Jean Clark, daughter of a Cambridge friend of Mary's. My best man was Walter Stables, a friend from 1920 when we first became near neighbours in Norwood. He was also a link with Jack, being of the same war-scarred generation. The chief usher was Falkner Allison, later to become Bishop of Chelmsford and then of Winchester, where I'm sure he was never so rash as was one of his predecessors in that see.

After the inevitable ordeal of the reception, Handley Hooper drove Mary and me all the way to Paddington, the kind of gracious, thoughtful, action that was characteristic of him. We spent our honeymoon at Avebury, from where we made two excursions, one to Marlborough to show Mary the school and introduce her to Mrs. O'Regan, Mrs. 'Pat' to us, then and always; and one to Stratford-on-Avon to see *A Midsummer-Night's Dream*. We had nine days of honeymoon and then to our first home in Boscombe.

The first apprenticeship was to marriage.

It may have anticipated the beginning of the second apprenticeship by a fortnight, if one goes by the calendar, but in fact it had begun five years before. We had proved that 'Love's not Time's fool' and could recite the rest of the sonnet without apology. But now we had to test it out in the light of common day, to discover each other as man, as woman, to explore the meaning of a partnership in which physical and mental and spiritual made for wholeness. And it did not happen in a minute or smoothly. I suspect that in every happy marriage the process and the progress have a key word, the word patience, called for in different fashions by both partners. So we found it, enjoyed the finding and are continuing to enjoy it. To be exasperated in love, 'exasperated', yes, and yet 'in love' —that is the secret alchemy in marriage which transmutes all its baser metals into gold. Needless to say, we didn't discover all this in the first fortnight, but our feet were on the road.

Of course it helped enormously that we had come to marriage through the kind of testing in which two minds, however differently patterned, had discovered a unity so deep that differences could be made the ministers of a deeper unity still, a theological reality which applies to other unities than marriage.

From the start we were clear that ours was going to be a partnership in which each was always indispensable to the other, indispensable not in an emotional sense but in hard practicality. All our decisions, and we have had many to make, some of far-reaching importance, have been made together. The question of 'who decides?' has never arisen in our experience. Sometimes one has been the leader, sometimes the other, but always it has been a case of which, while holding hands, started running first. Spheres of operations have obviously been recognised, but no sphere has had a 'no entry' sign for the other partner. Kitchen and study have both been shared under the sign '*sursum corda*'.

Believing as we did that this first apprenticeship was a preparation for the second, we shared a further theological conviction — the parity of ministries. This is the real meaning of the priesthood of all believers, that cardinal doctrine of truly evangelical practice. In that most vital of all priestly acts, the bringing of the assurance of the grace of God into some troubled mind and heart, we have both been used, Mary as extensively and variously as any one I have known.

Again from the very start we knew that our home was to be 'open house'. So it has been down the years. Our 'visitors' books' are fascinating reading but only record those who have actually shared board and lodging. Those who have just taken pot luck are legion. It has been huge fun, made possible, I admit, only because Mary has always been blessedly strong. This alone has made possible her phenomenal achievements as a hostess. But being hostess to countless young people in Boscombe, to hundreds of undergraduates in Cambridge, to young married couples in Blackheath, to the tidal waves of visitors in Westminster, and bringing up children and being an unfailing partner in ministry, supervising almost every sermon I preached, all this called for wider gifts than presiding with distinction over a teapot. It called for organising skill, adaptability, and the philosophy of 'have-to does it', which makes the really great administrator, or, as I would prefer to call it, being a Martha without ever losing the touch of Mary.

Let that testimony stand. It need not be repeated provided it is borne in mind in all that follows that that has been the setting of our everyday life for more than forty years.

Two years after our wedding Rosemary was born, bringing with herself a wonderful piece of fresh self-discovery of ourselves also, not as two but as three. Here, surely, is part of the magic of childhood. Here is a new self which is indisputably its own self, and yet is part of yourself too, to be loved for itself, but also loved as giving back to you something of yourself. All this shared by the original two is one of the experiences by which we look into heaven. We found it so. And Rosemary has gone on meaning this to us all her life, and in her turn discovered the same miracle. Two years later, in 1936, Pat came along to make a foursome, adding her own distinctive magic to the wonder of life, and in her turn also entering into the mystery.

All this is not a romantic view of marriage. It is reality, and to miss it is to miss the many-splendoured thing. In writing this I am not forgetting for one moment the many of my much-loved friends, men and women, who have remained single —I will not say unmarried for that is a wholly negative view of what a dedicated single life can be. These men and women and others who, being married, have not enjoyed the gift and heritage of children, have been 'fathers and mothers in Israel', giving an enrichment to the lives of all they touch, 'very members incorporate' in Christ's family, for whom he in his blessed humanity must have a very special love and understanding.

Here perhaps is the place to record both a conviction and an experience. To love one woman supremely and without reserve is to be free to enjoy the friendship and affection of other women, young and old. And the same, it stands to reason, goes for the other partner similarly committed. This is one of the mountain-top experiences of Christian marriage. Of course, sex is involved, but it is sex enjoyed in a disciplined relationship. Dangerous? Again, of course. Life lived fully is dangerous. But given the conditions I have stipulated, together with what St. Paul called the *epieikeia* of Christ, his courtesy, his respect for personality, the dangers can be transmuted. On a lighter vein, I treasure an inscription in a book given me one Christmas by my office staff at C.M.S. and signed by each of them, one of them, indeed, has typed the manuscript of this book with great devotion —

> Max is not a Muslim
> He has only one wife!
> But this comes with much love
> From five 'girls' in his life!

It is time to move on. The second apprenticeship began on Sunday, 22nd May, 1932, when with others I was made a deacon in Winchester Cathedral, Bishop Boutflower officiating, as Bishop Theodore Woods had died some months before.

A change of Bishop might well have signified a complete upset of our plans but Bishop Garbett very generously accepted the arrangement already made, though, shrewd man that he was, he took the precaution of appointing his chaplain to be joint Secretary with me for the youth work of the diocese. I have a suspicion that Bishop Garbett was not normally inclined to appoint men without a previous interview.

By way of preparation for my diaconate I was invited by the Vicar of Romsey Abbey, Canon Corban, to spend a few days of retreat in his clergy house. This had been strongly urged upon me by one

Mud house at Zaria, where the author had the top flat, 1927-8

Bayero Dan Nuhu, the house-boy
who became a Pro-Chancellor

Guy Bullen

The author and Mary dressed in centenary cloth with the elephant's tusk presented to C.M.S. on the occasion of the centenary of the Niger Mission, 1957

Mary saying thank you for the gift of a sari at a ceremony in Meerut, 21st December, 1959

of his curates, Douglas Horsley, a friend of Cambridge and of C.S.S.M. days, the son of Admiral Horsley mentioned earlier. Douglas was always a High Churchman, but a most happy ingredient in the 'pie' that had made up our house-party at the Eastbourne C.S.S.M. Later to become Bishop first of Colombo and then of Gibraltar, he took his duties of friendship seriously. Hence his anxious insistence that I should have a spell of quiet before that Trinity Sunday in the Cathedral.

The value of being quiet has never needed to be argued with me and I agreed very willingly. Those few days at Romsey were a good preparation for the days ahead. I was glad to share with the others the orderly routine of church services, though I cannot pretend that this routine has ever been the mainspring of my Christian experience or of much inspiration for the Christian life. What I have always valued immensely is the balance of the Book of Common Prayer and the pattern of its worship, a pattern which, as far as Matins and Evensong are concerned, includes all the elements needed for corporate as for private worship. Yet I believe this pattern yields its fruit best by adaptation. The phrase 'doing what the Church does' has never held much content for me because the Church Universal, being so infinitely varied, the phrase has little genuine meaning. Even the Church of England is not exactly monotonous in its uniformity. I can gladly follow a principle once I am gripped by its validity. I have to be satisfied with a reason before I surrender myself to a rubric.

All that said, I owe to Douglas Horsley in special measure my essential Anglicanism, a certain ethos not easily to be defined but which finds expression in the liturgical expression 'decent order and godly discipline'.

My first Vicar was George Foster Carter, and this was a great privilege. He was one of the hardest-working parish priests I have met, yet infinitely considerate to his curates, and treating that greenest of green things, a newly fledged deacon, with most gracious courtesy. He was the most assiduous house-visiting parson imaginable. He never seemed to be off his bike and was out in all weathers. Sensitive and gentle, he had a genius with the sick. He expected his curates to visit, and to report on their visits, and also to play their part in the ministry to the local hospital.

I cannot pretend that I ever enjoyed knocking on doors. My capacity for quick contact with people is very limited indeed, and unlike Mary who can extract a stranger's life-story within minutes, I agonise trying to think of something to say. And as I never enjoyed being visited when I was ill I found it difficult to believe that the sick derived much happiness by being visited by me. In taking ward services on a Sunday afternoon I was always impressed with the high percentage of patients who slept through my exhortations or snored more loudly than was natural otherwise than as a protest! However, the Vicar gently but firmly insisted on these duties being fulfilled.

In being obedient I had two remarkable experiences. In reply to my knock one day a rather harassed-looking elderly lady opened the door. She was obviously fussed and bothered and I discovered that her son was ill. I asked if I might see him. Rather reluctantly she agreed and led the way upstairs. The man was obviously very ill indeed. I asked about the family. His wife was dead but he had a little daughter, and now his mother was looking after both of them. I just told them I knew a little about illness myself. Some instinct kept my mouth shut about any religious subject and I made no attempt to say a prayer. A few days later I called again and was rather pleased that they seemed glad to see me. It was, I think, at the third or fourth visit that the old mother asked me if I would read them something from the Bible. I had a pocket New Testament with me and, getting a nod from the man, I read a few verses, and asked if I might say a prayer. To this they eagerly agreed. I visited that house regularly and was with him not long before he died. I think my very halting ministry helped him and his mother. I remember so clearly one day his saying to me, 'Do you remember that day you first called? You know if you had started any parson's talk, or said a prayer, you would never have been allowed in this house again.' That was a lesson I never forgot. In my own pastoral experience with people of every kind I have found that, if one is ready to take the opening when it is given, the things of the Spirit come naturally. The real mistake is to imagine one is responsible for making the opening. For myself, at any rate, I have proved that I am far too gauche to be trusted with the initiative. All too often when I have taken it I have been wrong. In the pastoral ministry I am convinced that the beginning and the middle and the end is 'listening'. It is 'with listening ear thy servant stands'. The call to speak may come early or late. What matters is to be to the great service 'dedicate'.

The second unforgettable experience came when I walked into a small men's outfitters shop. I introduced myself to the young man behind the counter. I found he lived above the shop and he asked me to come into their living room and meet his wife. We began a friendship which was sealed about eighteen months later when during an evangelistic campaign both of them entered into a decisive Christian experience by which their lives were dramatically revolutionised. It was only a matter of time before their sitting room behind the shop was filled with young people who, consciously or unconsciously, were seeking what they had found. Bill White and Gladys his wife were and are a remarkable pair. He had two apparently irreconcilable hobbies, a passion for Bach *and* for hot jazz. In his own inimitable way Bill brought the two into the service of the Gospel. One evening a week came the young who liked Bach or were learning to like him. On another evening the room was filled with hot jazz enthusiasts. Each session ended with tea and biscuits, and somehow or other Bill and Gladys were found quite naturally talking about Jesus Christ and being listened to.

These were two experiences which would never have come my way if the Vicar had not insisted on my doing systematic visiting, and reporting back to him at Staff Meetings what I had done. The home with death in it and the home with new life in it are no bad epitome of the ministry of a parish priest. It was no small thing to discover this early on in my apprenticeship.

In the Winchester diocese junior clergy had to send in a written sermon once a month to one of the senior clergy in the diocese. I have always been grateful to the man who took great pains to help me. One lesson he taught me was that I should always write out my sermons in full, and preach from the full text. He was quite prepared for me to 'ad lib' at this point or that; he was quite ready for me to know my material so well that I need hardly glance at it; but have the whole text with you in the pulpit, he insisted. I am sure he was right. Among other advantages it meant that there was some chance of the grammar being correct. Again, it prevented those irritating hesitations punctuated by the 'ers' and other monstrosities which can so easily deform a sermon. What is more, the discipline of careful preparation equipped one to meet those occasions, and they have been many, when one has had to speak extempore with virtually no notice. If one has learnt to think on paper one can think on one's feet. In the process I learnt that the rules of spoken English, allowing for modulations of voice and purposeful pauses, are the same as for written English. There are those spell-binders, men like William Temple, Charles Raven, Donald Soper and Studdert Kennedy, artists of the spoken word, who can speak from notes or, as I have frequently seen, speak without them. More earthen clay demand 'five finger exercises' till concert days are done.

But besides being taught the art of sermon construction there was the equally important matter of delivery. Here my tutor was my Vicar who showed me that in preaching there are varying levels of intensity appropriate to different occasions. I was a very impatient young man, perhaps in part because I was in a hurry to make up for lost time. Very easily I overstepped the limits of what a young man can properly say to a congregation which our organist, usually with a grimace, described as 'autumnal'! After one of my more exuberant outbursts the Vicar said to me quietly in the vestry, when no one else was present—'Max, thank you for your sermon, but if I may dare to suggest it try a little more *suaviter in modo* and a little less *fortiter in re.*' That gentle, kindly, witty and well-deserved rebuke has lived with me ever since. I have not always observed it, but I have never forgotten it.

Besides my own beloved Vicar there were two other parish priests, among not a few, who won my especial devotion. One was A. W. Hopkinson, Vicar of St. Augustine's, Bournemouth. Very deaf and altogether radiant, the author of two books, *Be Merry* and *Confessions of an Optimist*, he was a superb blend of Christianity and common sense shining through Tractarian windows. His never-failing welcome whenever I called, his interest in all I was doing and thinking, is one of the happiest memories of my apprenticeship in the ministry. He, like my own Vicar, was a holy man. From them I learnt thus early that holiness is not only the most interesting, but also the most exciting and stimulating quality one can ever encounter.

The second parish priest who meant much to me had charge of a small parish in the New Forest. R. H. W. Roberts, later to become a canon of Truro and Director of Education for the diocese, gave me most generously of his friendship. Keenly interested in the Industrial Christian Fellowship, he made as certain as he could that I should come to an understanding of the social, economic and political context within which the Gospel had to be interpreted.

I was marvellously fortunate in these parish priests who, with my Vicar, had with all their great experience retained the buoyancy of hope, a hope which could look the devil in the face and not for one moment believe that he was other than defeated. The devil has not stopped going about roaring during the last forty years, but the noise he makes is the noise of frustration in the face of certain defeat. That conviction I learnt from these men who were in the great succession of the undefeated.

In looking back on this apprenticeship I cannot forget what I learnt from Bishop Garbett—three priceless lessons of which he was the living exponent, not so much by what he said as by what he was and what he did.

First, I think of him as a master in the art of working out a meticulous programme of living, disciplined yet flexible. Charles Smyth's superb biography* amply documents this characteristic. To a stranger this could be somewhat intimidating, and very much so to anyone tempted to waste his time. One soon learnt that he expected from those who

*Charles Smyth, *Cyril Forster Garbett — Archbishop of York* (Hodder and Stoughton, 1959).

served him the same kind of discipline he imposed upon himself. This could be very unnerving but also very bracing.

Then there was his superb sense of justice—his fair-mindedness. I remember very vividly a case where a man had been delated to him on a false charge. As Bishop he had to take the matter seriously. *Prima facie* evidence was strongly against the man. As it happened I knew the man well, knew the situation and was convinced that he had been 'framed'. I presented this case to Bishop Garbett and convinced him of its probability. He had, of course, to take some immediate appropriate action. This he did. But within a year he had offered the man another chance, demonstrating his trust in him. This was great-ness. Having decided that a man was innocent, he decided to treat him as innocent. This does not always happen in society generally, nor even in the Church.

Finally there was the confidence which he put in anyone when he was satisfied of their competence. I had ample proof that he trusted me as one of his junior clergy. Later I was to get more dramatic proof. When he was Archbishop of York and I was at C.M.S. he would sometimes, at very short notice, ask me to brief him on a subject dealing with foreign affairs upon which he intended to intervene in a debate in the House of Lords. On these occasions he accepted my briefing without question, accepting all the risks involved. Perhaps it is not surprising that for these three reasons alone, and there were others, he was for me the chief among those who know.

My third apprenticeship was into the polychromatic society of the Church of England as represented in the Rural Deanery of Bourne-mouth. The entire spectrum of churchmanship, as known in the Church of England, was there represented in wild but exciting profusion. There was a church in which I was invited to preach in which as far as I could see and hear a large part of the service of Holy Communion was not only inaudible but, where audible, was in Latin. This could be balanced by another church where the liturgy of 1662 was presented plain, and unadorned by any adventitious aids whatever. Instead of leaving everything to the imagination nothing was left to the imagina-tion. And, of course, between these two extremes there were any number of variations. It was into this liturgically pluralistic society that I was plunged as one of the diocesan Secretaries for Youth. It proved a marvellous preparation for future visits to almost all of the Provinces of the Anglican Communion.

In our division of labour as Youth Secretaries, the Bishop's Chaplain, A. S. Reeve, later to be Bishop of Lichfield, and a good friend always, took the north of the diocese and I was responsible for the programme

everywhere south of Winchester. So I had an official excuse for
exploring all the liturgical byways of Bournemouth, Southampton,
and the countryside. My first duty was to make my number with the
Vicars. Both in Bournemouth and elsewhere the reception was inevitably mixed. What credentials, after all, did I possess? *L'audace et
toujours l'audace* being Raymond Scantlebury's motto, I adopted it
as my own. Sometimes, I am sure, stunned by my effrontery, yet
remaining unfailingly courteous, the Vicars to whom I presented
myself were astonishingly kind, even if in many cases cautiously non-
committal. Most were prepared to watch and see if 'this thing were
of God'. But I met my Waterloo in one small country town. Invited
in by the Vicar, he sat me down in a chair and asked me to explain
what I imagined the Youth Movement was going to do. At that stage
I had only a very hazy idea myself, but I outlined a possible programme.
He received this with the encouraging comment, 'My dear boy, all
these things were tried more than forty years ago and they have all
failed!' Not surprisingly that proved to be a parish from which no
support was ever forthcoming. But this was an isolated experience.
What was obvious was that we had to prove ourselves in one way or
another. At that moment in history a diocesan-sponsored Youth
Movement was a novelty, otherwise than in the form of the traditional
uniformed organisations. We had to work our passage. The break-
through came unexpectedly.

  Early in 1933 I was asked to discover if an evangelistic campaign
directed towards young people would be welcomed by the clergy of
Bournemouth, the missioners being undergraduates from Oxford
and Cambridge, assisted by a number of older men, and under the
general leadership of the Rev. Bryan Green from Oxford. Having
by this time visited all the Vicars, I was given a friendly hearing by
the Chapter. On my being able to assure them that among the older
men were two Mirfield Fathers, and that the campaign would be an
Anglican one based on the parish churches, a general blessing was
given to the enterprise. Only one parish contracted out of the
campaign.

  As for the Bournemouth end of the planning, the detailed organisation, publicity, hospitality and the arranging of times and places for
the meeting, the responsibility was mine, fortunately shared by Mary
who undertook the immensely complex task of finding hospitality
for a total party of 120 men and women, only one of whom, Bryan
Green, did we know. Persuading people to give hospitality for ten
days to total strangers called for diplomacy of a high order. But
Mary's capacity for wheedling the unwanted out of the unlikely was
already a highly developed skill, and all was successfully arranged.

Equally delicate a task, though much less demanding in time, was allocating the senior missioners to parishes where they would be welcomed and be assured of co-operation. At this kind of diplomacy I was a tyro. Many years later I was to be given the exciting assignment of collecting a team of Christians of many different allegiances, all resident in the Middle East, to collaborate in describing Christianity in that region. That the project proved a success and that I made no enemies but only friends, I attribute to some of the lessons in tact, discretion, and the capacity to skate very rapidly over thin ice, which I learnt in preparing for the Bournemouth campaign! For it was, indeed, a liberal education in overcoming initial suspicions and doubts, 'jollying along' parish priests far older than myself, who had no initial grounds for trusting me on so important a matter, while entering into the very proper anxieties of men of very varied schools of churchman-ship, and with perhaps even more varied views of the form an evangel-istic campaign should take.

This is not the place to tell the story of what happened. Suffice it here to say that the whole experience for Mary and myself gave us an almost overwhelming sense of the genuine underlying unity of the Church of England, and of the remarkable loyalty and generosity of spirit which can co-exist with great theological differences. There are those who affect to despise the comprehensiveness of the Church of England, who dismiss it as based upon nothing more than theological confusion and an inability to argue from first principles. I am not so sure. Britain today is a far more mixed society than it was when Cranmer successfully introduced a Book of Common Prayer, Richard *Anglicanism* Hooker described a form of Ecclesiastical Polity suitable for our nation, and Launcelot Andrewes gave a fresh impetus to the activity of private prayer. Yet upon that three-fold basis a spiritual fellowship was created which has stood the test of time and which, I firmly believe, offers, in the much more complex Britain of today, a vital contribution, shared of course with others, towards the creation of a Christian society which is, at once, ordered and free.

The fourth apprenticeship of these years was to a new way of fulfilling our missionary commitment from which we were both equally convinced that God did not intend to release us. Africa in particular, and the rest of the world in general, was always on the horizon. Where we could not go ourselves others might go if the idea was once suggested to them. And some did. But one of the lessons which we absorbed from R. H. W. Roberts was that 'Mission' is not *mission* primarily a geographical expression at all. It signifies God sending his Son to share our human condition. Nowhere where man is found is outside the range of Mission. When, later, we were together to be once again preoccupied with the world outside these islands, it was to prove invaluable that we had learnt this lesson. Without it there could have been no true perspective. What could we seek, what dare we seek, for the men and women of Africa and Asia if we were not as deeply concerned to seek the same things for the men and women of Britain? Thanks to Roland Roberts we were set free to learn all we could from the young men and women who were caught up with us into the Youth Movement.

Our *modus operandi* in the Youth Movement was based on a few simplicities. We aimed to establish 'cells' for Bible Study and Prayer in parishes where the clergy were sympathetic and where a nucleus of young people existed. We held 'Youth Weekends' in various deaneries, or in a convenient centre to which speakers of distinction would be invited. Some of these 'weekends' would bring together sixty or seventy or even more of men and girls in the age group sixteen to thirty. The whole purpose of the 'cells' and the 'weekends' was to train for Mission, that is for reaching those outside the Church, and in the process to train lay leadership. Then, in addition, each summer we ran a Youth Camp, sometimes in Dorset and sometimes in North Wales. The organiser and inspiring genius for these camps was Raymond Scantlebury who acted as Commandant. They brought together a hundred or more young people for a fortnight. They were hilarious times of real holiday-making, while at the end of the day one or other of us, or some visitor like Brother Douglas, or Prebendary Cash, would lift the eyes of the company to the wider world, and to the Life of the Spirit. It was all very informal, but for many it was an introduction to a degree of commitment, and to an idea of the Christian life, which came as a thrilling surprise—that and nothing less.

Experience taught us one lesson very quickly. If you want people to 'grow' in their thinking, in their grasp of the Faith, in their ability to lead, then the more the parson keeps his mouth shut in gatherings of young people, such as we were exploring, the better. There is no quicker way of learning about people, and people learning about themselves, than letting them do the talking. This will not happen if the parson fancies that he has to be giving tongue all the time. Nor ought he to imagine that only he can draw wisdom out of the Bible. There are insights which the youngest disciple can offer, and that offering will often mean far more to the individual, and to others in the group, than the words of the 'professional'. Apart from what the 'professional' himself is learning, among other things the art of listening, there is the great increase of fellowship, of corporateness, when everyone is contributing. We learnt these lessons quickly in the Youth Movement.

That great parish priest, Peter Green of Salford, once said that he never felt sure that he had really got anywhere with a young fellow or girl 'until he had got them down on their knees to pray to Christ and up on their feet to speak for him'. Coming from the tradition from which we did we said 'Amen' to that. At first to join in an open prayer-meeting is for some people very difficult. We encouraged the hesitant to write out their prayers and read them. Many began like this. To be able to pray extempore, to talk naturally and spontaneously to God, by oneself or with others, contains a great many volumes of divinity. You are at the very least equipped to deal with some of life's emergencies and its spiritual opportunities.

Naturally our deepest experiences were with the Youth Fellowship in our own parish. Ten years after we left we went back for a reunion, the meetings being chaired by the young man in the men's outfitters shop whom we met earlier. Thirty-five young people were present, many of course new to us, many still well known, and not a few of the original company abroad in India, in Fiji, in Kenya, in the Mediterranean and in Jamaica, some in government service, some as missionaries, one just about to join the U.N. Secretariat. It was a bracing experience to see what one 'cell' could produce.

A question remains. Was this very flexible and essentially unregimented approach to the younger generation a success? What are the criteria of success in the affairs of the Spirit? We were pioneering. To the best of my knowledge no other diocese in England was, at the time, attempting anything similar. Such free and easy ways are commonplace today. They were, in church circles, novel then. We were in no way following the methods of the Oxford Group, as Moral Re-Armament was then known. That is not said in criticism. Our approach, with all the limitations that are implicit in the fact, was an experiment made within the parochial system of the Church of England. We were all the while concerned to send people back into their parishes, there to work out their 'reasonable service' from that base. What we can claim is that we are still in touch with many who, in different places in England and abroad, have gone on to prove a discipleship begun in one of those 'cells', or at one of those youth 'weekends', or at a summer camp.

In our third year at Boscombe our Vicar moved to a parish in Hereford. There was a six months interregnum when, as senior curate, I had the main responsibility for the parochial round, ably assisted by Dick Gillman, since then a Vicar in Reading and later in the Potteries. Married to Raymond Scantlebury's sister Norah, their friendship is another unbroken link with that spring-time of our Ministry. The new Vicar, the Rev. A. W. Parsons, was most friendly and could not have been more kind to us both. But already we were reckoning that after we had completed four years we would be ready to move. This reckoning, true to our vow, we kept to ourselves.

At this very moment Bishop Garbett invited us to consider a parish in Southampton. That might have been the signal for which we were waiting. But we did not see ourselves as committed to the parochial ministry as that is traditionally understood. Somewhere within us was a pull, deeply felt but quite undefinable, that somewhere in the future God might yet use us in the overseas service of the Church. Bishop Garbett fully respected our decision. But I was proud that he should have thought us worthy of consideration. It was a sort of accolade.

Then suddenly 'out of the blue' came the invitation to go to Holy Trinity, Cambridge, anything but a traditional cure of souls.

6

1936 - 1942

Holy Trinity Church, Cambridge

All men are ready to invest their money
But most expect dividends.
I say to you: *Make perfect your will.*
I say: take no thought of the harvest,
But only of proper sowing.

T. S. ELIOT

The Rock

ANY Evangelical called to serve as Vicar of Holy Trinity Church, Cambridge, could hardly accept the summons other than with a sense of awe and trembling and a deep sense of wonder. Here, for fifty-four years, Charles Simeon had exercised a ministry which, for its repercussions then and since, can have had few, if any, parallels in the history of our Church.* Yet in another sense, and I hope not contrary, Mary and I had the happiness of feeling that we were coming 'home'; home to a church with so many undergraduate memories; home to a Cambridge which had meant so much to us both. We had no hesitation, should the interview with the Trustees confirm their choice, about knowing that we would accept.

The interview took place in No. 1 The Sanctuary at Westminster, and it set the seal on our acceptance of the invitation: for the Trustees made it clear that they expected us to concentrate our ministry on work with undergraduates. This meant a very real continuity with the work in which we had been so largely engaged in the last four years at Boscombe. Our youthfulness would be an asset as ensuring that we were within range of the thinking of another group of young men and women in their late teens and early twenties. This happy assurance for ourselves did not prevent Jack Morton, the retiring Vicar, from whistling with astonishment when he discovered my age. But with his natural charm and grace he disguised his anxiety and put me wise to many things. Probably no less anxious but equally kind were the two Churchwardens, H. M. Brock, one of *Punch*'s artists, and Walter Francis, a leading solicitor in the town.

What I quickly discovered from all three was that the Trustees had a somewhat inadequate view of the role of Holy Trinity Church in both town and diocese. That it had a flourishing congregation of local citizens and paid the highest parochial contribution to the diocesan quota made it quickly apparent that there were going to be two whole-time jobs in the days ahead. Some practice in riding two horses, not always inclined in the same direction, had been gained in the previous years, but this was a far more formidable proposition.

Historically it was true that, thanks to an early established 'Lectureship' in the seventeenth century, Holy Trinity had had a continuous link with the life of the University. Sibbes, one of the most eminent of the Puritans, had during the Commonwealth ministered here. And Holy Trinity Church had offered the Cambridge Platonists a pulpit. But no less was it historically true that the church occupied a significant place in the life of Cambridge long before there was a uni-

*Charles Smyth, *Simeon and Church Order* (C.U.P. 1940) gives a balanced and measured portrait set within the context of the Evangelical Revival in Cambridge in the eighteenth century.

versity at all. The earliest mention is of its total destruction in 1174. Rebuilt in 1188, it became a focus during medieval times for a local devotion to St. Erasmus. Whether he was the thirteenth-century Spanish saint or one of the martyrs under Diocletian is unknown. But for me his unexpected name had an intriguing association and one much to my liking. For this was a church which since Simeon's time had had a great missionary tradition. And was it not Erasmus of Rotterdam, the great humanist of the Reformation, who through his book on 'Preaching' got some Englishmen, notably Dr. Bray, thinking seriously about Missions to the heathen?

I make this historical reference, not only because of my own delight in history but because it made its own contribution towards my sense of responsibility to my parochial ministry, as distinct from the work with undergraduates.

Obviously there was plenty of work ahead on two fronts, and an urgent need was to find a curate who could share the task with me. E. T. Killick, the Cambridge and Middlesex cricketer, a happy legacy from Jack Morton, 'played me in' before going off to a parish in Letchworth. I was very fortunate in persuading Alan Cooper, later to be Vicar of St. Andrew's, Plymouth, and then Provost of Bradford, to join me. Alan was a genius with the younger generation and in an incredibly short time had built up a 'King's own' Bible Class for teenage boys and girls which nearly reached two hundred. He also had a wonderful talent with small children. The 'Children's Church' on Sunday mornings, to which many dons sent their children, became one of the most vigorous features of the church. Thanks to Alan, parish and congregation were not neglected.

A veteran member of the congregation, a lady with a formidable capacity for being outspoken, was overheard to say, 'We have a new *young* Vicar and we are very happy!' So were the young Vicar and his wife. From the very start the Church Council and the older folk generally, who might so easily have been suspicious, gave us a generous welcome and sustained support, support that meant everything in the very testing days that lay ahead for us all. Symbolic of this whole attitude of out-going friendliness was Maisie Cattley, Headmistress of the Perse Girls' School. A close and intimate friend of the Mortons, she did not wait to find out what we were like, but from the very beginning gave us a friendship which was to prove one of the richest and happiest we have known, rich beyond exaggeration in that kind of friendship which, Bacon says, 'redoubleth joys and cutteth griefs in halves'.

Here again was the richly-coloured thread running through all of life's pattern of the generosity lavished upon us by people older and more experienced than ourselves, who might have put a damper on our spirits but instead urged us on, often, I am sure, not without misgivings.

In the first meeting with Jack Morton he told me of one immediate task which lay ahead — the celebration, during the coming autumn, of the centenary of the death of Charles Simeon. He had begun making plans and had already secured a promise from the Archbishop of Canterbury, Dr. Lang, to preach on the Sunday nearest the day (13th November). I saw this, at once, as an occasion not to be missed. With the active encouragement of the Parochial Church Council and of other Cambridge friends, we planned a week extending from Sunday to Sunday when special speakers would give an interpretation of Simeon and his significance. Eleven leading churchmen took part, including the Bishops of Ely, Worcester, Truro, and Croydon, a future Bishop of Rochester and a future Bishop of Worcester. Archbishop Lang paid a notable tribute to the Simeon Trustees for their fidelity to their terms of reference and their unfailing sense of responsibility to the whole Church. The last address was given with his characteristic verve by the greatly beloved former Vicar, Edward Woods. Needless to say Jack Morton, now Rector of Hackney, also gave one of the addresses, appropriately enough on 'Simeon and the Parish'.*

This week of celebration attracted a remarkable amount of attention in the national, provincial and local press, and a flood of press-cuttings flowed in. The occasion reminded Cambridge, both Town and University, of a man who, though dead one hundred years, still had something vital to say. And partly because the celebration had so fully realised the plans for which Jack Morton had taken the initiative, it sealed the friendship of the old guard with the new Vicar. They felt reassured that while a new chapter was beginning there was a close continuity with what had gone before.

Meanwhile there was that charge laid upon me quite explicitly by the Trustees, and eagerly accepted, to pay especial attention to undergraduates. There had been in existence for a great many years what was known as the Cambridge Pastorate. The chairman of this was the Principal of Ridley Hall, the secretary the Vicar of Holy Trinity, and, associated with them, one or two college chaplains. The Principal of Ridley during my time as Vicar was Paul Gibson, a one-time C.M.S. missionary in Ceylon. He and his wife Kathleen were always at our service, ready with affection and advice The puckish glint of humour in Paul's eyes was a never-failing reminder that laughter and joy are

*The Addresses were published by the Lutterworth Press under the title *Charles Simeon — an Interpretation* within a matter of days after the celebrations.

Christian virtues no less than pagan. At the start of this time in Cambridge the college chaplains of the Pastorate were R. S. K. Seeley of St. John's, later to be Provost of Trinity College, Toronto, and I. D. Edwards of Christ's, later to be Dean of Wells. There was also a Pastorate Committee which included in its membership Charles Raven, Regius Professor of Divinity, and Dr. A. B. Cook, Emeritus Professor of Classical Archaeology, affectionately known as 'Zeus', from his fabulous researches into that divinity. There was no problem therefore of gaining entrance to the University.

In Cambridge few college chapels had any morning service, other than Holy Communion and that at an early hour. I therefore concentrated, during full-term, on securing preachers who, I knew, had something to say that was worth hearing. To ensure that undergraduates knew what was being offered I printed a terminal card. This was widely circulated, and before long as many as a thousand undergraduates were receiving a copy every term, most Colleges having a representative who saw to the circulation. At Oxford, in an earlier day, the great Canon Christopher had followed a similar technique but with this variation—he gave a box of cigars to the head porter of each college and asked him to distribute the cards. By my time cigars were much too expensive! Volunteer undergraduate labour was a cheaper and, I think, a more effective method.

With the beginning of the Lent term of 1937 I decided to experiment with courses of sermons, one for each of the eight Sundays of term, at each of which one aspect or another of the common theme was expounded. Never forgetting the words on Charles Simeon's memorial tablet in the chancel—who 'as the subject of all his ministrations determined to know nothing but Jesus Christ and him crucified'—I was determined that I would only invite into Simeon's pulpit men who would, in one way or another, illuminate this inexhaustible theme. During my six years at Holy Trinity I do not remember any of my preachers failing to reach this goal. The range of the theme did indeed prove inexhaustible. I hope that when one term, greatly daring, I preached a course of six sermons myself, I came somewhere near my objective.

Besides the Sunday mornings in Holy Trinity which, increasingly, attracted large numbers of undergraduates, there were many other activities. College chaplains were most generous in inviting me to preach in their chapels on Sunday evenings. There were also many informal groups which I was invited to attend. And in some terms special courses, other than on Sundays, were arranged. In the Lent term of 1938, for instance, Charles Raven gave a course of eight talks on Sunday evenings.

Here I must pause to pay tribute to that beloved man, prophet, preceptor and friend, whose generous backing for everything I tried to do in Cambridge was an unfailing thrill and unimaginable support. In those years immediately before the war and during it I would dare to assert that the most powerful single Christian influence in Cambridge, bar none, was Charles Raven. I am not thinking of religious coteries which had their own powerful sources of inspiration, but of the generality of undergraduates mostly agnostic or, at best, on the fringe of Christian belief. I was in touch with so many of these myself that I know I speak truly of Charles Raven.

A man trained in science and theology, he could speak to a very agnostic generation as could no one else in Cambridge. And precisely because he could command the respect of agnostics, he was able to confirm in the Christian Faith countless young men and women who but for his inspiration and intellectual power might have lapsed from the Faith altogether.

In thus speaking of Raven I am necessarily saying something about myself. I am testifying to his own profound and permanent influence on my own life and thinking. I loved the man for his courage and humility, for the sheer brilliance of his mind and the width of his interests, but above all for the fact that deep at the heart of his being was a profound love for and loyalty to Jesus Christ. For him discipleship was everything. What was so exciting was to see how all-embracing that discipleship proved to be. *Nihil humani a me alienum puto* could have been, may have been, for all I know, his private motto. He constantly demonstrated it in his life and teaching. What was so arresting was that everything human, everything in the natural order, he related to Christ, whether as its redeemer from evil, or its fulfilment as good.*

'A faithful friend is the medicine of life', says the Apocrypha. How rich then in *materia medica* is our own personal pharmacopeia. There are those warm intimate friendships between near equals in age: there are those which are born from involvement in some shared task, coloured by the common commitment: again, there are those in which discrepancy in age, experience and ability, impose no barrier of enjoyment at least for the younger, less experienced and less able of the friends. Such a friendship was it my good fortune to enjoy with Charles Raven from 1936 until his death in 1964. One characteristic of the man, among many, still warms my heart when I look at a letter he sent me in 1944. I had recently written a small book of historical essays and had asked him if I might dedicate it to him. After

---

*While writing this story of my own experiences I read in typescript a full-length life of Charles Raven by Dr. F. W. Dillistone, a brilliant, sensitive, and perceptive study, worthy of the subject.

an absurdly generous opening paragraph in reply, he added, 'But if (and only if) you feel that it will not endanger the influence or circulation of your book, of course I should love to have my name associated with it.' During the war years his spirit was clouded not only by the war as a tragedy, but also because he felt so unwanted, being forbidden any opportunity for broadcasting, chiefly on the grounds that he was known for his pacifist sympathies. That explains the sentence from his letter which I have quoted. I wish the people who thus penalised him, and the wider public, could have heard the innumerable times during the war when he spoke in Holy Trinity without once exploiting the opportunity to air what were some of his deepest convictions. Giant that he was, he knew that there were other subjects about which to prophesy. I was immensely proud to pay this small public tribute to him. I only wish the book had been worthier.

Sunday afternoon at Holy Trinity Vicarage was when Mary came into her own as hostess to innumerable undergraduates. You never knew how many would turn up. One Sunday it might be only twenty. The next Sunday for no particular reason there would be sixty. But somehow there was always enough to eat, even in war-time. Life at the Vicarage was a whole-time activity even before the war filled the house with refugees and evacuees. A Vicar's wife can make the necessity of being hospitable not just a virtue but an exhilaration to all who enter the house. But in addition to undergraduates and refugees there were two small daughters who needed attention, for Pat had arrived to join Rosemary in 1936.

Perhaps there is some significance that, whatever her other duties might be, Mary, during the years of their childhood, never allowed anything to keep her away from the children at their bed-time, which was also prayer-time. This unfailing dependability was the sheet-anchor of that home, from which of necessity I was so often away. What this dependability of Mum meant to Rosemary and Pat only they can say, but their future was to prove eloquent of what mother-hood could mean to their own children because of what it had meant to them. Certainly it also meant for me that whatever the wear and tear of the day I would come back to a home full of peace. I do not forget that the home-maker of that peace had had her full share of wear and tear on her own account, which made the peace more miraculous.

Throughout my time at Holy Trinity I was most fortunate in the men who came to help me. After two years Alan Cooper went off to

Lagos as diocesan missioner. I was then joined by Berners-Wilson, 1938–1939, who, after war service as a Chaplain R.A.F.V.R., was to become the Officer for Religious training of the National Association of Boys' Clubs. In his place Basil Watson came as a deacon. This, from his point of view, though not from mine, was a mistake. No one could have been a nicer colleague, but Holy Trinity Church did not offer a good training ground for the first steps in the ministry. And I was in no way qualified to 'train' a deacon. Basil's friendship has proved strong enough to outlast my failure of him. He went on to a curacy in Northumberland and then to a distinguished career as a Naval Chaplain. He was succeeded by Connop Price, now Provost of Chelmsford, with whom we have had continuous and grateful contact when, later, we were in London and he was a member of the Church Assembly. After I had left the parish he saw the new Vicar in and then served as a Chaplain in the Air Force.

All of these men were friends as well as colleagues. They lifted a great burden off my shoulders, for the response from undergraduates was becoming overwhelming. The vast uncertainties in the international scene were challenging men and women of the undergraduate generation to think at depth, and they were hungry for understanding and guidance. With all this there was, as well, the preparation of the congregation for war. Here were two conflicting sets of demands often impossible to meet at one and the same time, although closely related. Where I was extraordinarily fortunate was in the unstinting help of Evered Lunt, Chaplain of Downing. Later he was to be Rector of St. Aldate's, Oxford, Dean of Bristol and Bishop of Stepney, in all of which spheres he exercised a devoted ministry. But I will always believe that the most distinctive of his achievements was his little-known ministry behind the scenes with senior members of the University during the ten years when he was at Downing. As a pastor of souls he was one of the wisest men I have known, humane in his profound understanding of human weakness, utterly self-sacrificing in his readiness to meet any human weakness without counting the cost to himself. I myself owe him a spiritual debt quite impossible to repay. He steadied me in many a difficult situation and accompanied me through many a desert patch.

Very soon after our arrival in Cambridge the clouds of war began to bank up on the horizon. In 1937 came the overture to the *gotter-dammerung* of the West with the Spanish Civil War. After Munich 1938 it became clear to anyone not politically and morally purblind that 'out of this nettle danger' all that had been plucked was a few months' breathing space. Arguably, that breathing space saved us.

What at least seemed crystal clear to this parish priest was that he must bend his energies into preparing his congregation for war, and for entering into it as far as might be possible in a mood as different from 1914 as possible. Hysteria about the enemy is a bad way of making war and an insurance against making peace at the end of it. Oliver Cromwell's reported advice, 'Put your trust in God, my boys, and keep your powder dry', does not compass the whole of theology, but it takes in quite a lot of it. While I had no responsibility for coping with the nation's supply of powder, I had every responsibility for helping some hundreds of men and women, young and old, to discover what trusting God meant; and more than that, discovering more about God in whom to trust.

'Munich' drove me back to the great prophets of the Old Testament. Here were men upon whom, as they saw it, the end of the world had come. The bottom had fallen out of things. The great deep was breaking up. Yet at that very time and in those very circumstances these courageous men fashioned an interpretation of history, found for themselves a meaning in the nonsense of events. In them I found inspiration and a wonderfully steadying influence which, under God, was to be a real anchor in the seven years that lay ahead.

That was my private anchor. But I had a graver responsibility. I had a congregation whose own world was about to be broken up. Was there a word for them? If there was then it would have to be found in the worship in church.

Here I must digress and explain my own philosophy of corporate worship. As I see it the task of a parish priest is, supremely, to ensure in so far as he can that the worship of God in church, Sunday by Sunday, is intelligible and positive. As an Anglican I started off with the enormous advantage that the Prayer Book pattern of worship for Matins and Evensong, the services to which the great majority of people came, particularly the less instructed and the less committed, do contain in balance the main ingredients of corporate worship. To this pattern I have always been devotedly loyal. That loyalty has convinced me that it is the 'intention' of the Prayer Book that matters. In practice this means a selectivity which cannot be controlled by any generalised lectionary, whether of lessons or psalter. We are no longer a Bible-reading people and this applies to church people only slightly less than it does to unbelievers. Large parts of the Bible, even the New Testament, call for a commentary for their understanding, or at least an expository sermon. Only a few of the Psalms, perhaps thirty, can be sung profitably *and* to edification by a congregation today. A high percentage of hymns ought never to be sung at all. Prayers need very careful choosing.

With these convictions, but adhering closely to the familiar pattern of the services, I aimed at a selectivity by which in each service lessons, psalm, hymns, prayers and sermon were related to one dominant theme. I made one very careful change. Each service began with a hymn of adoration, as objectively worded as possible. I believe that this, in terms of corporate worship, provides the only possible theological basis for expecting a congregation to enter seriously upon the General Confession at 11.0 a.m. on a Sunday morning.

There is one very obvious danger in following such a procedure and that is for the parish priest to choose only favourite passages for lessons; to forget that, in a hymn, bad poetry and even a bad but well-loved tune can yet convey truth; to overdo the number of unfamiliar prayers, beyond the capacity of the congregation to follow. On this last point I was early grateful to Mervyn Stockwood for telling me his view that four prayers in the space following the hymn after the third collect, were a maximum and, if there were no hymn, then only two. I'm sure he was right.

As a check on my own eccentricities and prejudices I kept a careful 'log' of every detail of every service during my six years at Holy Trinity, hymns, hymn tunes, psalms, lessons and prayers. After each service I did a careful post-mortem and recorded such comments as I might receive. The three thick volumes filled with this mass of detail are evidence that I did not trifle with this side of my ministry.

Further, by way of helping the congregation to understand the services, I produced a series of small pamphlets. The first of these explained in simple terms the rationale of Matins and Evensong. This was followed after a few months by other pamphlets on Psalms and Hymns and the Creed. Over the years, thousands of these were purchased by members of the congregation and by visitors. I am sure that they helped to make our worship truly corporate, and also the offering of minds as well as hearts.

Although, over the years, we had many a visiting preacher of eloquence and power, although the sermon was always taken with the utmost seriousness, I treasure above all the many letters I received from regular members of the congregation, from undergraduates, and from visitors, all testifying that what had most deeply moved them in Holy Trinity Church was the spirit of worship.

If I have here concentrated on Matins and Evensong it is because in the task at Holy Trinity, in the years when I was there, these were the services to which large numbers of people came who would never have come to Holy Communion. *Autres temps autres moeurs*, perhaps. But I wish that I felt absolutely certain that the current fashion of concentrating everything on the Family Communion was reaching that eighty per cent of our nation which is not hostile but which is nowhere near ready for committed discipleship. As so many clergy have, for the last thirty years, been dedicated to debunking Matins and Evensong, any revival of these services may be impossible, except in a few places. The increasing number of stunts of every kind, rarely inspired by any liturgical awareness, suggests nevertheless that the vacuum created by the displacement of Matins and Evensong has not been filled.

There is, of course, no reason whatever why a sermon at Matins or Evensong cannot be devoted to interpreting the meaning, purpose, and vital importance for the Christian life of the Holy Communion. One year at Holy Trinity the sermons every Sunday Evensong from Advent Sunday to Whitsunday without exception were based on the Epistle or Gospel for the day. But, of course, they were twenty-minute sermons in which a lot of teaching can be done, and people taught to know their Bible.

I have dwelt at length on this subject of worship because I have ample evidence that it was this primary emphasis upon the corporate act of worship, of which the sermon was an integral part, which in the deep places of the human heart and mind prepared that congregation for the stresses and agonies and tests of war.

There was, as well, another factor which played a great part in knitting the congregation together. From 1937 onwards Cambridge became a reception centre for an increasing number of victims of Hitler's paranoia about the Jews. Among those who came to be resident in Cambridge was Franz Hildebrandt, one-time colleague of Dr. Niemöller at his church in Berlin-Dahlem. Franz became the Pastor of the German Lutheran congregation in Cambridge. With the unanimous support of the Parochial Church Council I was able to welcome that congregation to a regular late Sunday evening service according to the Lutheran rite.

This was to have an historic sequel. In the week before 3rd September, 1939, when all prospect of a peaceful end to the threat of war had faded, we realised that it would be impossible to have the late Sunday evening service for the German congregation, because the church could not be blacked-out in time. Franz came to enquire what could be done. I shall always be glad that the year of preparation for war had been a preparation for myself, as well as for others, and so I was quick-witted enough to say that I could think of no better way of starting the war than by having a joint service of our two congregations, part of it in English, part of it in German. Franz warmly welcomed the idea. Using Evensong as the framework, we simply doubled each part, the Invitation in both languages, the Confession and Absolution in both languages, one lesson in English, one in German, the Creed said simultaneously, prayers alternating, and two short addresses. It was one of the most moving services I have ever attended. The occasion, in all conscience, was moving enough. Further to this mutual strengthening, the fact that two congregations of two nationalities at war could meet together in common worship at such a moment was a pledge that here, at any rate, the anti-German hysteria which disgraced Church and Nation in 1914 would not occur. By the mercy of God this hysteria hardly occurred anywhere. We were the privileged ones to be able to have this unique service because a German congregation was already using our church.

Not long after the outbreak of war our congregation became intimately involved with others in the establishment of a club for the German community, a club which they would run for themselves but for which congregations in the town provided a rota of helpers—the whole very complicated enterprise being superbly co-ordinated by an indefatigable Quaker Lady, Miss Sturge. In this way personal friendships were made which helped to tide the Germans over many of the anxieties they were to experience.

Joint German-English services continued to be held until 1940 when, with few exceptions, all the men were taken off to internment in the Isle of Man. This was one of those unimaginatively stupid actions of the kind which happen in a time of emergency when a group is penalised on grounds of guilt by association—they were Germans. Tragically, this form of mental sickness is today spreading all over the world. The round-up of those Germans took place on Whitsunday morning. That evening Franz was due to preach at one of the joint services. He rang me up to say he was under detention. At once I got through to the Chief Constable, asking permission for Franz to be allowed to preach, and accepting responsibility for his return to custody. Permission was readily given. The Chief Constable and others in Cambridge, who had had ample opportunity to know the little German community, were all acutely embarrassed by the stupidity of the 'blanket' internment order. Of course it was the summer of 1940. Of course we knew all about 'fifth columns'. What was forgotten was that the notorious 'fifth column' consisted of a defeatist or traitorous element in a nation itself. We had our 'fifth column', no doubt of it, but it did not consist of German refugees!

After Franz Hildebrandt and most of the men had been interned we continued to welcome the German women and such men as remained, to our services, but only when Professor Dodd came to preach was it possible to have a sermon in German. This provided an amusing incident on one occasion when Dr. Dodd was preaching. In the middle of his sermon a lady not unknown for eccentricity got up and left the church, slamming the door. A letter appeared in the Cambridge local paper protesting at a German being allowed to preach in 'that language' at such a critical moment in the war. It was indeed a critical moment, but I had the utmost joy of writing to the paper to advise the readers that the horrible German language had been spoken by one of the most distinguished English theologians alive, none other than Dr. C. H. Dodd, Norris-Hulse Professor of Divinity in the University of Cambridge.

On 30th August, 1940 I received a telegram from the camp in the Isle of Man which read:

> Cambridge refugees remember first anniversary of joint services with greatful thanks to the vicar, organist and congregation of Holy Trinity Church. Christ is our peace who hath made both one.

What I liked about that telegram was its recognition that it was the congregation of Holy Trinity not just an individual that had been responsible. And I was especially glad that the organist was singled out. Harold Fleet, who had given me the fullest support in all I had tried to attempt with regard to the worship at Holy Trinity, was enthusiastic in helping the German congregation, just as his wife Kathleen was in the work at the club.

A letter, also received during 1940, came from a German who had escaped internment, perhaps through longer residence and the acquisition of British nationality. It came in acknowledgement of a note of sympathy which I had written to him when so many of his friends were being interned. He wrote:

> What a relief in these days of hostility and misunderstanding to be welcomed so heartily by you and by Holy Trinity parish as a friend. Having no possibility to carry on with our own German services we shall thoroughly enjoy to join in those of Holy Trinity Church we learned to love since we came to Cambridge and where we are at home now.

The breathing space after Munich had not been wasted.

But we must retrace our steps to 7th January, of that year 1940. On that Sunday Canon S. J. Marriott of Westminster broadcast an address with the title 'The Day of the Layman has come'. Among his hearers was a young Cambridge business man, Kenneth Cooper. He, with a number of other men in reserved occupations, had been meeting together from time to time to wrestle with some of the spiritual and moral problems of war-time. None were churchgoers. Kenneth wrote to Canon Marriott to ask if he would be willing to follow up his address by coming to Cambridge to meet the group. Canon Marriott came and they had a most profitable evening. At the end of it Kenneth Cooper, ever practical, asked how they could continue along the lines the Canon had suggested. Surely, said Canon Marriott, there must be someone in Cambridge who would gladly come and meet the group. What prompted Kenneth to ring me up and so start another priceless friendship I do not know. But at his invitation I gladly agreed to go up and meet the group, and this I did from time to time. Kenneth, who took everything he did with immense seriousness, and worried at truth like a dog at a bone, started coming to Holy Trinity Church.

This seemed to me to be the opportunity of a life-time. Here was a layman very much still on the edge of things, having no religious commitment and, as yet, little that the orthodox would call Faith. And he was coming regularly to Church. We had 'clicked' as to friendship, seeing the funny side of serious things, and recognising that we were both explorers. So I asked his help. Would he, on Sunday mornings, when he reckoned I was back from church, give me a ring and in the frankest possible way tell me what he thought about the service and the sermon and, if I was preaching, tell me if for him I had 'rung a bell' or just completely 'missed the boat', to conjoin two metaphors which every reader will understand! He agreed. And from the next Sunday, until I left Holy Trinity, Kenneth and I were in a partnership which, for me, was one of the most exciting and worthwhile I have known. And life has not been dull in the way of partnerships.

He was the most faithful and valuable of friends because he pulled no punches. If he reckoned that I had failed to register anything that convinced him he said so. When he sometimes registered a hope that I was improving I knew I was getting somewhere. I wonder if a parish priest can possess a more valuable asset in his congregation than this kind of candid friend. You must, of course, be willing to come back, after pouring out your soul to the congregation, to hear a cheerful voice saying, 'Max, you were missing on a couple of cylinders this morning, what was wrong?' But those who are prepared to listen can learn. I covet such a friend for every parish priest I know, and every bishop!

Twenty-three years later I was to succeed Canon Marriott at Westminster Abbey. I wish I thought that any of my sermons in the Abbey had had comparable repercussions to that one on 7th January 1940.

Meanwhile, as from the outbreak of war, Cambridge, in terms of population, was almost bursting at the seams. Many evacuees from London were billeted in Cambridge, Mary being busy as one of the volunteer billeting officers. Our Vicarage family doubled overnight to thirteen. My mother had come to live with us immediately after Munich, and Sheelagh was now at the Perse School for Girls. The five of us and our much-prized nurse-housemaid, 'Mea', were fully stretched in coping with the crush, though in fact it did not last at this pressure for long. The 'phoney war' soon saw some of the evacuees from London gratefully returning to their own familiar haunts.

In other ways, however, Cambridge became more and more crowded. Being the war-time regional capital of East Anglia it became the base for an army of civil servants, together with members of some of the constituent Colleges of London University. All this meant a wholly unexpected opportunity for Holy Trinity. The original large numbers of undergraduates rapidly disappeared, but were more than replaced by the new population. It became normal practice to arrive at the church half-an-hour before the service to find a long queue of people waiting to get in, after the end of the children's service, to make sure of a seat.

One immediate problem was to discover how these 'temporary visitors' could be made to feel at home and, what was more important, be caught up into the spirit of the regular congregation and so become aware of the character of the spiritual warfare in which as a congregation we were engaged.

Obviously it was physically impossible to make personal contact with all these visitors. But a means did present itself through the printed word. With the beginning of the war we had scrapped the old-style parish magazine and now had a four-page quarto-sized leaflet. There was, however, no reason why this should not have inserted in it a supplement, varying from month to month. Our aim became that of using these supplements to help lift the eyes of readers above their local situation and the pressing nature of their own concerns and anxieties.

With permission, articles from *The Times* were reproduced: several important issues of Dr. Oldham's *Christian News-Letter* in this way got a wide local circulation: Canon Marriott's sermon of 7th January, 1940, was reprinted from *The Listener:* one of Dr. Cash's C.M.S. News-Letters was reproduced: a letter from Lord Halifax urging the great importance of Christian people refusing for one moment to relax their support of the missionary work of the Church overseas was included, a notable document, indeed, to appear in October 1940 during the great blitz on London: the Industrial Christian Fellowship,

and other societies which our congregation supported, in this way
also got their stories across: once I squeezed in a sermon of my own
on 'Preparation for Death' which was anything but morbid but at least
apposite. We were also getting people to think about 'after the war'
three years before we had won it. The United Council of Christian
Witness in Cambridge under the magnificent leadership of Dr. G. A.
Chase, later to be Bishop of Ripon, produced a powerful leaflet entitled
'Controlled Food Relief or Famine' dealing with the occupied countries
of Europe. This formed one supplement. Problems of evacuation, and
its significance as a social landmark, formed another subject. And there
was one fascinating supplement on 'China's Guerilla Industry' which
certainly took in some remote horizons. Nearer home we asked, 'Why
Christian Education Matters', which was, from the point of view of the
Churches, a preparation for the Butler Education Act. But of all these
supplements the one I myself most enjoyed came at a very dark
moment indeed in the spring of 1942 when nothing was going right.
It was an article in the *Spectator* by the Editor, Wilson Harris. It was
a great appeal for spiritual leadership referring to 'the new Primate,
whose lips a live coal from off the altar touches'. But it was more
than an appeal for leadership from the top. It was a word to everyone
of us to be ourselves leaders. On reading it I wrote at once asking
permission to reprint. It can easily be imagined what I felt when I
got the reply:

Dear Sir,
    I shall of course be more than glad for you to reprint our article
'Braced and Compact'. I used to go to Holy Trinity on Sunday
evenings as an undergraduate nearly forty years ago, and con-
ceivably some remote connection might be traced between that and
the article in question.
                                    Yours very faithfully,
                                        H. Wilson Harris
                                            Editor

There were many other articles, some by men like George McLeod,
all of which went toward this sustained effort to keep people's eyes
above the limitation of the present and lift their hearts and minds to
discern the greater spiritual struggle of which the war was no more
than a prologue.
    But all this printing was costing a lot of money. I remember putting
the situation to the Parochial Church Council. At one moment it
looked as if the discussion was tending towards retrenchment and
therefore a reduction of the programme. At the crucial moment one

of our ablest business men, a leading farmer in the Fens, Godfrey Wright, made a fighting speech on the enormous importance of publicity and urging the fullest support for any expenditure I liked to undertake! He carried the P.C.C. without a contrary vote. That in the middle of war-time, and at a very dark moment too, was no bad way in which a layman could give expression to what a 'theologian' would include under 'faith'!

One interesting project in which I was involved was the organising of 'The New Order Exhibition' in April 1941. This was an effort put on by the Cambridge United Council of Christian Witness. We hired the Town Hall (Cambridge had not yet qualified as a city) and planned a demonstration on how Christians could envisage a New Order wholly different from the one that Hitler was offering. We wanted to show what we thought we, as a nation, were fighting for: but more than that, a vision of a world community which might come to be once the war was over. Asking the question 'After Hitler What?' we covered the walls with a montage of photographs, paintings, and a patchwork patterning of cuttings from newspapers. This was the work of enthusiastic young artists, including my own secretary, Peggy Dolphin, and undergraduates qualifying in medicine like Ilsley Ingram, now a Professor of Experimental Haematology at St. Thomas's Hospital, and Peter Thompson, shortly to go to China with the Friends' Ambulance Unit—all working against time under the critical eye of Kenneth Cooper who was determined to allow no easy sentiment to get in. This was, so to speak, the backcloth against which documentary films were shown dealing with Iran, Africa, Malaya, etc. A galaxy of speakers was secured, including men like Sir Leonard Rogers, K.C.S.I., Dr. James Welch, Dr. William Paton, Professor Victor Murray, Canon Broomfield, and Prebendary Cash.

Our vision has not been realised—*Yet.* But it was good to see it. Because it held out no easy promises it strengthened all who took part to take the ugliness of life seriously and to glimpse something of the hidden beauty. We were not asking for dividends or even a quick harvest. We knew that that was not for asking. But we hoped we were doing a proper sowing.

In common with many other people we had been asked at an early stage in the war if we would send our children to Canada for 'the duration'. Many did. For us the issue was easily settled. For one thing we were determined to see the future through *together* as a family. For another, I was Vicar of a church which had been preparing for the test of war. Apart from that, the majority of people in Cambridge could not send their children to Canada. For us, for all these reasons, it was not an option.

This whole question of 'safety' led to one curious incident. The Vice-Chancellor of the University asked me to go and see him. He expressed himself as somewhat anxious at the number of senior members of the University who appeared to be thinking that Cambridge was too dangerous a place for their families. How justified he was in his anxiety I have no idea, but his talk led me to preach a sermon on the subject of panic. I took as my text 1 Corinthians 16:13 'Stand fast in the faith, quit you like men, be strong'. I made some play on the Greek word used for 'stand fast' — *stekete*, which I rendered 'stick it'. I think this was legitimate on that occasion. The 'pun' was not to the liking of the Emeritus Professor of Archaeology, Dr. Cook, who, as he left the church shook his head sadly at me. 'Zeus' did not approve. But there was no thunderbolt.

It is impossible to do justice to those crowded years at Cambridge. As one looks back, so many hundreds of faces pass before the mind's eye conjuring up so many occasions grave and gay, of tears and laughter, of doubt and perplexity and of seeing the light of faith suddenly illuminate an enquiring man or woman. And there was plenty of sorrow to face, not least when the Cambridgeshire regiment landed in Singapore just in time to be captured by the Japanese. But not one minute of that time, of grief and tragedy as well as of gaiety and high adventure, would either of us have missed.

Nor is it possible adequately to express our gratitude to the congregation who were so superb in their support. But one man must be noted. A parish priest who failed to pay tribute to a verger as remarkable as Charles Bennett would demonstrate his failure to grasp priorities. The man upon whose fidelity in matters of detail the whole machinery of a church depends is the verger. Such men, where they still survive, do by their care for detail, by their adaptability to the foibles of successive vicars and curates, by their cheerfulness, and by the way they welcome people into the church, provide that ordered background of harmony which makes everything else fall into place. They are of that breed of men referred to in the book of Ecclesiasticus 'who maintain the fabric of the world, and their daily work is their prayer'.

7

1942 - 1963

Background to Office

We are the Pilgrims, master; we shall go
    Always a little further: it may be
Beyond that last blue mountain barred with snow,
    Across that angry or that glittering sea,
White on a throne or guarded in a cave
    There lives a prophet who can understand
Why men were born: but surely we are brave,
    Who make the Golden Journey to Samarkand.

JAMES ELROY FLECKER

The Golden Journey to Samarkand

I can best introduce my twenty-one years as a Secretary of the Church Missionary Society by describing two journeys which I took during the remaining three years of the war. One journey was repeated many times and took me from Cambridge to Liverpool Street Station. The other was the first of many visits to the U.S.A. and Canada.

On leaving the Vicarage we were able to rent a house within short walking distance of the station. War-time travel was such that this meant catching the 6.41 from Cambridge each morning and arriving at Liverpool Street about 9.30. From there I walked across the blitzed desert between Liverpool Street Station and St. Paul's Cathedral and then down Ludgate Hill to Salisbury Square.

What made this journey so important for me and unforgettable was that I did not take it alone. Kenneth Cooper had to catch the same train, as did others known to him. So we formed a 'carriage club', six of us starting the journey at Cambridge and two joining us at Bishop's Stortford. The group were all young business executives in reserved occupations. One, for instance, was in a firm making diving material for the Navy, one was a constructional engineer working on air-fields. As to age, we were all in our thirties.

This early start, especially in the dark mornings of autumn and winter, was chilly work. Often we began by scraping off the frost from inside the windows of the carriage. The lights being dimmed, blacked out or non-existent, there was not much scope for reading. Fortified with our thermos flasks of coffee, and sandwiches, we settled ourselves for talk. And what talk it was! We ranged over every subject imaginable. Kenneth Cooper, in his own inimitable way, again and again threw in some provocative remark which brought the talk round to religion. I was the only parson in the carriage. Kenneth was, I think, the only other committed Christian.

The value of this daily debate with a group of active intelligent men, who quickly realised they need pull no punches because a parson was present, was that I started my day at the headquarters of a missionary society acutely aware of how very 'odd' my occupation was. If what I was doing was not to be seen as quite peripheral to the world of the men with whom I travelled I had to see the nature of Mission in terms of the world in which they moved. I had to be asking myself whether what I was doing could have any meaning at all for them. Yet it may have been of some indirect service to the Kingdom that we came to spend so many hours together during which problems of the Christian Faith could be discussed without hurry, with friendliness, and with no questions evaded because the answers were difficult. Kenneth was near enough to the others to refuse to allow me to cut any corners! Anyway I learnt a lot and I did not forget what I had heard on the train when opening my mail from Nigeria or Kenya, from Iran or India, when I got to the office.

There was one day early in 1943 which I will not easily forget. The war was going badly. There was widespread disillusionment in the nation. The high-spirited response of the whole people in 1940 and 1941 had been dissipated. Instead of a community of sacrifice, that carriageful of men had grim stories to tell of racketeering and pro-fiteering from the war. The talk was often cynical in the extreme. And so it was that morning. We turned to ask ourselves what leader-ship we must look for when the war was over, leadership which could lift the nation out of the morass in which we were wallowing. One of the company threw in the following —'There is only one man cap-able of rallying this country, and leading it, and that is William Temple.' Everyone in the carriage, after a moment's silence to digest the idea, agreed.

I quote that unexpected comment, and the general assent to it, as being more than just a tribute to William Temple, intensely sincere though it was, but as showing that a related Christianity can find an echo in unlikely places. William Temple was nothing if not relevant. Perhaps our debates over the months in that railway carriage had, also, been seen to be related to humdrum human experience. William Temple served as the symbol of the beginning of a corporate self-discovery. The fact that such a comment could be made, even wist-fully, by such a company was some measure of the disaster suffered by Church and Nation when, a year later, he was dead.

The other journey took me from London to Glasgow on a murky December day and then by the *Queen Mary* to New York. The great liner was stripped for war service as a troop carrier. So the stateroom to which I was directed was found to contain six double-bunk beds and nothing else, except the evidence that I was to share it with four un-known companions.

Dinner over, I went down to learn with whom I was going to travel. Entering the hall-way of the suite I saw four men sitting round two suitcases playing cards. One of them looked up and cheerily wel-comed me with 'Hullo, Padre, come and take a hand.' This was im-pressive. It must have been no small shock to realise they were to be cooped up with a parson for the six-day crossing. We quickly made our number with each other. One of them, the welcoming voice, was a steel-smelter from Irlam near Manchester, with whom I was to stay in the following year. One was a quick-spoken man from County Durham working for I.C.I. One was an Irishman, born in the same vintage year as myself and now a shop steward in a de Havilland aircraft factory, anything but a quiet man. The fourth, a Yorkshireman and the oldest of the four, was working on aircraft in Coventry. They were a delegation of Trades Unionists going over to the U.S.A. by way of a return visit from four American opposite numbers who were travelling on the same ship.

The weather was far too cold to be up on deck so, apart from meals and the evening cinema show, we stayed in our stateroom and talked. And grand talk it was. For the first three days I was just a fascinated listener as the four men argued the toss about the economic problems in their several industries and how they believed industry ought to be organised after the war.

These men had never met each other before, so question and answer, interruption and argument, went on hour after hour. As I listened I learnt more about the industrial set-up of England and what it looks like from the shop floor than I could have learnt from a dozen books or a course in economics.

I think they were rather pleasantly surprised that I obviously enjoyed listening to their arguments and, beyond asking an occasional question, had said nothing.

Then came the morning when they clustered round my bunk and said they wanted to tell me what religion meant to them, and after this I was to have my innings. That was how they put it! It was an education to listen to their experiences. One owed everything to his father's example, and he was sure his father had been right and he wanted to find the way back. Another had been in a church choir, had been confirmed, but the sheer pressure of life had caught him up. Yet the whole attitude which he had brought to the subjects about which they had been arguing showed that the Faith he had abandoned lay behind the ethics he obviously practised. The Irishman had an alert enquiring mind, and had abandoned his ancestral faith because he could not get serious answers to serious questions.

Not one of these men was hostile to the Christian Faith. But all had been more or less alienated. Here was my chance. I decided to start with the story of the Garden of Eden. I treated the story as being, in its very simplest essentials, a description of man in a relationship of dependence—drawing out from it that the attempt to be independent was an escape from reality. And I worked this round to the basic human need for mutual inter-dependence. It was very simple stuff. I can think of many other ways of tackling the story. But it was an interpretation which related directly to the arguments of the previous days. The response was astonishing. 'Why have we never been told anything like this before?' Well, I expect they had been told many times, though in rather different surroundings and it had not registered. Anyway, from now on till the end of the voyage there was no getting away from how religion had to be related to life.

As the talk went on all day and far into the night how grateful I was to the men like Roland Roberts, Charles Raven, William Temple, Mervyn Stockwood and Kenneth Cooper, who had all set my eyes looking in the direction of trying to see that the Christian Faith was painfully and costingly tied in with every single aspect of human life. But how was the connection to be established? Well, I am wrestling with that question still. There is no sort of easy answer. The exciting thing for me was that those four trade-unionists were immediately interested in what I had to tell them about the new job which I had just started at C.M.S. It was an unusual audience to which to explain what the missionary movement was all about. To them it was as much an opening up of a new world as their industrial debates had been to me.

News of our discussions had got round and by the last evening we had twenty-three people crammed in to the cabin, including the four U.S.A. labour delegates, a cotton manufacturer, a film actor, a Canadian soldier, an American architect, a man from our own Foreign Office and, for good measure, a girl on the staff of *Life* magazine.

One of our Trade Unionists, the steel-smelter, took the chair and I was asked to open up on colonial questions. How often I was to do this in the next twenty-one years! Crossing the Atlantic in the third winter of the war was the unexpected setting for my first attempt to look into the future and to think aloud about race relations, burgeoning nationalism, and the Gospel.

The talk waxed fast and fine, everyone joining in. We ranged over half creation and, at one point, nearly had a free-for-all between the four Irish present because that 'distressful country' had come into the discussion by way of someone's illustration. It was very funny because all four of us Irish happened to be agreed about the issue in question, but four Irishmen in agreement is what any other crowd would call a fight. It was an odd 'missionary meeting'. It went on till midnight. Among those present were an American padre and a Salvation Army Captain. Our chairman, winding up, said that as Christmas was only a few days away he thought it would be a good idea if the three 'padres' each said a short word about Christmas.

The evening over, I went up on deck for a breather and a further talk with the cotton manufacturer and the shop steward, a trio not wholly lacking in symbolic significance for me. I was 'in the middle' of the industrial complex of our time. This was where I was determined that, in thought and imagination, I would remain and learn what it meant that our western, industrialised, technological revolution was spilling over into Africa and Asia.

We were all rather sorry the journey was over. I was not a little thrilled when the man who had welcomed me into their company on the first evening said that for him the trip would have been worthwhile if it never went beyond New York. 'The same goes for me,' I said.

Those journeys which I have described did, in a subtle and fundamental way, determine how I was to interpret my work in C.M.S. Somehow, as I saw it, I had to share my understanding of the context in which the modern missionary had to work, help the missionary to understand it, and go on understanding it better myself. At the same time I had to try, as far as possible, to help the devoted and dedicated members of the Society at home to welcome the brave and strange new world in which the Gospel had to be interpreted. I was fortunate in having to hand one invaluable instrument. Dr. Cash, my predecessor as General Secretary, had, at the outset of war, started the C.M.S. News-Letter as a medium of communication, particularly for laymen. The next 232 News-Letters were to be my way of showing that I had learnt something from those journeys.

I must, however, go back and begin this part of the story in rather more conventional fashion, though how it began has a piquancy of its own. In 1938 the General Committee of the Society appointed me to the Executive Committee. A year or so later the Secretaries put forward my name for membership of the Executive Committee's sub-committee for Appointments. This sub-committee, chaired by the President of the Society, was responsible for nominating for appointment the Officers of the Society, the Secretaries and the Under-Secretaries. So it was that, when in 1941 Dr. Cash became Bishop of Worcester, I was summoned, with the others, to a meeting which would nominate a successor to Dr. Cash as General Secretary. The then President, Sir Robert Williams, being ill, the chair was taken by the Treasurer of the Society, Kingsley Tubbs, twenty-nine years before a new boy with me at Heddon Court.

The Treasurer opened proceedings by saying that he had before him a list of some thirty names of persons suggested as possible successors to Dr. Cash. What was our pleasure? Our pleasure was unmistakable. We all wanted our curiosity satisfied as to who the thirty might be. The list was, I think, in alphabetical order. Certainly it was somewhere towards the end that I was thunderstruck to hear my name in the list. The silence which followed the reading of the names did not last long. Indeed, I broke it almost at once by saying that it would reduce the list by one if my name was removed. My love for C.M.S. and my respect for Dr. Cash and his achievements made it, in my judgment, quite ludicrous for my name to be considered, and I said so. The

Treasurer asked me if I was serious. I said I was and my name was scratched. Discussion then became general. Unanimity was early reached on one outstanding name, a man not only of great scholarship but of notable missionary experience. He was, however, abroad. War-time communications being very uncertain, the next meeting of the Appointments Committee was fixed for some time ahead.

When the Committee did meet next time I was in bed with influenza. They had before them a letter of refusal from their first choice. What transpired at that meeting I do not know. What I do know is that I received the astonishing information that the Committee wished to nominate me for appointment as the new General Secretary.

I took twelve days to reply, feeling it imperative to discover if my future colleagues, the other Secretaries of the Society, really approved. I met them as a group a few days later. Then I went down to Worcester to see Bishop Cash. He gave me his blessing in more than an episcopal sense. Back in Cambridge, I consulted the three wisest men I knew — Paul Gibson, Evered Lunt and Charles Raven. All approved. Likewise, I took the earliest opportunity of seeing the Bishop of Ely, Dr. Edward Wynn, a friend of many years. With his blessing and that of all the others, I wrote to accept the nomination. On 3rd March, 1942, the Executive Committee approved it, and on 19th March I was elected by the General Committee. On 1st June, for the first time, I sat down at my desk in No. 6 Salisbury Square. C.M.S. House, Salisbury Square, itself had been familiar to me since boyhood when I often visited my father in his office just along the passage from where I was now sitting. But there was nothing familiar about that chair. What prevented it from being a 'hot seat' was the unreserved welcome given me by the whole staff. Even so it was the quiet, self-effacing, meticulously careful, and always efficient businesslike ability of George Cooper, my office assistant, which really made my job possible, not only in those early days, but on until his retirement in 1957, when a similar loyalty and friendship and efficiency were given me by his successor, Margaret Rome.

I came into office with a very deep respect for my predecessor. What attracted me above all was the spirit of the man. Throughout a large part of his time as General Secretary he had been occupied with an unhappy theological controversy in which the Society was involved. What profoundly impressed me, as it did many others, was that he never allowed controversy to dirty his soul. Bilious comment he always refused to respond to with bile. This was the gentleness not of a weak man but of a very strong one. Later, in a different context, I was to be much involved in controversy myself. From Dr. Cash I learnt that it is possible to disagree without bitterness even about the } most deeply held convictions: to disagree and yet to remain in spiritual fellowship.

Again, I was fortunate in that Dr. Cash's far-sighted statesmanship had ensured that the Society entered the war years in a financial position which was basically as sound as possible, that of being out of debt.

It was also no small asset that I had been on the Executive Committee for four years and had had abundant opportunity of watching the interaction of a General Secretary with a very independent-minded Committee. Leadership of a Committee of laymen and clergy, all men and women of experience in their own fields, and all equally committed to the welfare of the Society as they saw it, calls for adroitness and an awareness that victories in argument can be Pyrrhic, that defeat is not disaster, that *reculer pour mieux sauter* is not only a practical policy on the battlefield, but often the key to arrival at that kind of *consensus* which makes committee work a satisfying exercise in co-operation. Dr. Cash also taught me this.

How did I see my task as I began to find my feet in Salisbury Square? The two journeys already described gave a sense of direction. Somehow in the years ahead we had to discover how to relate the commission to preach the Gospel with the no less urgent commission to preach it with understanding, to communicate it in a world where its personal values and corporate insights were increasingly under attack or contemptuously ignored. This would certainly mean giving the missionary movement a different image from its traditional one, without, if possible, losing its traditional bases of support.

The 'New Order' Exhibition at Cambridge in 1941 had attracted the attention of wider circles. The range of Christian witness was increasingly seen to be very much more extensive than preaching, more even than the forms of 'preaching' already familiar through the media of education and medicine. Men's minds were being radically altered by the pressures of the technological revolution. What was no less obvious was that the war was enormously increasing the head of steam already generated against the old-style colonialism. Japan's new 'Co-Prosperity sphere' in Asia might not be destined to endure. What was as nearly certain as could be was that, when Japan was defeated, there would be no going back to the old imperialisms.

Writing this now is not hindsight. Those hours-long discussions on the *Queen Mary*, and all my reading, had convinced me that the missionary movement was moving forward into an unknown world.

Meanwhile, England was suffering from war-weariness. My immediate responsibility was for a staff which was not only depleted in size but exhausted by the complications involved in much of its work. This had had to be divided between Salisbury Square, and that part of it which had been evacuated to Chislehurst. And it did not call for much imagination to see how tired my secretarial colleagues were, or to guess that whenever the war ended—and no end was in sight— there would be a great many desperately tired missionaries returning from long-extended terms of service abroad.

Long tradition going back at least as far as Henry Venn (1841–1872), had determined the pattern of the role I had to play. By virtue of office I was Secretary of the Society's main committees. As to my immediate colleagues, I was *primus inter pares,* a position in which the *primus* must gain consent from a team of *pares* who were in this case, in terms of experience, far more my superiors than equals—a delicate situation. Nevertheless, and inescapably, I had to be the chief interpreter of the Society to the Church in this country and to the Church overseas. Henry Venn had also insisted that it was the prerogative of the 'Chief Secretary' to communicate with the Archbishop of Canterbury and with Bishops generally. Also, to circles which knew little or nothing about Mission, the General Secretary was accepted as the spokesman of the Society.

Such was my assignment, and such was the way in which I saw the unfolding future of the Society's work, necessarily vague as to details but clear as to general direction. Something of how I saw my personal responsibility can be seen from my diary. During the early part of 1942 I had been reading Bishop Lightfoot's revised texts and English trans- lations of the Apostolic Fathers. In my diary for 9th June of that year I had copied out the following extract from the letter of Saint Ignatius to Saint Polycarp:

> Vindicate thine office in all diligence of flesh and of spirit. Have a care for union, than which there is nothing better. Bear all men, as the Lord also beareth thee. Suffer all men in love, as also thou doest. Give thyself to unceasing prayers. Ask for larger wisdom than thou hast. Be watchful, and keep thy spirit from slumbering. Speak to each man severally after the manner of God. Bear the maladies of all, as a perfect athlete. Where there is more toil, there is much gain.

Was it very presumptuous to copy that passage into my diary within ten days of coming to Salisbury Square? If so, it was in a degree safe- guarded from *hubris* by the fact that I have never had any sympathy for what is called the Ignatian view of episcopacy. But it seemed to me that apart from his adjuration to address other men 'after the manner of God' —an ambiguous piece of advice —it did appear that the passage had some profound advice to give to anyone who, after whatever fashion, had been called to exercise *episcope*.

An immediate task, however, which allowed of no postponement was in finding my place in the team of Secretaries who carried the day-to-day responsibility for the affairs of the Society. It so happened that at the time of my appointment there was also a vacancy in the office of Home Secretary. With very great imagination and not a little courage the Committee encouraged me to find the man of my own choice. I chose Tom Isherwood, at the time Vicar of Christ Church, Claughton. We were of one mind on every issue and it was an immense joy to have his gay and witty comradeship for four years. What is more, he helped me to learn how to feel my way with colleagues so much more experienced than myself. Handley Hooper, the Africa Secretary, had been Africa Secretary when I went out as a missionary in 1927. Gurney Barclay, the East Asia Secretary, was a veteran of work in Japan, as was that generous saintly figure, John Mann, one-time Bishop of Kyushu. Geoffrey Cranswick as India Secretary had done yeoman service in the Nadia district of Bengal. Harold Anderson, with years of missionary service in China behind him, was Medical Secretary. Oliver Turton, with business experience in Pakistan, was Financial Secretary. Ethel Doggett, a mine of historical knowledge, was Editorial Secretary. Soon to join us, at my urgent insistence, as Woman Secretary, was Ena Price, already knowledgeable of the Society's work as Women Candidates' Secretary, but like Tom Isherwood and myself a tyro at the Secretaries' Table.

This was a formidable team. That they should have been willing to welcome me was itself a considerable miracle of grace. The principal instruments of that miracle, in which nevertheless all shared, including their successors as the membership changed with the years, were Ena Price and Handley Hooper. Ena, who was to see me through my whole time at Salisbury Square, was one of an age with myself. She became my closest friend in this friendly circle, in effect my 'office wife', a woman of wisdom and tact to whom I could always turn for guidance in many a complicated human problem, whether within the Secretariat or on the staff. We had also this in common that neither of us had departmental responsibilities. Each of us by definition had a general concern, she very particularly for the women on the staff and for the women missionaries. She was a consummate pastor exercising a continuous ministry of reconciliation, a veritable priesthood to her fellow-secretaries and the whole staff.

Handley Hooper, in the very nature of things so much my senior in age and experience, was in an almost fatherly relationship. He had encouraged me as a missionary recruit; he had had me as one of his more impetuous missionaries; he had stood by Mary in the years of my illness; he had married us. He had a deep concern that I should 'make it' in my job. And he had the faithfulness of a true friend.

A letter of his to me in 1948 is at once a measure of that faithfulness and of how slow I was to learn the art of chairmanship, to discipline } my own sense of urgency, and to acquire a degree of patience. I had recently returned from a journey round the world and a book of mine *The Truth of Vision* had just been published. He wrote:

I want you to know with what great satisfaction I have been reading *The Truth of Vision*. As you know, I hope, I have never seriously doubted that in all essentials our outlook on C.M.S. work was identical, but your own anxiety over a point of variation in the expression of those views left me wondering whether, after all, there was some deep-rooted conviction directing your own reading of events, which I had not grasped and, therefore, could not share: from time to time a particular incident evoked from you an emphasis, which seemed overriding past the point of extreme tension, and I have waited to see whether other considerations still had the power to reassert themselves in your judgment. In the end, you've always had the grace and humility to respect a demurring voice, and to give it a hearing: so that I was strengthened in my belief that it was in method rather than substance that any divergence occurred.

If I had wanted any further assurance, you have given it to me in your book, and I do thank God for the deeper confidence it has engendered in your leadership: while it was positively exciting to find inchoate ideas which had been milling round in my own mind clothed in clear-cut observations in your book.

I never reach ideas by cool logic: they grow for me in intuition, or rather the subconscious until they burst into the light of day. It's why reading is such a succession of thrills for me, as a sentence here and there cracks the shell for a small chicken to emerge!

A lorry engine is always likely to be an exasperating medium of locomotion to one who is accustomed to jet propulsion, but with the good sense to recognise that what will not drive a plane will yet prove a means of transport, I'm happy to think that my slow movement may not utterly dismay you.

I'm more concerned lest the intensity with which you meet each issue should wear you down. May the end in view stablish your heart against the breakdown on a rough road.

My love to you, Max, and very tender sympathy as well as deep gratitude for the pangs which must have attended the birth of this book.

I quote that letter in full because it reveals two things. It shows the tact and the gentle skill with which an older man could pull up a younger one, correct a grave fault in his practice, and the while tell the truth in love. That letter also illustrates the quality and depth of fellowship within the Secretariat of the Society.

Because that fellowship was so rich in its spiritual dynamic I want to make clear its secret. To do this I quote some words from a friend who has also been for many years my revered teacher in the New Testament, Professor C. F. D. Moule (Charlie to his innumerable friends). In a small book, *Christ's Messengers**, he answers the question as to what character marked the first Christian community.

> We noticed, (he wrote), that 'forthrightness' was a quality of the individual Christian before his opponents. Within the community the same thing appears as 'simplicity of heart' (Acts 2:46). This is the only place in the whole New Testament where this particular word occurs; but there are similar ideas elsewhere—'sincerity' (for instance, in 1 Cor. 5:8; Phil. 1:10), and 'singlemindedness' (as in Rom. 12:8). It is a quality which marks every real Christian brotherhood—a quality which we simply cannot create in ourselves: it is a gift of the Holy Spirit. The phrase seems to mean a complete transparency of motive, a condition in which acts and thoughts alike are controlled by one, single, dominating motive—that of pleasing the Lord.

I aver that for twenty-one years I lived in a community of a similar 'simplicity of heart'. I believe that all the others would give the same testimony. Pilgrimage in such a company is exciting living in which it is possible to go 'always a little further' than any one of us could venture alone.

I do not pretend that we did not know occasions of great strain within the group of Secretaries. Disagreements between one and another sometimes ran very deep indeed. Often I got up from a Secretaries' meeting physically exhausted and deeply worried. In saying this I am not thinking so much of those failures in myself which Handley Hooper had so faithfully pointed out, and of which there were many. I am thinking rather of the fear, which I sometimes had,

*C. F. D. Moule, op. cit. (Lutterworth Press—World Christian Books, 1957), pp. 91-92

that a clash of temperament might lead to a breakdown in relationships, such as would paralyse some part of our work, with incalculable repercussions. If a team is geared to co-operation then non-co-operation can disintegrate the team. We never reached that point but we did, on occasion, get perilously near it.

Again, I remember a sickness of heart which was almost overwhelming when I thought that I was carrying none of my colleagues with me in my understanding of imminent developments abroad, still less of the appropriate means by which the Society could turn them to advantage. Time, often, seemed as if it was 'five minutes to twelve'. Despair was, sometimes, only just round the corner.

But I am glad that as a team of Secretaries we knew the rough side of being on pilgrimage, that is the company of the other pilgrims! Perhaps only by taking the rough with the smooth could we discover that, in spite of ourselves, we were held by the Holy Spirit, that *koinonia* of the New Testament kind was not only for fair-weather travelling.

I have written of that first company which met each Thursday to deal with the Society's business. If I do not here catalogue the others who succeeded them it does not mean that the quality of the fellowship diminished. In many ways it became enhanced.

But there is one more whom I will mention here for, after Tom Isherwood had gone to Canada in 1946, Leslie Fisher joined us as Home Secretary, coming to us from being Rector of Bermondsey. He and I were close colleagues for seventeen years, closer to each other in some ways than most of the others because so very much depended on the completeness of our partnership. As General Secretary I was often abroad. But at all times it was my responsibility to be scanning the horizon, marking the direction of events in the world and their bearing on our enterprise, and in broad outline indicating what it must mean for the Society. Leslie had the tremendous task of translating these hopes and fears into terms which could be understood in the parishes, and their often unattractive implications accepted by the Society's membership, upon whose continued and increasing support in understanding prayer and self-sacrificing giving the work depended. Leslie and I did not always see eye-to-eye in regard to tactics. That we could, nevertheless, be in such close accord owed much to the fact that often he was able to call for me in his car, and, as we drove up to the office, we could discuss the best way of doing the work of interpretation. And it was through Leslie that I got my main opportunities of discovering the sterling worth of the 'bagmen' of the Society, our Area Secretaries, and being privileged, in at least some cases, of enjoying their friendship. They themselves were a remarkable company at the heart of which was Leslie himself. Leslie worked them hard but never harder than he worked himself. He had his difficulties. He knew what it was to face a crisis of confidence. For there came times when strong leadership in an uncongenial direction was quite essential. The Area Secretaries were not 'yes' men. But Leslie won through. Part of his secret was his deep compassion for a world in need of the Gospel. No one could doubt that. Part of his secret also was that he never allowed that compassion to be generalised. It found its immediate focus in these men and their families for whom he was directly responsible.

Earlier, I have referred to the war-weariness of the staff. Once again those journeys by train and ship gave me a clue to what was needed. The senior members of the staff, the back-room boys who carried the routine of the administration, needed encouragement. Not least they needed to be as fully advised as possible of the changes ahead in the work of the Society. Many of these men had been with C.M.S. since boyhood, coming in at fourteen years of age. Some had already completed almost fifty years of service. A number remembered me as a schoolboy coming in to visit my father. Their confidence in the steering of the ship had to be won. So at the earliest possible moment I began to take parties of six or seven of them away for a weekend to St. Julian's.* There we would have some time for Bible Study, a period of interpretation about the work of the Society as it seemed likely to develop, and then one or two sessions in which everyone was encouraged to let his hair down and ventilate his worries and anxieties, whether about the Society, or the way the work at Salisbury Square was organised. We did not call it workers' participation. But we were feeling our way towards it. I reckon this was as important for the Society as anything I did in my first five years. And Ena Price was also taking to St. Julian's similar groups from the women of the staff with the same object in view.

These weekends did not achieve all I hoped. A few of the old guard found new ideas more than they could stomach. Many years later I was given evidence of under-cover rebellion of which I knew nothing at the time. Nevertheless, something was achieved. They gave renewed vigour to hard-working tired men. They served to bring some of the younger ones forward towards the day when they would be the seniors upon whom the morale of the entire staff would in fact depend.

All that I have written so far might well suggest a 'junta' running the affairs of the Society in magnificent isolation. The facts were far

*See page 222

otherwise. We were, as Secretaries, very much men and women under authority. Anything less like a company of acquiescent 'know nothings' than the Society's Executive Committee,* or for that matter any of its Committees, it would be difficult to find. Here, lessons learnt under Dr. Cash were of value. I had more than once watched some carefully cherished plan put forward by Dr. Cash referred back. I also had observed that, perhaps six months later, the same plan, virtually unchanged, would be approved unanimously. I had the same experience. But I would gladly bear witness to the fact that whenever the Committee rejected some proposal of the Secretaries it was not out of cussedness, but out of a shrewd idea that the proposals had not been given the detached consideration they needed. More time and thought were needed. When the Committee so judged they were always } right.

We sometimes found Committees exasperating; yet they were our governing bodies and they were our direct link with the Membership scattered all over the country. Furthermore they brought in the judgment of the well-informed 'amateur' as a check on the specialised knowledge of their salaried 'professionals'. As Secretaries we could easily miss the wood for the trees. The very able group of laity and clergy on our Committees kept the balance and prevented us disappearing out of sight! And they were quite extraordinarily generous in the trust they reposed in us. By way of illustration I can recall that, though my monthly News-Letters were often anything but congenial reading, and often raised major issues of missionary policy without any prior consultation with any Committee, I was never once taken to task for having over-stepped the limits, or unwisely committed the Society. I very much doubt if there was any other General Secretary of a Mission Board in North America, Australia or the continent of Europe who was allowed a freedom comparable to that which I myself enjoyed. A committee with that courage could rely on absolute loyalty. In my twenty-one years we had many a lively and vigorous debate, some shaking of heads, and not a few cases of business being referred back, but never a row, and, to the best of my recollection, never a single resignation.

I have only one regret, as I look back, and that is that it was not until I was actually writing this book that I made the discovery that my great-great-grandfather, William Day, curate of Bengeworth in Worcestershire, was on 2nd December, 1799, elected a country mem-

*In 1973 some alterations were made in the Committee structure of the Society. The Executive Committee of fifty members was replaced by a Standing Committee of thirty. In relation to what has been said above let us hope that *plus ça change plus c'est la même chose*!

ber of the Society's Committee, and is named in the Society's first subscription list! It would have been such fun to pull out this bit of information while intervening in some debate, or using it as a final peroration in proposing some novel departure in the Society's policy!

Duty as well as pleasure demands that I reflect on the Officers of the Society, in particular the President and Treasurer under whom I served. Sir Robert Williams, the President when I was appointed, was a sick man at the time and died shortly afterwards. I shall always reckon that one of the most useful things I ever did was to bring forward the name of Mr. Kenneth Grubb as the man we needed as our new President. In *Crypts of Power** in which he records some of his own memories he has written most kindly about me so that it would be embarrassing if I had to say frankly how much I disliked him. It was, however, far otherwise. Our first meeting had been in 1920 when he was my tent officer at a boys' camp. From time to time I had read of him in the intervening years when he was in South and Central America, and we had corresponded briefly. I knew him as a man with a missionary background, his father having been one of the Society's Assistant-Secretaries for twelve years at the end of the last century. He himself had been a pioneer missionary in South America, and had established a great reputation for his contribution to thorough research, reported in the publications of the World Dominion Trust. Meanwhile I knew something of his work with the Ministry of Information during the war.

Everything that I was anticipating about the likely situation at the end of the war pointed to the need for a President with great administrative capacity and a very wide knowledge of the world and of the 'corridors of power'. I was delighted when he was offered the appointment and accepted it.

This began for me a very stimulating partnership. For here was a man upon whom I could try out every new idea and know that he would bring to it a critical judgment born of a vast and varied experience. Also he was one to whom I could turn for advice on how best to approach authorities in the State, both in this country and abroad. Indeed he was invaluable in undertaking most of these approaches himself. The generosity with which he gave his time and thought to the Society was the more remarkable in that, with each year that passed, my own demands upon him for time and thought increased enormously, precisely when he was being increasingly caught up in countless other activities, not least those of the Church Assembly. But I never turned to him in vain.

*Sir Kenneth Grubb, K.C.M.G., *Crypts of Power—An Autobiography*, (Hodder and Stoughton, 1971).

I will not pretend that he was the easiest person to work for. A glutton for work himself and a master of orderly procedure, he expected to be met with a similar appetite for work and an equal mastery of procedure. I can work fairly fast myself, when this is necessary, and in that respect I kept up with him. But I was no master of procedure. Further to that, I matched his laconic style of writing with a prolixity which must often have distressed him. From time to time he expressed his distaste, and drafts, when returned to me, while always improved, were rich in the blue pencillings which eliminated any word or passage of even the faintest hue of heliotrope, let alone purple! Nonetheless it was vastly invigorating and a continuous education. I must add, what a future historian restricted to correspondence and memoranda might miss. Kenneth Grubb brought to his work for C.M.S. a devotion based on a dedicated discipleship to Jesus Christ and the missionary commission. There were those who only knew the man of affairs, the shrewd business mind, the somewhat cynical observer of ecclesiastical machinery in operation. I knew the man of faith. There is no possible accounting of the debt the Society owes to his wisdom, his statesmanship and unremitting attention to its affairs. When his knighthood was to be gazetted he was asked under what heading he would wish the recognition to be made. He had a wide variety of choice. It was characteristic of Sir Kenneth that he asked for the heading, 'President of the Church Missionary Society'.

The other chief Officer of the Society was Kingsley Tubbs, a member of a firm of chartered accountants in the City, who for thirty-two years served the Society as its Treasurer. As Treasurer he was Chairman of the Finance Committee. Although the Financial Secretary of the Society was secretary of this committee, the General Secretary was expected to be present. In no sense of the word competent to deal with financial matters, I could admire superb and courageous chairmanship. No time was ever wasted and yet no important decision was ever rushed. During these years there were many occasions when the financial situation of the Society was critical in the extreme. But I never knew Kingsley Tubbs lose his nerve or just play for safety. He often used to insist that he was a plain layman and did not understand theological issues. Nevertheless, knowing what the Society was about he was determined to ensure that the material sinews for its spiritual warfare were available.

I give two brief illustrations of his vision. At a critical juncture in the Society's affairs shortly after the war, when the deficit in the income and expenditure account was nearly fifty thousand pounds, the Home Secretary had the temerity to ask for an extra publicity fund, to enable the Society's case for greater support to be more adequately presented.

Kingsley Tubbs quickly saw the point, successfully pressed for ten thousand pounds to be added to the Society's budgeted expenditure, and saw to it that it was repeated in the following year. He also proved himself a no less staunch supporter of the Initiative Fund, whose operation was left to the discretion of the Secretaries, one of the most valuable departures from precedent in my time.

In Henry Venn's day the Society was described as a 'lay-society'. This was a technical legal term. We were proud to use it as denoting a Society whose decisive leadership in the persons of its Officers and, with one exception, the chairmen of its sub-committees, was vested in laymen or, equally, lay women. In C.M.S. bishops and clergy had their honoured place. But they did not dominate.

During my time and after the Society had the services of an able group of men and women who, while not carrying Secretarial responsibility, were doing work that was every whit as important. Again, I cannot list them all, but there are some I must mention for in a particular degree they made possible the realisation of many of my dreams.

I mention first, Leslie Stubbings. A man at the top of his profession in the highly competitive field of commercial advertising, he had played a leading part in the advertising campaign of the Ministry of Agriculture during the war. With the end of the war he wanted to do something different. Nothing if not an adventurer, he offered his services to C.M.S., threw up a secure position and a fine salary, and came to us with no certainty of more than a two-year appointment.

I was one of those immediately responsible for the appointment and he came to me for interview. For long I had been profoundly dissatisfied with the quality of missionary publicity in general, and with the Society's publicity in particular. It so happened that just before the interview a paperback of mine had been published with a bright and bold design for a cover. I was rather pleased with it. I showed it to Leslie Stubbings, who exploded, 'This is terrible. It is plain dishonest. Look at the contrast between the fine bold cover and the dull unimaginative print inside, the narrow margins, the ugliness of it all.' That was quite a slap in the face for an author. Leslie Stubbings didn't know me from Adam, and was on interview for a job. What I recognised at once was that here was the man we wanted —a man of integrity who would never willingly allow an outside cover to tell an inside lie.

Leslie Stubbings transformed the Society's publicity. He did more. He set a pattern and a standard for the other Societies both Anglican and Free Church. As a well-informed observer has stated:

His 1946 report *Invitation to Adventure* had, within a decade or so, permeated all Christian thinking and publicity and standards of presentation. Bringing him into the Society in 1946 was not the least significant event for the Church of England in the mid-twentieth century of Anglican affairs.

That may sound like exaggeration. Having been interested in typography for many years, and having seen the impact of the 'New Order' Exhibition in Cambridge in 1941, I am satisfied that although Leslie Stubbings is unknown to fame that quotation is a sober assessment. His works do follow him.

In 1945 Bernard Nicholls, a member of the staff of the Associated Press, working in Reuter's building, walked across Salisbury Square to ask if there was a possibility of employment with C.M.S. The war had tested his capacity for adventure when as a convinced pacifist working in the shelters throughout the blitz on London he saw as much of the front line of danger as many a man in the armed forces. He likewise, with the full support of his wife Doris, was prepared, after the war, for the leap of faith involved in the loss of a secure job and the consequent loss of salary. C.M.S. at the time had nothing to offer except a junior post in the editorial department. But he brought to that department an experience possessed by no one else on the staff. Very quickly he became a close collaborator with Leslie Stubbings. He was the obvious man to become our Public Relations Officer and, as such, was a member of Leslie Fisher's team which so brilliantly prepared for and carried through the Society's 'Third Jubilee' programme in 1948–1949.

Kenneth Cooper, the 'argumentative cuss' and expert disperser of any tendency to complacency, was no longer so accessible. Bernard took his place with unfailing zest. How often at the close of the office day he would come into my room, and within minutes he would be taking up some half-baked idea of mine and shaking it like a terrier dealing with a rat. After an hour or so of this I was pulverised, physically exhausted, yet stimulated beyond measure. We didn't always agree. Bernard wasn't concerned about agreement. He wanted to make sure I had looked all round a question before going forward to plot a course of action. The errors from which he saved me were legion. As important, he was a continual assurance that I hadn't been wasting my time on those journeys by train and ship. They had taught me the value of men like Bernard Nicholls and Leslie Stubbings so that when these men came over my horizon I was equipped to learn what they had to teach. It was an invaluable education. Being myself by nature an academic, it was men like Kenneth Cooper, Leslie Stubbings and

Bernard Nicholls who kept my feet on the ground and my head not wholly lost in theological clouds.

In 1953 Douglas Webster, later to be a Canon of St. Paul's Cathedral, joined us as Education Secretary. So rapidly did he make his mark by his lucid interpretations of the Bible and the freshness of his presentation of the Gospel, well illustrated in such books as *In Debt to Christ* and '*What is Evangelism?*'* that he became in constant demand all over the country. In 1961 the Committee agreed to support him in a much wider ministry. He was appointed 'Theologian Missioner', and encouraged to accept invitations not only from dioceses in which C.M.S. was at work, but from other dioceses and Provinces, making in this way a contribution as wide as the Anglican Communion.

Douglas Webster and his predecessor as Education Secretary, John Drewett, were the two men whose deep theological insights and uncomprising concern to relate these to the wider life of society, worked on parallel lines with Leslie Stubbings and Bernard Nicholls, to keep our direction clear. It was such men who kept the rest of us from losing our way or, as was to become so fashionable in the Church in later years, from losing our nerve.

No one who had to do as much writing of memoranda and books, not to mention the monthly News-Letter, as proved to be an essential part of my work, could have hoped to do without the continuous help of a research assistant. Once again I was fortunate. In a later chapter I will be referring to the remarkable contribution made by Elizabeth France (now Mrs. Harold Anderson). Here I would pay tribute to Greta Preston who came as research assistant in 1955 and, in time, became the almost omniscient source of information, not only for members of the staff but for everyone else who could reach her by telephone. I modestly claim a share in this 'build up'. While I rarely ever recommended anyone to read a book I had not first read myself—this was an absolute rule as regards those recommended in the monthly C.M.S. News-Letter—yet all my writing depended on a mass of other and detailed information being collected, assimilated, and arranged in order. This was Greta's work and she never failed to have everything ready for me the moment I wanted it. We worked together to a careful programme and she knew up to four or five months ahead the kind of material I would need. Often she suggested the theme for a News-Letter. Always she was thinking ahead. Partnership of this quality is very exciting. It is some satisfaction to know that she enjoyed it as much as I did. I have been very lucky with the 'girls in my life'.

A General Secretary, in the nature of his office, receives a very great

*D. Webster, *In Debt to Christ* (Highway Press, 1957), '*What is Evangelism?*', (Highway Press, 1959).

deal of confidential information, much of it of temporary significance, but still confidential, and some of it of very serious import. His private office staff must be persons of utter reliability with whom a confidence is a confidence without qualification. I never had a moment's uneasiness on this score in twenty-one years. I have already mentioned George Cooper and Margaret Rome, my two assistants, repositories of dynamite which never exploded. From Dr. Cash I inherited, as private secretary, Mrs. May. In 1944 she was succeeded by Madge Lea who retired in 1957 to be in turn succeeded by Gwyneth Hawkins, Mary Kimber and lastly by Susan Turner (now Mrs. Harverson). They all had the same discretion, as did Ella Jennings who kept the Society's Committee records and indefatigably typed almost all my travel diaries, of which there are thirty-seven. What was as valuable as their discretion was the cunning way in which Madge Lea and Susan Turner, in particular, were able to convey, without saying a word, that they disapproved of some passage in a letter I was dictating. The smooth running of the pencil over the notebook did not stop. But a palpable silence began to fill the room. I realised quickly that I had allowed exasperation or temper to find expression in language calculated to hurt, not to help. 'Was that too tough?' I would ask. 'Well, perhaps a little,' came the reply. That passage was scrubbed.

That I have been throughout my life the most fortunate of men must by now be obvious. If in this chapter I have dealt at some length with some of the men and women with whom it was my good fortune to work it has been of set purpose. There is a degree in which leadership is always lonely, and inevitably exhausting physically, while being a continuous threat to the spiritual life. If during those years I did not fail more than I did it was due not only to my immediate family, but also to the family in Salisbury Square. To be completely happy over so long a period with both families was an experience which deserves to be noted. It is not all that commonplace.

This is perhaps the place to refer to a letter which I received in May 1946, a letter which I found as disturbing as it was unexpected. Mr. Attlee, the Prime Minister, wrote asking me to accept nomination to a diocesan bishopric. Mr. Attlee cannot possibly have known anything about me but I guessed who had put the idea into his head. Sure enough, next day there came a letter from an episcopal palace pressing me to accept the invitation.

What so disturbed me about this suggestion was that it should have been made before I had completed even four years at C.M.S. To have accepted would have been an act of complete irresponsibility. I had scarcely begun to learn my job as General Secretary. Furthermore, on being appointed it had been unofficially but clearly stressed that I would be expected to stay with the Society for at least ten years.

Courtesy demanded a not too abrupt refusal but I had no difficulty in explaining my position to both my correspondents. For me my commitment to the overseas missionary work of the Church was my real vocation, a vocation temporarily interrupted through illness and now, in such an unexpected way, once more offering a means of fulfilment.

During the second half of my period of office my reading of the riddle of the future argued the wisdom of aiming at a much smaller number of missionaries, whose activities, for the most part, would not be the traditional ones in schools and hospitals. Events, as I understood them, were pointing in this direction. This prospect I did not find in any way depressing. A right deployment of a smaller number of missionaries, more carefully selected and trained, could mean far more than the wrong deployment of double the number. The great problem was how to convey this idea to the members of the Society in the parishes in Britain. This is still the problem. Here was, and is, a genuine dilemma. All the probabilities suggested that the parochial pattern of Church life was about to undergo intolerable strains and stresses in the years ahead. The Society, I felt, was in danger of being very seriously limited in its operations in so far as it was tied in to this parochial pattern, with all that that pattern represented of conservatism in regard to the need for change. The supreme need of the future of evangelism, at home as well as abroad, was for flexibility.

Much of my time and thought was concerned with persuading others of these two interlocking concerns. As things have developed since then I think that my reading of the riddle of the future was substantially accurate. I did not see then, nor do I see now, any reason whatever why the Society, with its long experience of Mission in changing circumstances, should not use its own characteristic freedom as a Voluntary Society to match the needs of Mission in the dramatically different world which is coming to be.

19/8/77
Perceptive!

8

1942 - 1963

The Missionaries

'The Future I may face now I have proved the Past'.

For more is not reserved
To man, with soul just nerved
To act tomorrow what he learns today:
Here, work enough to watch
The Master work, and catch
Hints of the proper craft, tricks of the tool's true play.

ROBERT BROWNING

Rabbi Ben Ezra

IN the contemporary twilight of Christian confidence, amid the widespread confusion among Christians as to the purpose of the Church, the word 'missionary', the very activity of missionaries, is under a cloud. However, to be 'under a cloud' is to be in good Biblical company in this, as in other respects.

I make no apology for the word 'missionary', for which at least in the English language there is, in fact, no possible substitute. For this word alone accurately translates the one used in the New Testament to indicate a 'person sent with a message', someone commissioned.

I was once present at a gathering of the leaders of the Anglican Communion. We were meeting during the summer in a land where the summer is very hot indeed. That particular morning the heat was intense. A distinguished scholar, himself of the hierarchy, spoke of his wish that the word 'missionary', not being a New Testament word, might be banished from our vocabulary. The speaker went on to make the remarkable statement that while, of course, the New Testament spoke of people being 'sent', it had no noun to express the idea. In the silence which followed this magisterial utterance I plucked up my courage to ask if I might be allowed to speak. Permission was graciously accorded. I then asked, in all innocence, if there were not a noun in the New Testament which did mean precisely 'a man sent'—the word *apostolos*? In the circumstances of that gathering there was only one possible answer to that question. The smiles on the faces of those in the gathering who claimed at least 'tactual descent' from the original 'Twelve' indicated that the point had been taken.

No, I make no apology for the word 'missionary'.

I am, of course, open to the charge of being *parti pris* when I go on to say that I am not prepared lightly to assent to the fashionable charges made against the activities of missionaries. The son of missionary parents, for a short time a missionary myself, the father of one missionary, the uncle of another, I must in fairness 'declare my interest'. But sometimes the 'insider' knows most about the game.

Trained in the school of history at Cambridge, I know that one must never be content with second-hand sources but must, whenever possible, get back to the originals. This, over many years of studying the history of the missionary movement, I have tried to do. Another lesson which Cambridge taught me was that, in interpreting the past, one must imaginatively put oneself into that past, get as far as possible under the skins of the protagonists of an earlier day, understand their environment in its widest sense, and see how they were affected by that environment.

It has, of course, been a decisive help to my study of the history of Missions that I have not been operating from an academic armchair.

All down the years I have been in the closest possible living contact with missionaries of many races, I have seen them at work under all conditions, I am without any illusions. Because I count among my friends African and Asian missionaries as well as Europeans and Americans, I know their common problems, their hopes and fears, their triumphs and disasters. I have a lively sympathy with African and Asian Christians who protest loudly at the terrible mistakes missionaries have made (and are still making, being human and fallible) —but I also remember the mistake they did not make. They did not mute the Gospel. Their most vociferous critics are the children, grandchildren, or great-grandchildren of those who were first introduced to Jesus Christ by foreign missionaries. To say this is not in any way to defend the limited horizons of much missionary thinking, the stupidities born of insensitivity to the feelings of others, the often shocking lack of imagination about the genuineness of alien religious experience. All of this amid much else has been well documented. It is part of the story. It must not only be acknowledged but 'felt'. For none of these blunders, 'Himalayan' ones sometimes, are beyond the possibility of repetition.

I have introduced these reflections at the beginning of this chapter because they go some way, not only towards explaining my own attitude to the word 'missionary', and to the activities of missionaries, but also to explaining the practice of C.M.S. in which I was involved.

The Society has always insisted that its main contribution has been the sending of missionaries. The aim from the earliest days has been the service *by* people, *with* people, *for* people in order to call into being a Christian community which should be self-supporting, self-governing, and self-extending. There is, of course, nothing whatever self-centred about this. It is implicit in the New Testament idea of the Church.

Now, if missionaries prepared to serve this end were to be the Society's main contribution, then everything would depend upon the quality of the men and women being sent. In the choice of missionaries we often made mistakes, failing to see that in this case or that a missionary vocation could be best fulfilled in this country rather than overseas. The urgency of the need overseas, and the pressure from local Church leaders for missionaries, often led us to go against our better judgment. In the result it was the misplaced recruit who suffered. The blame was ours. Yet I can also testify that there was many a case when it looked, at first, as if a mistake had been made and then the missionary triumphantly vindicated the decision. Some of the most remarkable careers of service that I have watched came close to shipwreck at the beginning.

What seemed obvious was that missionaries must be made as fully
aware as possible of the situations into which they were to go. My
responsibility was to look ahead. To be fore-warned is to be fore-
armed. Two illustrations may suffice

Already Japan had, by government decree, forbidden the use of
foreign money to support Japanese Bishops and clergy, who, at that
time, were largely dependent on money from the U.S.A. Here was a
warning, a foretaste of what might easily happen elsewhere. A Church
which, at least as regards its Ministry, was not self-supporting, was
precariously placed.

The Japanese Government's decree seemed to me to call for immediate action. With Committee approval I wrote to all the Bishops
overseas, for whose stipends the Society was responsible, asking them
to take serious note of the warning from Japan. I promised that the
Society would continue to maintain its present full support for three
years, and that thereafter the total commitment would be reduced by
one-tenth over a ten-year period, so that at the end of thirteen years
the local Church would be fully responsible for the stipend of its
Bishop. Of the more than thirty Bishops to whom I wrote, all except
one readily accepted the goal and most of them achieved it. That was
a practical issue.

Far otherwise was it to convince many of the missionaries of the
direction of events and what this would mean for them. But we were
all in this together. I was acutely aware that missionaries coming back
to England after the war, many physically and mentally exhausted,
some with a ten-year gap since last in England, would hardly be in a
mood for radical re-thinking. A few might realise that an England
whose resources, material and psychological, had been strained to the
limit, was in no condition to maintain an empire, even if it wished to
do so. Yet it had been under the umbrella of that empire's protection
and its fundamental, if sometimes muddle-headed, liberalism that the
missionary had worked. He might, and often did, disagree with the
local District Commissioner as to ways and means and timing. But the
missionary had no doubt as to the genuineness of that District Commissioner's concern for the people in his charge. Insensibly, the missionary absorbed and shared the benevolent paternalism of the Raj.
Rarely did the missionary or the District Commissioner sense the
mounting resentment of the governed at the whole concept of
'trusteeship', at a pupillage apparently to continue indefinitely, at the
humiliation of being under alien rule.

There was a very difficult task of interpretation to be undertaken
for the returning missionaries, apart altogether from the preparation
of recruits. By long tradition there was, every year, a conference of all

missionaries on furlough. The object of this, apart from spiritual refreshment and fellowship, was the establishing of real contact between missionaries and those of us working at Salisbury Square: that is, between two groups, each all too easily disposed to the subtle generalisations of 'us' and 'them'. The early missionaries' conferences which I had to chair were no small strain. It was not easy for men and women of long and ripe experience to accept any kind of direction for their thinking from one so much younger than themselves, one who certainly could not know their local situation. I had to listen to a lot of straight speaking. Some of the older warriors did not always 'say it with flowers'. But our common commitment held us together. And among the most senior were some who were good at reading the storm signals, more of them, if I remember aright, from Asia than Africa. The Japanese invasion to the borders of India, and some experience of Japanese internment camps, called for no commentary from me.

Obviously, however, with the future in mind, what was of paramount importance was the preparation of the men and women who had been through the experience of war either as civilians or in the armed forces, and who were to be missionaries in the post-war world. While half-aware that the world had changed and was changing fast, they had no yard-stick by which to measure the change. They were right-minded enough in their liberal instincts, but heredity was against them. An empire may pass away: imperial instincts do not pass away quite so quickly. Just as, in 1974, the conviction that the world owes us a living, and in particular owes us cheap food, is the native attitude of ninety-eight per cent of the people of Britain, so, thirty years ago, it was not easy for the heirs of nineteenth-century imperialism to envisage a political and religious situation in which they would no longer play the part of the natural leaders.

For them, then, there had to be some learning of the political and economic context in which their missionary vocation was to be worked out. There had to be a psychological conditioning to the sheer precariousness of being 'foreign' missionaries in the acutely sensitive nationalist mood of the Churches in which they would be working. And, theologically, they had to be helped to see just how vital was the contribution to the authentic *oikumene* of the Christian Church which they had to give, precisely by being 'foreign'.

Early on in my time in C.M.S. I was in Tanganyika (before it became Tanzania). I was dozing on my bed one afternoon when there came a knock on the door. There stood four Africans who asked if they might come in for a talk. There followed a wonderful hour of friendly conversation. What interested me was that all four were African missionaries from another African country. What was quite obvious was that they were as much 'foreign' missionaries as any European would be. In their foreignness lay part of their contribution. Missionary principles are of universal application and have nothing whatever to do with race.

yes!

Another theological task which had to be anticipated was that of entering into the spiritual experience of people of other Faiths. I myself was slow to learn what this meant. For long I followed the widespread custom of speaking of 'non-Christian' religions. In its own way this expressed an attitude which is one of the subtlest obstacles to entering into the spiritual experience of the man of another Faith. It starts off with a negative attitude towards the other man's own spiritual integrity: he is viewed as *not* something. What he is is not as important as what he is not. I had to learn, what every missionary has to learn, that this simply is not good enough. Unless the other man has an authentic spiritual experience he and I have no common language in which we can communicate that by which we live.

true

My first and most sustained attempt to look at this whole range of problems was made through the monthly C.M.S. News-Letter. These were always written with two groups in view, the missionaries, and those whose understanding prayer and sacrificial giving maintained them. That these News-Letters also secured so wide a circulation in North America, Australia and on the continent of Europe can only have been due to the recognition that they were a genuine attempt to come to terms with the real context within which the Christian Mission had to operate. Frequent travel abroad, twenty-one journeys in the twenty-one years, many of them enabling me to stay with missionaries, all served to ensure that what I wrote bore some resemblance to actual situations.

The Society had always been committed to the importance of pre-service training for its missionaries. This had for long been the rule for all women missionaries. This training had recently been overhauled and brilliantly directed toward the new world by that remarkable woman of spiritual insight, Florence Allshorn. Her own short experience as a missionary in Uganda had opened her eyes to what was involved in being a missionary.

Men's training had a much longer history, going back to the early days of the Society, but since the closing of the Training Institution at Islington in 1915 it had become something of a Cinderella. The curious idea had grown up, even in Henry Venn's time, that a university graduate did not need any special training for missionary service. The inherent fallacy in this view was that it assumed the acquisition of a university degree would carry with it a natural capacity for understanding the mind of a Brahmin, or a Pathan, or an Arab or a Nilotic tribesman. This was cultural imperialism at its worst, assuming as it did that the rest of mankind, or at any rate that part of it resident in the continents of Asia and Africa, would be content indefinitely with wisdom distilled from Oxbridge, or even with that distilled with the engaging accent of Trinity College, Dublin. Of the latter there is the attractive legend that where T.C.D. men were concentrated in considerable numbers, as in the diocese of Fukien in China, the products of the C.M.S. schools spoke their own language with a brogue! Legend that may be, but there is an element of truth concealed in it. It was always possible for western-trained Asians and Africans of ability to become so foreign-orientated as to be intellectually alien to their own people. A Chinese Bishop of our Church told me that he always wrote out his sermons in English before translating them into Chinese! British politicians, as well as missionaries, made many a miscalculation to their own grave loss over the next thirty years through misunderstanding this development.

If possible more curious was the idea that an English or Irish clergyman, by virtue of Ordination, was exempt from the necessity for specific missionary training. Indeed, many considered that the demand to experience it was an impertinence. A few moments' reflection should be sufficient to convince those still sceptical that two or three years in a curacy, idolised by the younger women of the parish, while being the accepted leader of the youth club, might engender a *folie de grandeur* in a young man. This would hardly be an ideal preparation for accepting a subordinate position under an Asian or African with some quite different values, and possibly fewer academic qualifications.

So we insisted that young clergymen as well as doctors and teachers, agriculturalists and technicians of varying expertise should all be trained together. At least a few corners were rubbed off before the abrasive experience of Asia and Africa. 'Come off it', addressed to a *ci-devant* curate by a laboratory technician in the training college, might be a 'moment of truth' which would save him from a later disaster in Nigeria or Pakistan.

We started our men's training again in 1946 in Blackheath with the Rev. Robert Young and his wife Edith in charge. They brought years of experience in Sierra Leone to their task and laid the foundations. Later, a site was found at Chislehurst close to the Women's Training College.

At Chislehurst the leadership devolved in 1951 on Douglas Sargent and his American wife Imogene, two experienced missionaries from

China, ably assisted by Wilfred and Joan Brown from India. When, in due course, Douglas was snatched away to become Bishop of Selby and Wilfred to a parish in the Southwark diocese, Dennis and Heather Runcorn from Hong Kong took over in 1962, their task shared with Jim and Saidie Hewitt from Pakistan.

Without in any way quarrelling with the later decision to transfer the training of C.M.S. missionaries to Selly Oak* in Birmingham, for which many good reasons can be adduced, I am extremely glad that in my time, when men's training was being re-started, and joint training of men and women explored, this could take place within easy range of Salisbury Square. It meant that Secretaries and staff at Salisbury Square, not to mention Officers of the Society and members of Committee, could be in close touch with the staff and students of the two colleges. To be able to do a day's work in the office and be down in Chislehurst for supper and the evening was an enormous saving of nervous energy. Frequency of mutual contact was another asset of propinquity; it made for the 'family' spirit of the Society. A contributory factor to this sense of 'belonging' to a family was a development, at which the Secretaries arrived spontaneously, of going away together as a group for two long weekends each year, to be quiet together and to think together over the Society's responsibilities. This 'nuclear' fellowship inevitably influenced the wider life of the Society.

This emphasis on personal relationships which puzzled a great many observers was, we believed, a vital antiseptic to the erosion of the spiritual life by the burdens of administration. I have no doubt myself that this emphasis on 'withdrawal' and on 'fellowship at a nuclear level' overflowed into the training of missionaries in innumerable subtle ways. All this made for a simplicity of relationship which was a very enriching experience.

At a later stage a further development took place for missionaries on furlough. We had tried, with uneven success, to ensure a measure of continued training 'on the field', with especial attention to language. But we had much more success with what Florence Allshorn had insisted was quite indispensable, the securing for missionaries on furlough of a time of rehabilitation, spiritual and intellectual and professional. This took very different forms with different people. For some it meant several months at St. Julian's; for others a time at Selly Oak; for yet others a professional course in addition; for many, attendance at a retreat. One very valuable experiment was made which we called a 'School of Missions'. At this, some dozen missionaries on

*An Ecumenical Training Centre for Mission.

furlough would meet with some of the Secretaries for three or four days and together wrestle with some of the major problems arising overseas, as well as making a corporate attempt to see more clearly the road ahead. These 'schools' were hard work. They were meant to be. But they also made for cohesion.

A succession of very able women, all former missionaries, had charge of the training of the women recruits during this period—Margaret Potts (Nigeria), Hilda Stovold (Kenya), Winifred McKeeman (Bengal), Irene Tatham (Bengal), and Mollie Kluht (Uganda)—each of them bringing her distinctive interpretation to the broad vision laid down by Florence Allshorn.

The Principals of the Training Colleges were fully responsible for the training, and it was at their discretion that visiting speakers were invited to meet the students. My own responsibility was the strictly limited one of being available to the Principals for discussion of particular problems which might arise and which called for counsel rather than official action. But I was also greatly privileged in being asked down several times each term to meet the recruits-in-training. As my travelling abroad increased I frequently went down to tell them of some of my experiences and discoveries. But in addition I had three main concerns, all directly related to the spiritual life of the individual missionary. As I travelled about the world I became increasingly disturbed at the way in which the evangelical tradition was communicated. Of genuine evangelism there was plenty, mediated in an infinite variety of ways and never stereotyped. There was ample evidence of lives transformed by a living experience of Christ. But when it came to corporate worship it was all too often a starvation diet. I was deeply convinced that an Evangelicalism which stressed reverence and care in the conduct of corporate worship, and was not afraid of beauty and symbolism, and which knew how to combine these with the word of interpretation, had a great contribution to give everywhere, not least overseas. To this end I did all I could to encourage a deeper understanding of Holy Communion, gratefully introducing the Clare College 'use' as pioneered by John Robinson, as well as interpreting the inner dynamic of sacramental worship as I understood it.

Knowing as I did how poverty-stricken was much of the worship they would encounter, and how extremely lonely their ministry would often be, I did all I could to get them enthused with the Bible as the 'meat' upon which they would have to feed if their lives were to stand the spiritual tests that would be inescapable. Once, we had a Bible School for four days on the Epistle to the Galatians, carefully prepared for by a printed programme giving a reading list and a synopsis of the six addresses. Then on the last evening we had a dramatic presentation of the message of the Epistle. Everyone had been so caught up into the message and spirit of St. Paul that with the minimum of rehearsal they gave an unforgettable picture of what the Epistle was about. On another occasion my niece Sheelagh, when in training, produced an exciting play on 'The House of Chloe' interpreting the opening chapter of St. Paul's first letter to the Corinthians. During one term, with a carefully prepared synopsis printed and in their hands, we studied together in eight successive weeks the Epistle to the Romans—'as affording a foundation of doctrine, a mirror of churchmanship, a guide to evangelism, for missionaries on service'.

In 1943 I worked out a harmony of St. John, Chapter 13, with St. Luke, Chapter 22, which was published under the title *The Master of Time—an experience of the Lordship of Christ.* The dedication read as follows: 'To all my fellow workers in Salisbury Square, and to all who, as missionaries, have known the pressure of time and have joined in the quest for its mastery.'

These very simple exercises were well supplemented over the years by Bible Schools conducted first by Maisie Cattley, formerly Headmistress of the Perse School for Girls, of whom I have already written, and then later for many years by Mary Child. While on the staff of the Blackheath High School for Girls she had successfully infected both our daughters, and many others, with an enthusiasm for the Bible. It was after ten years as a missionary in Nigeria that she brought this gift to the missionaries in training.

Prayer, *preces privatae*, for all the marvellous expositions that have been given by men and women of God all down the centuries, has always been for me a great mystery. I envy those for whom prayer is a deep entering into conscious communion with God. Of that I know little. In saying this I am thinking of something different from what can happen to me when reading my Bible. Then it has been God speaking to me. What I find so difficult is speaking to God. What a mystery prayer is! I sometimes wonder if we do not make it more difficult by trying to rationalise it, reduce it to a method. Am I just being lazy when I ask if the essence of prayer is not a relationship—something given, accepted and deliberately enjoyed? May not a visit be a prayer, a conversation a prayer, a letter a prayer, even writing a book a kind of intercession for those who will read it? In a book, if it comes from the heart, one is going out into the lives of others—one is establishing contact with their minds and imaginations and trying to move their wills Godward and manward, being thereby moved one-self. Isn't that prayer? Deep down I do not believe that this is being lazy. I wonder if it may not point the way to something rather exciting. 'He walked with God'—that might not, at first showing, be a definition of prayer. Is there a better one?

So I have meditated and so rather feebly I have tried, when asked, to share with others my own perplexities and my hopes.

Because I have always found myself thinking most coherently when I had a pen in my hand I had written and published in 1947 a small book with the title *Together with God—a programme for Prayer*. Offered first to my fellow-Secretaries as the basis for our devotional sessions at one Weekend, I was encouraged to make it available for missionaries.

I have written thus about prayer in this chapter because, however great the degree of our corporate and individual failure, we in C.M.S. have tried to keep in mind the words of one of our founding fathers, John Venn of Clapham, 'Follow God's leading: begin on a small scale: put money in the second place; let prayer, study and mutual converse precede its collection: depend wholly upon the Spirit of God.' In a word—'Put Prayer First.'

A long-continuing interest in international affairs drove me to ponder the extremely difficult circumstances into which, as foreigners, the missionaries were going. Earlier generations had faced the perils of disease, to a large extent mitigated today. The risk of violence has not varied significantly down the years if an over-all view is taken. Where the change is most marked is in the psychological situation confronting an alien of any race, but for the British, in particular, in territories in Asia and Africa where Britain has been the governing power. This is no place in which to detail the kind of sensitivity which a missionary in such a territory has to show today. What adds greatly to their problems is that what is often expected of them is a sentimental attitude towards the local Church, an uncritical attitude towards the local nationalism, and a happy acceptance of the role of a mat upon which everyone can wipe their feet. Let us face frankly that this is no more than a reversal of roles. But it was one thing to view the situation historically, to contemplate past *hubris* from the altitude of Geneva or New York or even Salisbury Square. It was quite another matter to confront a situation abroad in which your teeth were set on edge solely because of the sins of your fathers.

Part then of the preparation of missionaries for the 'shock' awaiting them was not only to commend the great Christian virtues of patience, humility, endurance, but also to indicate that 'speaking the truth in love' might be equally necessary, however unwelcome; that 'being tough' could be, in given circumstances, not only a Christian virtue but something of the greatest service to the community in which they served.

One of the most dramatic illustrations of what I mean by this is to be found in the life of that remarkable missionary Carey Francis.* Fellow of Peterhouse, Cambridge, a brilliant mathematician, no mean athlete, he found himself headmaster of the Alliance High School in Kenya. His devotion to his African students led him to refuse any compromise whatever on standards. Sometimes indeed it seemed as though he were demanding nothing less than an ability comparable to his own. But what he was doing was seeking for the future leaders of Kenya a quality of intellectual and moral integrity which would match their responsibilities.

The account of his funeral in Mr. Greaves' biography should be compulsory reading for all sentimentalists. The pall-bearers, with one exception all Africans, were leading political figures, members of the Government, and the leader of the Opposition party. The House of Representatives adjourned to enable members to attend the funeral— a remarkable testimony to a great Christian missionary who refused to allow sentiment to compromise principle.

The fact is, all who would serve their fellows, especially if their fellows are of a different race, need to be creatively tough. They need to meet men and women without illusion, because they have first learnt to face themselves without illusion: and then go on to build by faith something which only faith can anticipate. Here and there across the world I have met others who, like Carey Francis, were doing this. But they were rare. Is it possible to train missionaries for this? I am far from certain that it is. But we shall be saved from much disappointment, and some missionaries will be saved from bitter frustration, if we can make sure that all the missionary virtues which we inculcate are properly mixed.

Another psychological factor, a more subtle one, was brought home to me at an International Conference. We had been discussing finance, and I had tried to indicate the shrinking capacity of the Christian public in Britain to meet all the demands being made. As the issue was one of increasing contributions to the International Missionary Council for disposal through the Council I asked, as I thought, a quite innocent question— 'Should the Missionary Societies write out to the Churches in India, explain the situation, and offer the choice of more aid through the I.M.C. even if it meant less aid sent direct, because it was impossible to maintain direct aid *and* increase grants through the I.M.C.?' This produced a violent and somewhat emotional response from the leading Indian present who interpreted this suggestion as being a missionary society's attempt to control the Church in India.

*L. B. Greaves, *Carey Francis of Kenya*, (Rex Collings, London, 1969).

I had, of course, been entirely misunderstood. Now the fact that nothing was further from my mind, or from the minds of the others from the West for whom I was speaking, is not the point. I ought to have been able to out-do the Communist technique of 'double-think' and do a Christian 'quadruple-think'. 'Quadruple-thinking' is thinking out what I have to say, then thinking out how the other man will understand what I say, and then re-thinking what I have to say, so that, when I say it, he will think what I am thinking! That is perhaps a useful way of describing 'communication'. For without 'quadruple-thinking' the result is often confusion or worse. But, of course, 'quadruple-thinking' involves mental pain and great spiritual sensitivity. And that is not easily come by. Robert Browning began his poem *Easter Day* with the exclamation

'How very hard it is to be a Christian!'

If possible it is even harder if the Christian is also a missionary.

But the foreign missionary is not without helpers from among the citizens of the land in which he serves. I have myself learnt much about 'quadruple-thinking' as a Christian exercise from that very versatile Christian Indian, M. M. Thomas. Once, after hearing him speak many years ago, I commented that I thought listening to him was 'almost as good as a visit to India'. Even after visiting India twice since then I still think that really to 'hear' M. M. Thomas is to listen in to India—perhaps not to all the Indias but certainly to a very large number of them.

How hard it is to be a 'foreign' missionary, but how revealing it can be of the inner reality of the Gospel, I discovered again and again in every country I visited. One picture must suffice. It is of a small mud-walled compound in Omdurman which I visited in 1950. It was a little oasis of peace to which Sudanese women would come with their babies and talk to their friend Sophie Zenkovsky. Sophie was a Russian emigré. I never learnt the details of her adventures or how she came to be a C.M.S. missionary in Omdurman. But that is not important. To walk into her tiny sitting-room, see the curious objects on the wall, the beautifully embroidered cushions on divan and chairs, the bookshelf, itself a revelation of wide reading and much obscure learning, was to step straight into a world as apparently remote from anything else in Omdurman as it was possible to imagine. Immensely erudite, a vivid personality, she had a psychic sensitivity which one could feel almost before she spoke. And what speaking! I soon discovered her link with Omdurman. She knew the Sudanese woman, as perhaps only an exiled suffering Russian woman, with a Russian's earthy religious realism, could know her. She had penetrated their secrets. She knew what were the religious convictions by which they actually lived, which were as remote from Islam as it was possible to be, though they were all Muslims.

In order to enter into the lives of these illiterate Sudanese women Sophie had plumbed the wells of knowledge in the writings of countless scholars. That was the value she set on the human soul. An academic would not have called her a scholar. She was simply a person who believed that if you want anything enough you will pay the necessary price to get it. She was a living demonstration of a principle which I believe to be of universal validity for the Christian Mission. A missionary should aim to be a complete master of some field of knowledge, however small, which can be related to the missionary calling. It may be knowing how to plant tea shrubs like a Stephen Carr of Nigeria, Uganda and the Sudan, or demonology like Sophie!

I have seen many things in Africa, massed companies of Christians at worship, great cathedrals, imposing arrays of clergy, magnificent schools and colleges, and the promise of a harvest to come. For all these I thank God, but nowhere that I have been in Africa have I been so overwhelmed with a sense of the presence of God as in that little oasis in Omdurman. And it was a particular sense that I got; it was the sense of God crucified for men, and loving them in spite of endless rejection. There I saw the final victory of God as lying precisely in the fact that to the very end he gives himself utterly and entirely.

In the picture gallery of my memory there are a great number of 'portraits' of missionaries like Sophie. I am sure my collection is not a unique one. But it is comprehensive enough to make me very impatient with people who are ashamed of the word 'missionary'.

But you cannot build up a picture gallery like that without coming to certain very clear-cut convictions as to how best to 'service' these men and women. I believe that the pastoral care of the missionary is a primary responsibility upon those who recruit and in due course send them overseas. This means being available and ready for the unexpected. One day, early in my secretaryship, a doctor from a mission hospital in the Middle East came to lunch with me in our office canteen. Almost at the end of our talk he came to the real point he wanted to raise. He was puzzled and worried about the doctrine of the Atonement. I suggested he get a copy of Dr. Dillistone's *The Significance of the Cross* and that we should meet again and discuss it and see if it had clarified some of his problems. This we did a good many weeks later. But, as likely as not, such an encounter would have disclosed a problem at quite another level. A father and mother, desperately worried by the clash between their missionary vocation and the demands of parenthood, which seemed bound to bring them back to England, probably for good, wanted guidance. Only a real missionary knows the agony of that problem. One has got to have thought through the meaning of the vocation of parenthood for oneself if one is to get alongside a man and a woman in that dilemma. Two extremes, if you like, a doctrinal question and a domestic one—and a hundred thousand in between—what matters is being available to listen. It takes time. It involves nervous energy. It means thinking long about priorities. It means living with pain in your heart because always you are such an utterly unprofitable servant. But pastoral care for the missionary means nothing less. And, let it be categorically stated, a bureaucracy, under whatever sanctified title, cannot give it.

Perhaps something I wrote in my diary after one of my journeys round the world can make the point in another way. Referring to the joy it had been to get letters from home during a relatively long absence, I wrote that I was

more than ever determined to spend a regular amount of my time writing personal letters to missionaries. Official letters about business are no substitute for that personal keeping in touch, which letters that are not business achieve. I am convinced that we at headquarters do more for the morale of our missionaries and for the work of the Kingdom of God abroad by writing them personal letters of interest and inspiration and encouragement than by all our commissions and committees, our policy-making and our besieging of Government departments. Important as these things are, they should be wholly subordinated to the sustained equipment of our missionaries by prayer and personal contact . . . no amount of administrative labour, and even efficiency, is any substitute for the deeply human touch.

Through all my time in C.M.S. I had a recurrent nightmare that our administration should come to smack of the Civil Servant and not of the family of God. That is not to denigrate the Civil Service, indispensable in its place, but to refuse to confuse it with a missionary society. I am afraid the nightmare became too often a reality. We had too many missionaries for us to do our duty by them all.

Earlier in this chapter I have written of the four African missionaries I met in Tanganyika. Today in increasing numbers the Churches of Asia and Africa are beginning to send their own missionaries to other countries. This is exciting, and is the real evidence that the Gospel has struck its roots deep in the soil of the local community. I hope that those who are giving thought to this development, and in particular the leaders of this missionary initiative, are taking seriously the formidable nature of the service to which they are sending their missionaries; that they are sizing up the nature of the preparation called for; the task involved in mobilising the support of understanding and prayer by the 'home' Church; and the insistent demand for pastoral care for the men and women who are 'sent'.

I hope that it may also be remembered that a 'foreign' missionary, whatever the nature of his 'foreignness' needs to have available on occasion the relaxation of the company of his own race, to be able to turn for understanding help to someone who knows the background from which he has come. This is in no way to belittle the spiritual insights and imaginative capacity of leaders and members of the local Church. It is only to take our fragile human nature seriously.

What I have here written about missionaries, if it is valid at all, is valid for missionaries of every race, whatever their destination. It is equally valid when the mission is to some 'religious frontier' within their own country.

9

1942 - 1963

The Ecumenical Movement

The individuality is most intense where the greatest
dependence of the parts on the whole is combined
with the greatest dependence of the whole on the
parts.

S. T. COLERIDGE

The Theory of Life

'AN army moves on its stomach'—so Napoleon is reputed to have said. The same is equally true of the Ecumenical Movement, at least in its higher echelons. You cannot explore the *oikumene* without travelling. And you cannot travel ecumenically without eating what is set before you, though grace before meat is more than ever important.

A breakfast in New York, in December 1943, is one that lingers in the memory. In front of me was placed a large plate upon which rested three vast pancakes about eight inches in diameter and a quarter of an inch thick. Over this was poured a jugful of molasses. Then, superimposed upon this gastronomic monstrosity, were three sausages. I realised that I had reached the fringes of civilisation. This was confirmed a few hours later. An exhausting though interesting meeting found me, about 3.30 p.m., thirsting for a strong cup of tea. At that very moment our American hosts, with considerable pride at knowing the wishes of these natives from Britain, brought in a tray of tea things. Our eyes lit up, glistening with excitement, only to glaze over almost immediately though, I hope, not too obviously, when we found the cups already filled with water long off the boil into which we were each bidden to sink a tea-bag. We were to discover that this was part of a syndrome set off by the Boston Tea Party, which put this quaint idea of how to make tea into the American mind. It was a harsh beginning. In Canada I discovered, what I would never have thought possible, that a dietician, who was responsible for the provisioning of a sixteen-day conference, and whose previous experience must have been bought on a rabbit farm, could give us salad at breakfast, lunch and dinner every single day.

Elsewhere, a well-travelled stomach enjoyed more exotic fare. In Japan, there were seaweed and octopus to savour: in China, the easily acquired taste for bamboo shoots: in Tasmania there was shark. In Iran I learnt to pour a raw egg into boiling-hot rice and greatly enjoyed the result. Sheep's tail went down well in the Khyber Pass. Three days in a Gandhian Ashram in India accustomed without reconciling me to a vegetarian mess which, on high religious grounds, was deliberately designed to be tasteless. It was. Mashed bananas with gravy and chicken in Uganda, and palm oil chop in Nigeria were, by contrast, sheer delight. One ordeal was narrowly averted. In Jordan I sat down in front of a complete roasted sheep. Tradition demanded that the most honoured guest present should be offered the sheep's eyes. Providentially, there was an archbishop available! Only once have I completely disgraced myself and that was after eating curried goat in the Sudan. My excuse rests in the certainty that the goat must have been dead some time.

Yes, to have eaten the local food in six continents and never had a day in bed; and even been able to do many a hard morning's work on that farcical introduction to the day, a continental breakfast; all this demonstrates that I have qualified in one ecumenical respect if in no other.

This is not quite as frivolous a start to a serious subject as might at first sight appear. If once you have eaten salt with a desert Arab you have claims on his friendship. In Nigeria to 'break kola' and suck that unappetising nut is the first step towards establishing a relationship of mutual respect. Again, for a very long time, and for all I know, still, the serious work of governing Britain has been done round the dinner table and not in the Cabinet room at No. 10 or in the Houses of Parliament. This is life. Certainly, in my experience, I have learnt far more about the world and the things which make for ecumenicity while sitting over a meal than in any committee or gathering at a conference. I feel sure this is common experience.

This leads me to record what I believe to be the two most significant achievements of the Ecumenical Movement to date. In the first place it has broken through the race barrier. By this I mean that it has made possible a real meeting of minds. This has begun to take place between men and women from different cultures and traditions, bringing their different histories with them. I use the word 'begun' only of the period of which I am writing, when only a few could enjoy this experience, and before the great age of the migrations of the young. There had been great conferences before when Christians of many races had met. But what distinguished Whitby (1947), Willingen (1952), Evanston (1954) and Ghana (1957), was that, in a unique degree, two histories were meeting—the historical conditioning of imperial power and the historical conditioning of political dependence. Every single discussion at these conferences, in full session, in committee, or round a tea-table, or where two or three walked and talked together and were caught up in the silence of a moment of truth—every such occasion had for its background the conflicting perspectives of two histories. To realise this in relation to Asians and Africans was, for the European, a profound spiritual experience. We all shared in the very painful discovery of the radical changes called for, in our own unconscious assumptions as well as in the joyful discovery that 'in Christ' a *una sancta* is a growing reality. My diaries of these years faithfully reflect the pains and the joys of these discoveries.

And part of this first great achievement of the Ecumenical Movement was the scarcely less dramatic meeting between Europeans and North Americans. Here again were different histories, but there was more to it than that. Europe was very, very tired. The United States in particular was, at least at the Whitby Conference, sitting on top of the world. The trauma of China had not yet hit her. Her citizens felt that the world was their oyster, whereas Europe had had a surfeit of oysters for a very long time and had a much more apocalyptic attitude to the situation. The German delegates at Whitby expressed this theologically. The rest of us Europeans might put things a little differently, but we felt very much the same. The tension between these two fundamental attitudes was responsible for many of the tensions within the Ecumenical Movement, with Asians and Africans the somewhat uneasy spectators of something they did not and could not fully understand. Yet the meeting of minds was very real, full of pain and joy. When the U.S.A. came to her 'time of troubles', and it came with a vengeance, the ecumenical fellowship was a sustaining bond of understanding.

What I would call the second most important achievement of the Ecumenical Movement during this period was its success in bringing together representatives of nations in which the Christian Church was a minority, somewhat alien in flavour, and as yet contributing little to the national culture. For such men and women it was a great encouragement to find that they did not have to face their dilemmas alone. Furthermore they could share prospects as well as problems. Soon they demonstrated that there was a spiritual 'third world', not only a political one.

I well remember Dr. T. C. Chao insisting to me in private in Shanghai, what I had heard him say publicly at Whitby, that the Christian vocabulary was already infiltrating the Chinese consciousness. Readers of Chairman Mao's 'Little Red Book' can find evidence of this. Again, no one who knows anything of India will underestimate the impact over the generations of Christian schools and colleges. Arnold Toynbee's query should not be forgotten when, speaking of the worldwide technological revolution of today, an offspring of Europe's own spiritual development, he asks whether the rest of the world can permanently 'accept the husk and reject the kernel'.

In stressing these two achievements, or perhaps these two aspects of one achievement, I do so because they are commonly overlooked, or taken for granted, in comparison to the more pretentious claims often made for the Ecumenical Movement.

What is the Ecumenical Movement? I suggest that primarily it is an attitude of mind, a spirit in which Christians are learning to meet one another. As a movement it had long anticipated any kind of institutional expression. And when institutions to foster it came into existence they did so in myriad forms. Unions of Christian students paralleled the local conferences of members of different missionary societies. The latter prepared the way for national Christian Councils and, in due course, Councils of Churches, the International Missionary Council and the World Council of Churches. But there were much less stylised expressions, constructed quite differently, unburdened by the coils of committees which can so easily immobilise an institution. One could list many such unburdened expressions of ecumenicity, Iona for instance, the Ecumenical Sisterhood of Mary at Darmstadt, Othona, Taizé and St. Julian's, to mention only a handful. But the Ecumenical Movement is vastly wider and more embracing than all of these put together.

My own participation in the Ecumenical Movement, as I have defined it, began in undergraduate days at Cambridge. But it became part and parcel of my life when I arrived in Salisbury Square. Membership of the Standing Committee of the Conference of British Missionary Societies was automatic for the General Secretary of a Missionary Society. Very early I was given the privilege of being one of a delegation of three to the Jubilee meeting of the Foreign Missions Conference of North America held in Chicago in January 1944. It was to this conference that I was going on that unforgettable journey in the *Queen Mary* in December 1943.

Soon after this, the C.B.M.S. and the British Council of Churches formed a joint-committee to study the question of religious liberty. Professor Barker of Cambridge accepted the chairmanship and I was appointed Secretary. Here was a fascinating introduction to the complexities of international politics. The task of Secretary involved a considerable amount of work, mastering a wide variety of documents and some wide reading. What made this possible was the assistance of Elizabeth France, at that time my Research Assistant. With magnificent thoroughness she first absorbed the material herself and then presented it to me in a form in which I could assimilate it sufficiently to present a coherent picture, first to the Committee itself and, when the occasion demanded it, to the British Council of Churches and the Standing Committee at Edinburgh House. And Elizabeth did all this while wrestling with equally complicated matters more immediately connected with the Society. Blessed with a head for figures, she could make difficult financial problems almost easy enough for me to understand, in itself no mean achievement.

This Secretaryship, together with the growing friendship with Kenneth Grubb, proved a distinctive education. He was shortly to become Chairman of the Commission of the Churches on International Affairs, which, at Amsterdam in 1948, was established as a permanent agency of the World Council of Churches. Kenneth Grubb held this office for twenty years, throughout almost the whole of this period being also President of the C.M.S. In the sequel, it was impossible for me ever to consider the affairs of a Missionary Society or of the Ecumenical Movement as out of relation to the political world scene. I think it was this experience, as much as anything, which saved me from ever making the false distinction between the 'sacred' and the 'secular', which lies at the root of so much inadequate theology.

These two responsibilities proved an invaluable introduction to even wider ecumenical work when, almost at once, I was invited to become a member of the *ad interim* committee of the International Missionary Council, and so to be closely involved both in the I.M.C. Conferences at Whitby, Willingen and Ghana, but also as a member of the Joint-Committee of the I.M.C. and the World Council of Churches.

At the conference at Whitby (Ontario) in 1947 I was given the privilege of being responsible for the programme of worship, which entailed securing people of different traditions and races to play their part, while aiming to secure a pattern whose many threads formed a unity. I think that, together, we succeeded.

As Chaplain to the conference I was invited to join the Steering Committee, thus gaining a wealth of insights into the strains and stresses, frustrations and failures, hopes and fears, and genuine achievements of ecumenical thought and activity. As was my practice at all conferences, I kept a detailed daily diary. This was later to prove extremely valuable when comparing the actual course of debates as I had recorded them with the versions, duly edited, in the official reports. Such cannot convey atmosphere, nor is there space for the adequate reporting of debates. But when, in due course, the ecumenical activities of these years are seen in perspective and described objectively by historians, such diaries may prove interesting source material.

Joy was a feature of the Whitby Conference, joy in part born of relief at the end of the war, even if sobered by the manner of its ending: but joy also in the realisation of our real oneness, not in spite of our differences, but positively increased by our enjoyment of them. This sense of joyfulness was not due to any over-easy optimism. It was rather the expression of hope based upon the power of the Gospel. At one unforgettable session, six men spoke simply, directly and un-emotionally on 'How Christ found me'. All were first-generation Christians, one from a Brahmin background, one a former Confucianist, one a Muslim, one a secularist, one an agnostic, and one from a Latin-American culture whose formative Roman Catholic influence had somehow passed him by. It was a profoundly moving occasion. Equally Pentecostal, in the New Testament sense of the word, was what followed a speech by Professor Van Dusen of the U.S.A. when, without premeditation, he threw the conference open for a prayer meeting. This was, for me, the first occasion when I heard a great company speaking to God in prayer 'each in his own tongue'. Several African and Indian languages, Chinese, Batak, Burmese, Spanish and many others were used to praise the wonderful God of our salvation. Here was Babel redeemed for there could be no doubt that to each prayer all could say 'Amen'.

Here was the source of our joy and our hope. Dr. John Mackay gave focus to our thinking by framing a notable utterance round the picture-word 'Frontier'. It was an intensely realistic speech, frankly recognising that the old world divisions were changing, and that new frontiers of thought and action, political and economic, and religious were calling for men with the spirit of the frontier. Indeed, one of the great emphases of this conference was on pressing on to take the evangelistic opportunities of the moment, and to do so in a genuine partnership in obedience. A brilliant paper by Bishop Stephen Neill, 'The Christian Witness in a Revolutionary World' provided the theological and philosophical background for this idea of partnership.

In a very small way I was able to make a contribution to the mood of the conference. At the Steering Committee which preceded the full meeting, Dr. Goodsell of the U.S.A., Dr. C. G. Baëta of the Gold Coast and I were asked to draft a re-statement of the purpose of the International Missionary Council in the new situation. I got up extra early to prepare a draft which was accepted by the other two. Following a brief preamble I picked out as the primary object of the I.M.C. 'the active encouragement of an expectant evangelism' —an echo, was it, of that meeting in the Jerusalem Chamber in Westminster Abbey just twenty years before? In the debate which followed, our draft was substantially adopted.

By the time the I.M.C. met again in full conference, at Willingen in Germany in 1952, the mood was very different. The Report of the Conference, which contained the main addresses and also sundry statements and findings, had for its title, *Missions under the Cross*. In retrospect I wonder if that title was not ambiguous as to its meaning. Were we claiming that Missions, that the Churches, were carrying the Cross? Or did we picture them as standing at the foot of the Cross broken-hearted and in despair? Or were we accepting the judgment of the Cross on all our thinking and planning? I rather fancy there was something of all three.

Certainly, to those who were willing to see, there was already evident in many churches and in not a few missionary circles the first symptoms of a disastrous failure of nerve in the *western* missionary movement. Preoccupation with structures was becoming more and more an obsession in Christian circles of every persuasion. The movement towards Church unity was becoming bogged down, as its protagonists chased that will-o'-the-wisp of organic unity, unity interpreted in terms of common order. Organic unity can, of course, be discovered in other ways but no one then was exploring them.

Why was all this so? I suggest three reasons which reacted on one another. There was a shaking of the foundations of Faith: there was a deepening sense of insecurity reflecting the Cold War and economic instability: there was a developing siege mentality. The sickness, however diagnosed, was essentially spiritual. The Church seemed quite unable to disentangle itself from the machinery of a money-dominated economic order and from a social philosophy which was increasingly materialistic.

The traditional Churches and Missionary Societies found themselves confronted with a 'No-Church Movement'. Thoughtful westerners were increasingly voting with their feet. Pentecostalism, Revival Movements of many kinds, and, in Africa, the rapid growth of Independent churches, were all of them baffling phenomena to people who imagined that the Lambeth Quadrilateral or some Lutheran or Reformed Confession was a saving formula. All this strange new spiritual vitality was simply by-passing the traditional Churches.

I do not suggest that this was consciously appreciated at Willingen. But there were niggling doubts in the minds of everyone present. The glad confidence of Whitby had been dissipated.

But in one important respect Willingen struck a decisive note. Facing realistically the world-situation and the uncertainties which were threatening the missionary movement with paralysis, it proposed no easy solutions. Instead, there was a remarkable insistence on the paramount importance for Missions, and indeed for Churches, to define the why and wherefore of their activities. And this involves theology. The alternative to a theology of Mission is sheer opportunism of the kind that wastes resources, damps enthusiasm and finally fails for lack of recruits.

Willingen did all that a responsible conference could do by way of its findings and by remitting further work to the Research Department of the I.M.C. and to the Faith and Order Commission of the World Council of Churches. I noted in my diary that 'This long-range programme of study has an importance for the missionary movement which ought not to be measured in terms of observable results in any near future.' Events have justified and are justifying that cautious optimism.

What, however, we still await is a serious attempt to produce a theology which takes seriously the differences among Christians as being contributions to unity and not obstacles to it. Only when we can enjoy being different, because we really believe God, having made us so different, wants us to be ourselves, will we be able to experience unity. Only then will we be a demonstration of our Gospel to a world which seems bent on tearing itself to pieces.

I find it very difficult to write tidily about an essentially untidy, yet very consuming, element in my life. So many and varied have been the ecumenical activities in which I have been engaged that no ordered pattern is discernible. But courtesy, as well as gratitude, demands the insertion here of a privilege which I shared with Dr. Visser 't Hooft when, during our attendance at the ecumenical celebrations of the centenary of Protestant Missions in Japan, we were both given honorary doctorates by the University of Rikkyo in Tokyo. It was a great distinction to be honoured in such company.

Before turning to describe one vigorous and sustained argument in which for many years I was involved I must find space for two journeys, geographical and spiritual, which I undertook. One was to the All-African Lutheran Conference at Marangu in Tanganyika in November 1955, at which William Nagenda, the Ugandan evangelist and a prominent leader in the Revival Movement in East Africa, and I were both invited to speak on 'Revival in the Church'. The other journey took me to Buenos Aires for a Methodist Conference in February 1962 where I was asked to speak on 'The Nature, the Mission and the Message of the Church'.

What for me was so enriching in these two conferences was that I was allowed to sit in at a 'family' gathering, a 'family' of which I was not a member and yet in which I was made to feel completely at home. Here I was able to watch members of other Christian traditions wrestling with exactly the same problems as confronted Anglican Missions, watching their quite different approach to these problems and yet realising in a fresh way how close we all were to each other. These two most instructive as well as delightful meetings of minds made me more than ever impatient with the way in which the Sacrament of Unity has been theologically isolated from the whole range of Christian activity. It has been one of the devastating tragedies of the Ecumenical Movement that, out of a conscientious determination not to affront the conscience of any Christian in regard to the Sacrament of Holy Communion, that great instrument of unity has necessarily been relegated to the periphery of the Movement. We can meet each other everywhere except at the one place where it would appear from the

New Testament that our Lord intended that we should meet regularly.

Holding this opinion strongly I was happy to have a share in initiating the Open Letter to the Archbishops of Canterbury and York which was made public on All Saints' Day, 1961. The purport of the Open Letter was to insist that there is a strong body of opinion in the Church of England which does not accept the exclusive and excluding view that 'Anglicans conscientiously hold that the celebrant of the Eucharist should have been ordained by a bishop in the historic succession, and generally believe it to be their duty to bear witness to this principle by receiving Holy Communion only from those who have thus been ordained.' Thirty-two of us signed this carefully worded and very moderate appeal for progress towards a less intransigent position. Among the signatories were men of varying schools of churchmanship. They included some among the abler theologians of our Church. The immediate and important achievement of the Open Letter was to dispose of the widespread illusion among those of other Churches that there was only *one* received position within the Church of England. Our statement was warmly welcomed by many Free Church leaders, and by Church leaders on the Continent.

In 1966 a book of essays by a number of Roman Catholic scholars appeared.* In it there is a careful and appreciative study of the Open Letter in a long chapter on Intercommunion. From it I quote:

> ... if we are committed to reunion with non-episcopal as well as with episcopal churches (and the Decree on Ecumenism makes this commitment explicit), we are also committed to making the theological development which will make such a reunion possible; and, as I have argued, the lines of argument of the Anglican open letter, catalysed by the circumstances of a particular contemporary negotiation for reunion, and coupled with recent trends within our own theological tradition, show that such a development is indeed possible.

That, to put it mildly, is very interesting and encouraging. Things are moving.

One great issue which agitated the minds of those involved in the I.M.C. and the W.C.C. was the relationship between these two international organisations, one a body representative of Christian Councils, the other, a body representative of Christian Churches. There were many strong protagonists for the complete integration of the two

*Christians and World Freedom, Ed. L. Bright, OP (Sheed and Ward/Stag books, 1966), p. 94.

organisations. I believed this to be based on a misconception of their distinctive roles.

Shortly before one of the meetings of the Joint-Committee of the two bodies which met in Germany in 1956 I was asked by a member of the I.M.C. Secretariat if I was still as opposed as ever to the integration of the two organisations. I said I was, and we had a most interesting discussion. Because I believe a vital issue of far-reaching importance is involved, something far deeper in its spiritual significance than an administrative marriage, I must attempt an interpretation of the grounds of my opposition.

The more I have thought over this issue the more I am convinced that it was really bound up with how we envisage the dynamic character of society. If a society is to be genuinely dynamic then it must accept the inevitability of tension. But too much tension makes administration impossible. This means that a society like the Christian Church must make provision both for co-ordination of activity and for diffusion of power. How this is to be done is the great difficulty. At bottom it raises the whole issue of power. The desire to co-ordinate activity almost inevitably leads to the pursuit of power. Diffusion of power can degenerate into anarchy. I think that a possible solution can be worked out empirically, *not* theoretically, by drawing a distinction between organs of co-ordination and organs of voluntary action. Organs of co-ordination are necessary. Without them no community can exist beyond the smallest unit. But those who serve on these organs of co-ordination must be, in general, people whose 'bent' and 'spirit' drives them in the direction of co-ordination. It is an outlook on life which is a valid one and quite indispensable if the complexity of our world is to be brought under any effective control at all —if, theologically speaking, it is to be 'baptised into Christ'.

On the other hand, organs of voluntary action must exist if there is to be spiritual experimentation and initiative. The complexity of our world needs not only the co-ordinating mind. It also needs the critical mind. The critic, by definition, is the agent of judgment. And by virtue of this role of judgment new experiments are initiated. These organs of voluntary action call for a rather different temperament and attitude.

These two organs of Christian witness and activity are not inimical to one another. Those engaged in them can respect each other and value each other's distinctive contribution. But they serve each other best by 'being in tension'.

All this of course has far wider implications than the issue of I.M.C. and W.C.C. The whole function of the voluntary organisation in the Social Service State, the function of the Missionary Society in a diocesanised structure overseas, the place of a Missionary Society in the life of the Church at home, these are some of the areas of thought and action which are involved in any consideration of the place of the voluntary organisation in the modern world. How best can we secure an abiding place for a spiritual initiative, which will at the same time be itself safeguarded from degenerating into anarchy? Here, as I see it, is the role of the voluntary organisation. Needless to say, the voluntary organisation is not an end in itself. It exists to be a channel for the initiative of those who compose it. If it ceases to express this initiative it will die. In so far as it is responsible and Christian it will have intimate, though not necessarily constitutional, links with a Christian Church, either denominationally or ecumenically organised. Links can be effective without being constitutional. This is a fundamental principle of community. To see this and to make provision for it is one of the best ways of safeguarding the structures of society from being exploited by a power-drunk individual or a power-obsessed bureaucracy. This has been the discovery of democracy at its best.

Part of the ecclesiological basis for this view is the recognition that the Church really is a mixed society. It is not a community of saints and dedicated persons, but a society of sinners at every variety of spiritual development. When a Bishop interpreted the missionary theory of the Episcopal Church of the U.S.A. as being that every member of the Church is a member of the missionary society, he was really saying that 'baptism makes the individual a missionary'. But manifestly it does not do so. What it does do is to make the individual a member of a community called to Mission. But to be called and to be committed are two sadly different things. A community becomes committed precisely in proportion as it has a spiritual vanguard which is *committed*. It does not help towards strengthening this vanguard to pretend that every member of the Church is already part of it. Indeed, my own conviction is that to have a unified missionary organisation actually obscures the real situation and prevents the average person ever making any progress at all towards becoming one of the vanguard. This is best achieved by voluntary organisations consisting of persons who have joined together on some agreed basis to pursue an agreed aim by agreed methods. If one believes this with all one's heart one is of necessity opposed to the creation of monolithic structures.

So much then for my position and philosophy as I tried to expound it before that Joint-Committee met.

Being Irish, I am never unduly disturbed at sometimes being 'in opposition' or in any way cast down by sometimes being in a minority. At the Joint-Committee I was courteously allowed once again to state my case which I developed mainly on the ground of the need for maximum flexibility in the Missionary enterprise. Dr. Helen Kim of Korea warmly supported me, but we were overwhelmingly outvoted. As far as I was concerned I thought this was the end of the matter. I had persevered in stating my case, had been given a fair hearing, and had failed to carry conviction. Knowing that the I.M.C. Conference to be held in Ghana in the following year would be asked to endorse the decision of the Joint-Committee I intended to remain silent on the issue at that conference. There would be plenty of other important matters before us for consideration.

What I had not reckoned with was the fact that at the Ghana Conference there would be so many other people, particularly Germans and Scandinavians, who fully agreed with me. At Ghana, then, I found myself gravely embarrassed by being approached by these good friends and begged to state *their* convictions as their command of the English language was not adequate for the finer points of such a discussion.

I felt myself in an impossible position. But Dr. Mackay, the Chairman, having discovered the wide measure of resentment in the conference at the way the issue of Integration had been presented as a *chose jugé*, asked me to speak, knowing the line I would take, hoping that this would redress the balance somewhat. He was kind enough to tell me to speak for as long as I liked. I kept myself to thirty minutes. My main concern was to lower the tension in the Assembly as a good many present were really angry. I began as follows:

> I stand here in 'fear and trembling'—'fear' because I know that I may be misunderstood by many whose friendship I value, fear because I know that in some quarters I will be misreported. But these are experiences common to all who carry any public responsibility. It is an unworthy human fear and I will not allow it to inhibit me. But I also stand here in 'trembling' because we are dealing with great issues. We all stand under the Holy Spirit. I tremble lest, in speaking, 'I speak unadvisedly with my lips.'

I sensed that tension was relaxing. People were expecting fireworks. They did not get them. I went on to say that, subject to no new arguments being advanced in the subsequent debate, I would vote for Integration because 'things have gone far too far for the Assembly to draw back.' To reject the motion for Integration, about which the Officers of the I.M.C., we were assured, were united, would mean their wholesale resignation for they would be without a policy in which they believed. All this took only about three minutes. The rest of the time was spent in developing in other words what I have already described as my position and philosophy.

This was my swan song as far as the I.M.C. was concerned, but not as far as the Ecumenical Movement is concerned. That, in the mercy of God, is not wholly engrossed with structures.

As I look back on these years when I was very much at the heart of the Ecumenical Movement my main memory is of the great range of friendships which I enjoyed, and the great respect which I had for many of those who on one issue or another disagreed with me and I with them. And the unfailing kindness I received from those who did so disagree makes all the memories, even of disagreement, happy ones. Charles Morgan has a wise sentence which runs ' . . . a distinction necessary to civilisation—namely, the distinction between disagreeing with an opponent and treating his opposition as heretical'.* That is certainly what I understand as one essential part of the practice of ecumenicity. The number of friends in whose company I enjoyed this kind of civilisation is so vast that I dare single out only one —Norman Goodall. Of the many whom I had the privilege of knowing in the Ecumenical Movement no one was more representative of that Movement at its best. One time a Secretary of the London Missionary Society, and from 1955 to 1961 Secretary of the International Missionary Council, and the holder of many other important offices, Norman, from the Whitby Conference in 1947 until today has been a constant and inspiring friend, and never more so than when our judgments differed as to where the missionary movement was going. Among his many gifts he had one disarming quality which could easily trap the unwary. He possessed a gift of language which made him one of the most fascinating speakers to whom to listen. I have heard many great orators but none, I think, more persuasive than Norman. He could so spin words together, and lighten them with gentle humour, that one's critical faculties were lulled to sleep. Arguments would then be accepted which, expressed in more rugged terms and in a harsher voice, would have provoked immediate and even violent dissent. A dangerous man!

Yet I must testify that this dangerous gift was wisely deployed. It is a valuable talent for use in ecumenical conversations where abrasive speech, especially by those having to speak in other than their mother-tongue, can be combustible. The mellow, soothing quality of Norman's interjections have on many occasions, as I can testify, averted an unhappy and acrimonious conclusion to an important debate.

Norman has other great qualities, not least that of a generous understanding of the views of other people, and a deep respect for person-

*Charles Morgan, *Liberties of the Mind*, op. cit., p. 24.

ality, which he recognises as being itself part of every situation, every problem, every view-point. This has made him an ideal negotiator. He is no bulldozer, as have been not a few who have played a leading part in the Ecumenical Movement. In the acute tensions which have sometimes been generated between North Americans and those from the continent of Europe, he has played the mediating role of the British to perfection, with a foot affectionately placed in both camps. It is to the world's infinite loss that there has been no comparable British figure in the political field in the last twenty years.

I know that it is dangerous to single out an individual and treat him as a representative figure of a world-movement. But in these days when great movements, like great organisations, tend to dwarf individuals, it can sometimes restore perspective to see a movement epitomised in an individual. That is my justification for singling out Norman. And if he reads these words I hope he will forgive me, for, in doing so, I am expressing not only affection and admiration for an individual, but a lively devotion to all that is best and truest in the Ecumenical Movement.

10/20/77

1942 - 1963

The Church of England
and
The Anglican Communion

I have worshipped with the Church of England all
my life and believe that I have experienced in its
services things which are of eternal importance to all
men. I am thereby subject to a temptation which is
not peculiar either to Englishmen or to Anglicans.
What appears to be of absolute value, perhaps the very
message of eternity itself, comes to any particular man
in a way peculiar to himself — through particular
institutions, through particular types of people, by
means of particular types of devotion and expression;
the temptation is to confuse the medium with the
message it conveys, and then to believe that absolute
values can only be conveyed by those particular
methods and institutions, and then that in those
methods and institutions themselves lies absolute and
universal value. And this leads to the very common
sin of idolatry, the substitution of the particular for
the universal, the temporal for the eternal, the creature
for the creator.

G. KITSON CLARK

The Kingdom of Free Men

IN a speech on 12th December, 1826, George Canning, then
Foreign Secretary, made the oft-quoted remark, 'I called the New
World into existence, to redress the balance of the Old.' I had a
dramatic view of a contemporary attempt to redress that balance in
January 1944 when, on returning from the U.S.A. in the *Queen
Elizabeth*, one of a handful of civilians, we travelled with a complete
division of Amercian troops.

Already, in meeting with the officers of Mission Boards in New
York and at the Jubilee celebrations of the Foreign Missions Conference of North America in Chicago, I had had my first close-up view
of the dynamism of the American missionary enterprise. I had some
serious questions to ask. It was more than a little disturbing to note the
twentieth-century equivalent of the nineteenth-century slogan,
'Christianity and Civilisation', reappearing as 'Christianity and the
American Way of Life'. The emphasis on the evangelistic power of the
dollar was also disconcerting. But, with all the questions, there
remained a sense of something immensely vital waiting to be harnessed
in the post-war world. For myself, I was convinced that, for good or
ill, this vital force was going to shape the Ecumenical and Missionary
Movement of the next twenty-five years.

To that conference in Chicago I had taken a greeting from Archbishop William Temple, which showed how he was reading the signs
of American dynamism and the hopes it had raised in his own mind.
The letter which I read out in Chicago ran as follows:

> I am writing to ask you when in the United States to give my
> most cordial greetings to our friends there both in the Protestant
> Episcopal Church and in the Joint Missionary Boards. I believe that
> the future welfare of the world depends very largely upon the main-
> tenance of happy relationships between our two countries and that
> a lead in this should be taken by the Christians on both sides of the
> Atlantic. If we can be united in the spread of the Gospel through the
> world and of effective Christian principles in our two nations we
> shall at once have supplied a nucleus of Anglo-American friendship
> and have secured that our co-operation is influenced by those
> principles which can alone make it fruitful for good to ourselves or
> to others. May every blessing go with you.
>
> I send my special greetings to the Foreign Missions Conference as
> it celebrates its Jubilee. That Conference was the pioneer in Mis-
> sionary co-operation and we are all to an incalculable extent its
> debtors.
>
> William Cantuar

William Temple's vision and his hopes had to be interpreted at the grass roots on both sides of the Atlantic. And many on both sides applied themselves to what was to prove a much more difficult task than the possession of a common language, or, at least, two closely-related dialects, might suggest. As soon as Willard L. Sperry's *Religion in America* appeared in 1945 I ordered a good many copies and sold fifteen of them to members of the C.M.S. Executive Committee. At the time it was far and away the best means of getting people in this country to understand the American religious scene. Over the years I paid seven more visits to the United States and came, I think, to a measure of understanding of how they looked at the world.

I hazard the view that the ebullience of the many different forms of American Christianity had a direct bearing on one disturbing development which has played havoc with the earlier ideas of the Ecumenical Movement and its pioneers. For it soon became obvious that there was a powerful under-tow to the tide making for closer ecumenical relationships. This was the growing movement towards world-wide denominationalism. As Churches, in the persons of their *official* representatives, met together, the accent came increasingly to be laid on the things that distinguished them from each other, a re-emphasis on the grounds of their separation. It was, of course, put much more politely, with much bowing in the right direction. But it remained a fact that natural conservatism in all the Churches laid a new emphasis on each of them preserving its heritage intact.

This under-tow was as surely present in the Church of England, and in Anglicanism generally, as it was in the Lutheran, Calvinist, Baptist and Methodist Communions. For this reason, if for no other, it is impossible to consider the Church of England and its sister Churches in this era out of relation, both to the Ecumenical Movement and to its polar opposite, the growth of ecclesiastical empires. It is something of a tragedy that, precisely at the moment when political empires were being liquidated and Europe's fatal legacy of nationalism was to increase the world's divisions, the world-wide Christian Church could only speak with such ambiguity.

I write thus pungently because I was myself painfully involved in this ambiguity, both personally and as being the Secretary of a Missionary Society which was, at once, deeply committed to the Ecumenical Movement; intimately involved in the steps being taken in South India and elsewhere towards Church Union; the while remaining in conviction an Anglican Society.

It meant a very great deal to me that the two Archbishops of Canterbury with whom I had most to do in my capacity as General Secretary of C.M.S., William Temple and Geoffrey Fisher, both lived with this tension themselves, and could sympathetically understand the strains and stresses of a Society like C.M.S. I knew that I could always turn to them for guidance.

Of Archbishop Temple I have already written in other connections. Here let me add that no one could doubt his commitment both to Mission and to Ecumenism. It is often forgotten that his historic and widely-quoted remark about 'the great new fact of our era' in his enthronement sermon on St. George's Day, 23rd April, 1942, found its setting, not only in reference to the Missionary Movement, but equally to the Ecumenical Movement. His books, *The Church Looks Forward*,* containing as it does, besides much else, five addresses with that title; and *Basic Convictions*,† one of the four convictions being 'The Divine Constraint of Christian Missions'— may explain to a generation for whom he is becoming only a name, why so many of us leant on his mind, responded to his vision, loved his great humanity, and felt for him a reverence, an affection and a devotion we have never been able to give in quite the same way to anyone else. Because I knew something of the depth of his concern, I had no hesitation in asking him if he would be willing to come one Thursday to Salisbury Square to have lunch with the Society's Secretaries. He welcomed the invitation and, indeed, came twice. He obviously enjoyed himself and the discussion as much as we all enjoyed his company and his wisdom.

It is interesting to speculate as to what might have been his contribution to the interpretation of the Christian Faith in India, had he been allowed to pursue his offer of service to C.M.S. to join the staff at St. John's College, Agra. Rightly or wrongly, he was pressed by Archbishop Davidson to remain in this country. The 'ifs' of history may be profitless objects of contemplation. But they remain interesting none the less.

Necessarily, because over so much longer a period, I had the opportunity of seeing a great deal more of Geoffrey Fisher, and being allowed some degree of his confidence, not only on the missionary work of the Church overseas. By a strange coincidence, I was staying at St. Julian's while he was there for a few days of quiet before his enthronement at Canterbury. He had a private sitting room at his disposal, and I got a message that he wanted to see me. I found him surrounded by sheets of a proof of a Constitution for an overseas diocese of which he knew that I had some knowledge. He asked me a lot of questions, and I was astonished to find how quick he was to pick out the salient factors in a situation of which he had no personal experience.

*William Temple, op. cit. (Macmillan, 1944).
†William Temple, op. cit. (Hamish Hamilton, 1937).

I cite that incident, and the occasion of its occurrence, to illustrate the practical bent of his mind, and also the astonishing capacity he had for paying attention to detail. And it was typical of the man who was to make so profound an impact on the Anglican Communion, that in those few relaxed hours before taking up his great responsibilities at Canterbury he should be giving concentrated attention to the affairs of a diocese six thousand miles away. A similar concern for practical action showed itself in his famous Cambridge sermon on Church Union. Always he was the careful administrator, looking beyond ideas to see what might make them work. This did not mean that he was indifferent to theological issues though, unlike his predecessor and his successor, they were not a major object of his interest.

Disunity, however, disturbed him in so far as it prevented the Church from discharging its primary task of witness. This led him to seek a means of discovering what were the real theological grounds of dispute between Anglo-Catholics and Evangelicals in the Church of England. To this end he first invited a group of men of known Anglo-Catholic convictions to state their position. From this group came, in due course, a very important document, *Catholicity—a Study in the Conflict of Christian Traditions in the West*. After allowing this document to be digested for several years he invited another group, who could claim to speak for the Evangelical tradition within Anglicanism, to record their position also. This group, of which I was privileged to be one, produced a report with the title, *The Fulness of Christ— The Church's growth into Catholicity*. At about the same time, he asked a number of Free Church scholars to define, as they saw it, what were the grounds of conflict between the Catholic and Protestant traditions. This group produced a no less valuable document, *The Catholicity of Protestantism*.

The value of these invitations was that they frankly recognised that real theological issues were involved, while at the same time defusing them of partisan polemics. It was a very valuable initiative coinciding, as it did, with the continuing, and still unresolved debate, on the relations of the Church of England with the Church of South India.

I was particularly glad to be associated with this enterprise, as it served to demonstrate that the emphatic position taken by C.M.S. as to continuing support for the Church of South India was based on theological principles which could not be lightly dismissed.

But concern for a deeper unity in England never allowed Geoffrey Fisher to lower his sights. His remarkable series of visits to the Orthodox Patriarch in Jerusalem, to the Ecumenical Patriarch in Istanbul, and to Pope John XXIII in Rome was of very great value, and an important precedent for much subsequent travelling by Church leaders.

Over his proposed visit to the Vatican there was considerable controversy. For many weeks his mail contained a larger number of letters of vituperative denunciation. Geoffrey Fisher's humanity and capacity for detachment find here a nice illustration. A schoolboy of eleven, known to me, overheard his parents expressing their dismay at these attacks on the Archbishop. Without saying a word to them he wrote a letter to the Archbishop which in effect said 'Jolly good show! I'm on your side', to which he added some artless comment of life at school. A long time afterwards he handed to his mother a letter, by now grubby from being long cloistered in his pocket, which had come to him from Lambeth Palace —

My dear Peter

Please forgive me if I reply to your letter for myself and Mrs. Fisher by means of a typewriter. I wanted to write to you in my own hand, but just at present there are too few hours in each day for me to get through all that I have got to do. And so by dictation through a dictaphone I send you this note to thank you very greatly indeed for your letter and for your good wishes as I set out on this coming journey.

To tell you the truth I valued no less the cheerful information you gave me about the firework display and about rugger pitches deep in mud. They brought back to me happy memories of far-off days when I was free to play rugger and to send off fireworks and to laugh at the misfortunes of a master who sends it off wrong. I am quite sure from your letter that you are very happy indeed at Christ's Hospital and enjoying life to the full.

All good wishes,
Your sincerely,
Geoffrey Cantuar.

The man who could thus respond to a schoolboy's letter and enter into his enthusiasms could, on a wider stage, win the lasting respect and affection of men of many races who responded at once to his spontaneous friendliness and his sheer enjoyment in meeting people. Not the least of his contributions to the high office he held was that in an age when a premium is set upon the personal qualities of public men, he could be so disarmingly natural. This did not always make for popularity. If he was tired or upset he could become a 'headmaster' and this certainly caused friction, not least with the Press. But more people were won by the human being than were alienated by the head-master. Nowhere was this more obvious than in Africa, America and Australasia. And in Africa, in particular, his deep humanity was of paramount importance. In Geoffrey Fisher, Africans saw a great

Church leader, and a European at that, actually abdicating authority, in Africa an event as yet without precedent in the State.

Someday, so I believe, it will come to be recognised that the single most far-sighted piece of statesmanship during his archepiscopate, was his steady and deliberate diminution of the metropolitical authority of the Archbishop of Canterbury. The decisive step which he took in this connection was the hastening of the creation of new Ecclesiastical Provinces which were to enjoy virtually complete autonomy.

In Africa, this meant that the Church anticipated political independence, in itself a spiritually important demonstration of respect for and trust in the capacity of Africans to rule themselves. Provinces which embraced more than one national state were an ambitious symbol of the *una sancta*. Not always has national *amour propre* been willing, or strong enough, to make the necessary surrenders to achieve this ideal. But, if in some respects he proved ahead of his time, it was good that in Geoffrey Fisher there was a Church leader who could see the need in the twentieth century for courageous adventuring, and who, seeing the need, took appropriate action.

At a different level we in C.M.S. were also trying to be adventurous. I give an illustration of action we took which in due course was to be closely related to Geoffrey Fisher's own vision.

On 15th August, 1947, the historic day of India's Independence, Harry Wittenbach, the recently appointed East Asia Secretary of the Society, and I were in the city of Nanking. Early that morning we went to the Indian Embassy and must have been among the earliest visitors to felicitate the first Indian ambassador to China on the memorable character of the day. And memorable it was in more ways than one. If I need convincing, and I did not, this eagerly awaited day also spelt the inevitable and rapidly approaching end of the colonial empire in Africa. And with the passing of that empire, under which the Christian Churches had thriven, those Churches would find themselves 'on their own'—if one may speak the language of earth and not of heaven. Under the old colonial regime the Churches, and more particularly the Anglican Church, had been a privileged minority. Under the new Independent Nation States, which were to emerge, this would change, with incalculable consequences. No one could guess what might happen.

For me, and for my colleagues, it seemed an urgent matter for C.M.S. to be put in a posture where it could be of maximum service in the coming new political situation. Already such machinery as we possessed abroad was very simple, a corresponding secretary with an office. Conferences of missionaries, where they survived, were rapidly ceasing, or had ceased, to be the centres of power they had been in an earlier day. But even greater simplification was now being demanded. To this end we proposed a regional secretariat for East Africa which would be able, over a wide area, to relate the needs of the several dioceses to the strictly limited resources of the Society. It was as simple and innocuous an idea as that. However, we badly miscalculated the reactions of 'the man on the spot'. He, whether Bishop, Archdeacon or Mission Secretary, all of them English, together with many a missionary, interpreted this as an insidious attempt to establish control from Salisbury Square. Our purpose, in point of fact, was to abandon every vestige of such distant control as might still appear to exist. And we wanted to do this before all positions of authority were held by Africans, who might think that we were withdrawing support. But the presentation of our case was unconvincing. No doubt there were personality problems which were complicating factors. Furthermore, 'the man on the spot' saw only the 'spot'. Nowhere was he seriously facing the imminent end of colonial rule—I write of the late forties. In the sequel, the chance was lost of creating a readily adaptable machinery which would have helped to smooth the early years of that provincial development which the Archbishop was soon to initiate. We did, indeed, establish a regional framework but it was only given grudging local support. When provincial autonomy was established the necessity for just such provision of regional machinery was belatedly recognised as essential. But a great opportunity for a smooth transition had been thrown away.

It is a pity, but sadly true, as the Turkish proverb puts it, 'Experience is a precious comb which Providence only gives to men when their hair is gone.' All the parties concerned in this dispute became prematurely bald.

During these years I was also much involved in a vigorously conducted and prolonged debate between those who wanted to put more authority into the hands of the Missionary Council of the Church Assembly, with the long-term object of the Church becoming its 'own Missionary Society', and those of us who were firmly convinced that the need of the times was for a maximum of flexibility to enable new initiatives to be taken in evangelism in the rapidly changing situation overseas. I had struggled unsuccessfully to secure this flexibility for evangelism through the Ecumenical Movement, as I have noted in the previous chapter. It was the same issue, in a slightly different form, in the English scene. A proper independence for the Missionary Societies, while in every way possible increasing mutual consultation and co-operation, seemed the best safeguard to ensure the flexibility which I believed to be vital.

What very few people were ready to recognise was what the two reports commissioned by Archbishop Fisher, *Catholicity* and *The Fulness of Christ*, had revealed: that within the Church of England there are two valid theological positions which stem from equally valid, but quite distinct, premises. And these premises lead, in practice, to quite different forms of action, and in particular to very different policies animating, for instance, the U.S.P.G. and C.M.S. To say that is precisely *not* to say that one is right and the other wrong, but to insist that they really are different. Mutual recognition of this and mutual respect are calculated to lead to much invaluable consultation and, in many areas, to no less invaluable co-operation.

In this debate it was true, I suppose, that the General Secretary of the Missionary Council, Canon McLeod Campbell, and I were the two main proponents of the differing points of view. It was for me, and for him also, for all I knew, an experience of great nervous strain. The entire missionary situation throughout the world was changing with incredible rapidity in country after country. This was my concern and my primary interest and overwhelming anxiety. To have to waste months and years in a running battle on 'structures' was utterly exasperating. But I knew that I also was being utterly exasperating. Thanks to this awareness and McLeod Campbell's greatness of soul our personal friendship actually deepened over the years. In 1952 he and I were both at the I.M.C. Conference at Willingen in Germany. He was the 'House Father' of an international group in one of the lodging houses among which delegates were distributed. I was one of his 'children'. This explains the German references, for whose idiomatic correctness I make no claims, in some verses which I sent to him in the following year on the occasion of his seventieth birthday, 6th July, 1953:

No lovely Fraulein I
All dewy-eyed and eager
To greet this festal day
With tuneful *lieder*
Not with flowers I sing
Only with words on loan
Borrowed from Willin-gen
'Campbell *Wonderschon*'
Allow me then my pen
To proffer this reminder
How truly glad I am
For our *gemeinde*
Let not the sun rise high

E'er from its gleams a glint
Marks a halo around
our Septuagint

Back came his reply the same day, 'Brilliant, my dear Max, and a real joy — greatly exhilarating my birthday breakfast. How beyond words sweet of you. Yours, John McC.'

Who knows what atavistic memories born of our entitlement to the same old school tie softened the astringency of our debate? While still in slightly frivolous vein it remains to record a curious fact that for a part of this period the President of S.P.G. (Archbishop Fisher), the President of C.M.S. (Sir Kenneth Grubb), the General Secretary of S.P.G. (Bishop Roberts), the General Secretary of the Missionary Council (Canon McLeod Campbell), the General Secretary of the Mission to Delhi (Bishop Western), the West Asia Secretary of C.M.S. (Campbell Milford), the Africa Secretary of C.M.S. (Handley Hooper) and I had, at different times, all been at Marlborough.

Geoffrey Fisher had a curious habit of involving me in somewhat improbable activities, in most cases extraneous to my immediate concerns in matters missionary and ecumenical. In 1954, for instance, some while before the return of Queen Elizabeth from her first Commonwealth tour, he wrote me a letter beginning, 'You have experience in drafting prayers for public use.' Where he got the idea from I cannot imagine. But the letter ended by saying that he was asking three or four people, including myself, to draft a number of prayers for use by the clergy, at their discretion, on the Sunday after the Queen's return. The prayers were to be prayers of gratitude for her safe return, and of petition for blessing upon all that might issue of good from the tour. Obediently, I set to work and sent him three prayers which, if not quite up to the standard of Archbishop Cranmer, I hoped might merit consideration. Whether they did or not I do not know. They were not used in the church which I attended on Sunday, 16th May of that year.

Then came the Lambeth Conference of 1958 at which I made some contribution to the huge volume of reading matter provided for the attending bishops. The first document which was indeed intimately related to my main areas of activity had for its title, *Missionary Commitments of the Anglican Communion*. I had had the benefit of useful criticism of a preliminary draft, but I was left to embody these in my own way. Rather less obviously within my province was a commission appointed to consider *The Commemoration of Saints and Heroes of the Faith in the Anglican Communion*. It was chaired by Eric Milner-

White, the Dean of York, and had as its Secretary, Eric Kemp, then a Fellow of Exeter College, Oxford. The report contained a great deal of interesting information. Its recommendations were very cautious indeed. My contribution as a member of the Commission was minimal.

More serious by way of responsibility was the appointment of a commission to study *The Family in Contemporary Society*, of which I was asked to be chairman. The members were a very distinguished company. The laity included such eminent authorities as Sir Alexander Carr-Saunders, Professor T. S. Simey and Professor R. M. Titmuss. The clergy, who included Canon I. T. Ramsey, then a Professor at Oxford, Canon R. H. Preston of Manchester, Canon Bentley of St. George's, Windsor, and Dr. Sherwin Bailey, were no light-weights. I conceived my task as being to ensure that everyone had a full hearing of his views. In the sequel, the Commission presented a unanimous report. It decisively shaped the discussion of the subject at the ensuing Lambeth Conference and the form of the resolutions passed there, which were a signficant departure from the negative attitude on this subject of previous Lambeth Conferences. This time the note struck was positive and constructive with its stress on the 'responsible family'. The real credit for the report must go to the Rev. G. R. Dunstan of the Church of England Moral Welfare Council, now Professor of Moral Theology at King's College, London. The document, a very considerable one, was drafted by him. For me it was no small compliment that in the Introduction to the Report the Commission thought it appropriate to quote at length from a C.M.S. News-Letter.

I went to West Africa immediately after the Commission had finished its work; and it was there that I received a most warm letter from the Archbishop who wrote of this 'most exciting and impressive Report. It rests as few Reports do on carefully digested evidence . . . I thank you all most sincerely for a splendid piece of work.'

Because my work at C.M.S. took me so much abroad, my personal links with the life of the Church of England were relatively tenuous during this period. But I was examining Chaplain to three Bishops and this, with visits to most of the theological colleges in Britain, served in some degree to keep me in touch with the younger generation of clergy. And invitations to speak at diocesan conferences meant some awareness of the 'feel' of the Church in these islands. Yet to my inevitable loss I lacked much touch with the parochial clergy.

However, my 'age group', to cull an analogy from Africa, began to come to my aid. During these years the previously aberrant prejudice in favour of choosing Bishops almost exclusively from Oxford was happily being corrected. Some of my Cambridge contemporaries and friends found themselves in the hierarchy. This provided me with a happy entry behind the scenes in some dioceses. And there I began to appreciate the increasingly difficult nature of the office of a Bishop, as it has developed in the last half-century. The more one understood of this, the more one wished that nine-tenths of the energy devoted in some circles to establishing their descent from the original Twelve, might have been diverted to considering how, in the very different circumstances of today, they could be enabled effectively to be apostolic men, the passionate desire of them all.

That reflection, by the way, applies throughout the length and breadth of the Anglican Communion, and to those wider horizons I turn. Each journey abroad tended to serve a variety of purposes. Ecumenical business, missionary interests, and specifically Anglican concerns over-lapped with one another. One illustration of this may be found in the three-month period from June to September in the year 1954. The programme began with an interdenominational conference on Missions at Fayetteville in Arkansas. From there I moved to Meadville in Pennsylvania for a conference, arranged jointly by a number of Mission Boards, including the Episcopal Church, as an orientation course for missionaries going abroad for the first time. I was with them for a fortnight. This was followed immediately by a committee meeting of the I.M.C. on Staten Island, New York, which lasted a week. Straight from there I went to Green Lake in Wisconsin for a five-day conference with two hundred Lutheran ministers and their wives. A short two-day conference for ministers and laity at Lake Forest, Illinois, intervened before I found myself at Minneapolis for the Anglican Congress.

Those attending at Minneapolis had been divided into a number of groups, carefully representative of the different areas of the Anglican Communion. I was asked to chair one of these groups, a far from easy task as it had no cohesion, each member primarily concerned to chase his own private herring, which was commonly red. This congress was in fact, badly organised with far too much being attempted in far too short a time. The passion for filling the unforgiving minute with five minutes' worth of distance run is an American foible. It generally means that one has run round in a circle and got nowhere! From Minneapolis, jaded and weary, I went to a meeting of the C.C.I.A., in which I disgraced myself by falling asleep and snoring. At the Evanston meeting of the World Council of Churches which followed I was present as a consultant.

That somewhat over-filled three months included, of course, many most interesting, and some most inspiring, encounters with large numbers of people, and the beginning of friendships which have endured until today. One such 'enduring' I would here record. At the Meadville Conference for outgoing missionaries I had been asked to take the morning Bible-readings, relating each one to the contemporary scene. Masefield once wrote, 'The days that make us happy make us wise.' Certainly, this opportunity to expound Scripture to a group whose members, I soon discovered, were as hungry for exposition, as they were surprised and challenged by it, made me happy and, I think, gave me wisdom. I was given 'freedom' to speak from the heart. And, as happens in such cases, heart speaks to heart. With Bruce Copland and his wife Marnie who were *in loco parentis*, and with more than thirty of those American missionaries, I have been in touch regularly ever since. Many have stayed with us in our home in England, some I have met again on subsequent visits to the U.S.A. when they were on furlough. For me, this prolonged touch with American missionaries of many different Churches, has been an enormously enriching experience. It has given me an insight into America, into American life, and an affection for both, which I do not think I could have acquired at such depth in any other way.

My diary for those three months filled three volumes, comprising 716 quarto pages of type, approximately 170,000 words. That may give some idea of the wealth of that total experience and the sheer impossibility of doing justice to it.

In all my visits to the U.S.A., I was accorded the most generous friendship by the Bishops of the Episcopal Church and by Bishop Bentley and others of the Mission Board. I had the privilege of attending the Triennial Convention in Hawaii in 1955 and being very much 'on call' for the sessions of the Overseas Department of the National Council which were chaired by Bishop Block of the diocese of California. Conferences with Episcopal clergy in the Carolinas, Texas, California and New England, further helped me to understand a little of the peculiar problems of a Church which was grappling with the problems of a continent. Within that continent itself there were 'missionary dioceses' which were not self-governing. It was little wonder that, by and large, there was, otherwise than at the Virginia Theological Seminary with its long tradition of sending missionaries overseas, very little understanding of the world outside the U.S.A., little sense of compulsion to world Mission. World War II did not have any significant educative influence on the American public or the American Churches.

That may appear a rash statement. But I think many thoughtful Americans would endorse it. The traditional isolationism of American thinking, its internal frontiers only recently closed, is, at best, only just below the surface of the American mind. There was no psychological preparation for becoming a world power, and every kind of prejudice against the inescapable responsibilities of that power.

All this was reflected in the missionary approach of the Episcopal Church, as of most of the other Churches in the U.S.A. But within them there were many individuals who had accepted that America's 'manifest destiny' had now to take account of many unpleasant realities. It was such persons, within the Episcopal Church, including some influential bishops, who welcomed my attempts to interpret the world scene, made as sensitively as possible to friendly, but somewhat bemused, audiences. I soon discovered one important truth. Once an American audience recognises that you genuinely like them and are enjoying their company, and are not in any way 'high hat', you can say anything you like and be as frank as you wish.

What stood out a mile in any view of the missionary scene as it was being presented to the Episcopal Church was the lack of any serious attempt to communicate the realities of the world situation. Not, be it admitted, that there was over much effort in this direction in most missionary circles in Britain at that time. A missionary, years ago, said to me rather bitterly, that missionary publicity was strictly limited to 'babies on the window-sill'. I knew what she meant. The trouble is, you can photograph a baby on a window-sill and make it look 'cute'. The emotional appeal is good for quite a few dollars (or half-crowns, to use the language of another age). You cannot easily photograph nationalism in a Church synod; the under-payment of African clergy; the Asian and African resentment at paternalism; the intoxication of political independence; the suspicion of economic imperialism. Yet these are what have to be understood. Indeed even the 'baby on the window-sill' ought to raise the question of the population explosion, but it very rarely does!

Within the Episcopal Church during these years there was a small but increasing body of responsible people who were determined to try to do something about a realistic educational programme on the subject of Mission. The Overseas Mission Society was founded primarily for this purpose, and for some years it produced a *Review* which was of first-rate quality.

Ted Eastman, the organising spirit of this enterprise, became one of my most cherished American friends, and many an hour did we spend arguing how best the 'O.M.S.' could do its job. It was to become a casualty of the grim events within the U.S.A. itself in the sixties,

The C.M.S. Secretaries' group at a Thursday meeting, 1944. Left to right round the table: Harold Anderson, Ethel Doggett, Tom Isherwood, Geoffrey Cranswick, Oliver Turton, the author, Ena Price, Handley Hooper, Gurney Barclay, John Mann.

Briefing the Archbishop before a meeting

With the Rt. Hon. R. A. Njoku, Nigerian Minister of Trade and Industry,
Eastern Region, at a reception in C.M.S. House, 1957

Rosemary, Mary and Pat on holiday in Norfolk

Sheelagh Warren at Gayaza

and of the bitter self-questioning which began in American life, as a result of a deteriorating race situation and the horrors of Vietnam. It could, I think, only have survived if it could have maintained some human agency rooted in an overseas situation, rooted in such a way as to be a focus of prayer and interest. Within the Episcopal missionary organisation this, while not impossible, was difficult of achievement. A Mission Board with a continent-wide constituency, beset with internal constitutional problems, must act according to its own genius. What is unintelligent, though rather too common, is the drawing of an analogy from American organisation and applying it in the English scene.

I found a somewhat similar missionary condition in Canada, to which land of far-stretching distances I paid a number of visits. My journeys took me the whole length of the country, though I never had so intensive an experience as had come my way in the United States. Here again, was a virtual continent with all the internal problems posed by distances, as real for the Church as for the nation. As a nation, Canada, twenty years ago, had not emerged, as she has today, as an economic colossus and a powerful diplomatic influence in world affairs. Likewise, at that time, the Church was heavily preoccupied with her own vast door-step. There was a missionary situation in the immediate foreground which obscured the wider world overseas.

What is common to all continent-wide organisations, unless very deep conviction and imagination are at work, is that support for missionary work will tend to be seen almost exclusively in financial terms, and very little, if at all, in terms of understanding prayer and personal responsibility for the missionaries. And, no less obviously, missionaries returning on furlough will be far less accessible for those personal contacts which make for a living link between them and those who pray for them, than if those prayers were informed with some degree of real understanding of the context within which the missionary works.

All this I saw, I hope with sympathetic understanding. I was quite unprepared for what was for me an unexpected experience in visiting one Canadian diocese. I was not there on any official business but simply passing through. I paid a courtesy visit on the Bishop and he insisted on taking me out the next morning to visit some of the beauty spots in his diocese. I was busy absorbing a view of quite matchless beauty when the Bishop, apropos of nothing that we had been talking about, suddenly said, 'I hear there is a movement in Britain towards having the Church its own Missionary Society. Don't you have anything to do with it! We once had a variety of missionary agencies here and they were all amalgamated by what was heralded as a great act of statesmanship. It killed missionary interest. No personal interest survives to spur people on.' At the end of the day the Bishop dropped me at my hotel. As we shook hands and I tried to thank him for his kindness he just said, 'Don't you let them put one umbrella over you all. Keep the Societies. We've tried the other way and we know it is a failure.' Immediately on getting to my room I copied out the Bishop's remarks into my diary, where they remain to record one of the more intriguing experiences in Canada.

The problem of writing years after the events being recollected makes continual references to diaries imperative. Only in this way can I be sure that I am not either misrecording events and conversations or allowing hindsight to fudge the edges of memory.

That conversation, however, cannot be my last word about Canada where I received so much kindness and quite undeserved honours. I had only been a short time at C.M.S. when I was invited to give the Convocation Address at Wycliffe College in the University of Toronto, and to receive an Honorary D.D. This was in January 1944. I am sure I am right in thinking that this was an expression of the desire to maintain the link of the College with C.M.S. But for me it carried, also, the greatly cherished friendship of the Principal, Dr. Ramsay Armitage, and his wife, Mollie. From each visit to England he returned home with sundry bits of the Roman Wall, St. Paul's Cathedral, Westminster Abbey, and such-like notable structures to ensure that there would be one place in Canada which held 'a chip of the old block'.

And at the other end of my service with C.M.S. I was invited in 1963 to give the Convocation Address at Huron College in the University of Ontario, and again to be rewarded with an Honorary D.D. 'To him that hath shall be given' has been an embarrassing but enjoyable experience, and it would be churlish to underplay the enjoyment.

Other visits were to be paid to Australia and New Zealand, there to discover a different pattern of missionary support from those which obtained in Britain or in North America.

For reasons which are historical and which cannot be described in brief, the Ecumenical Movement in Australasia had, at that time, made very little progress. In many Anglican circles it was viewed with the greatest suspicion, a suspicion to which the complicating factor was added in Australia of very considerable theological tension within the Church. This tension was curiously fused by a unique feature in the Australian scene. Federally united, and with a strong Federal Government, the several States were far more jealous of their individuality than was even the case in the U.S.A. And, if it so happened that one state, by historical accident, had a Church life overwhelmingly dominated by Evangelicals, and therefore, again on historical grounds, closely linked with C.M.S., that was quite sufficient ground for other states, theologically orientated in a different direction, to view Evangelicals in general and the C.M.S. in particular as regrettable intrusions, serpents in an ecclesiastical Eden. At any rate, that was what the 'serpents' felt like! I am not suggesting for a moment that all the fault was on one side. I had all too much evidence that the 'serpents' often displayed an unnatural lack of that wisdom associated with their kind, which in turn prejudiced their reputation for being as innocent as doves.

Things are, so I am assured, better now as regards mutual respect between those who conscientiously differ. Meanwhile both Australia and New Zealand have increasingly realised their own nationhood, have ceased to feel 'dependants' of Britain, and, as nations, are themselves active in world affairs. A parallel sense of outward-looking interest has expressed itself in very vigorous missionary work, not only in Papua and the Pacific, but also in Asia and Africa. The Ecumenical Movement has also made rapid strides.

Once again, travel has proved for me an education in the enormous variety of the Anglican Communion. What only travel can teach one, in the sense of getting the fact well anchored in the consciousness, is the strictly limited extent of the Anglican Communion. Over vast areas of the earth's surface, over the continent of Europe, throughout the dominions of the U.S.S.R. and in the greater part of Asia, in almost all the former territories of the French Empire, and in most of Latin America, its influence has been at most slight, when not non-existent. This is a reference only to Anglicanism. In the mercy of God the preaching of the Gospel and the expansion of the Church have not been limited to our Communion, though a one-time map of the world divided into Anglican dioceses, might have deceived the the simple. The fact is, Anglicanism either anticipated the flag and encouraged it, or followed it. Where it and the flag coincided long enough for the Church to take root, there you will find impressive Anglican Churches today, or a significant contribution to United Churches. But, outside the one-time British Empire and the United States, where is Anglicanism a numerically significant factor? It has followed either the Union Jack or the Stars and Stripes. China was no real exception. While never a colony, its treaty ports and their environs were the main centres of Anglican development. Commodore Perry opened Japan at the point of a gun. But the Anglican Church played a very limited part in exploiting that particular open door.

None of this is to say that the Anglican Church has not exercised a spiritual influence where neither the Union Jack nor the Stars and Stripes has ever been flown. It most certainly has done so, but on a very modest scale, though no one can evaluate the work of individuals or of ecumenical activities in which it has shared.

But to this must be added two factors which are strictly ambivalent, providing as they do, both benefits and liabilities. With those two flags have gone the English language *and* a curious, largely indefinable quality of 'Englishness' or 'Americanness'.

The English language still enables more people of more races and cultures to meet together and talk than does any other. The literature of the English-speaking world is more widely available than any other, and it is English books and papers which are most widely translated into other languages. It is, then, easier to bring together more Christians whose common language is English than is possible in the case of any other group. This does not, in itself, give any particular advantage to Anglicans over Christians of other allegiances. But it does provide a major bond of unity between the leaders of Anglican Churches around the world. With the rapid passing of the Book of Common Prayer as a common point of reference and the expression of a common worship, the English language and the collegiality of its episcopate are the two remaining human factors which keep the Anglican Communion together—these two, *and* the continuing contribution of Anglican missionaries from all over the world, and not only from the 'white islands'!

But 'Englishness', or 'Americanness' is another matter. Anglican missionaries, whether from Britain, the U.S.A., or Canada and Australasia have, in giving themselves, given the best they knew. The best they knew about how to organise Church life was the only one with which they were familiar. What is more, when they started giving it in the nineteenth century, social anthropology was an unknown subject of study. Often there appeared to be nothing on to which their own Church ideas could be grafted. The result is an extraordinary sense of the 'un-natural' about so much of the Anglican expression in Asia and Africa. It is diminishing but it is still there. These are, of course, still very early days. A cultural renaissance may produce an Asian or an African poet, a Cranmer even, whose imagination will body forth 'the forms of things unknown' and give to Anglicanism there 'a local habitation and a name'. That could be very exciting. But we will be wise if we accept the possibility that the Anglican experiment has been a temporary phenomenon. It will survive for generations yet, no doubt, for human nature is, in matters religious, very conservative. But the forces of nationalism show no signs of abatement. There are formidable precedents for the compulsive union of Churches. Caesar, even if for the wrong reasons, has commonly been rather more eager for Church unity than Christians! Nor dare we underestimate the degree to which the reassertion of traditional cultures can make otiose what is reminiscent of the colonial era. The rapid growth of Independent Churches in Africa is one portent. 'No-Church Movements' resentful of imported religious divisions are not limited to Japan. They also are a portent. These signs need to be read very carefully, their meaning studied, their progress watched, if possible with sympathy. Those who smell heresies should take counsel with Gamaliel.

In passing, it may be observed that if anything like this estimate of likely developments is true, it should mean two things—far stricter selectivity in regard to the missionaries who are sent abroad (whatever their native country) than is as yet anywhere being contemplated: and a far more thorough training of those selected than is, as yet, anywhere in practice except in the Roman Catholic Church. This will not be easy to explain to the faithful, devoted, praying people in the home countries. But it will be even harder to explain the cruder selectivity of alien regimes.

Much travelling, and the many discoveries made on the road, the many rich friendships which have resulted, the enormous widening of horizons —all these have led me to a conviction which I can best convey as follows. My mind plays with the fancy of how valuable it might be if men marked out for leadership anywhere in the Anglican communion could be encouraged to make, at some period in their careers, a twentieth-century development of the eighteenth-century idea of the 'Grand Tour'. During this expedition they would stay, only occasionally, with fellow-Anglicans. Rather, they would be encouraged to travel mainly outside the Anglican pale. There they would discover the relative insignificance of Anglicanism almost everywhere. There they would enjoy living and moving among Christians of other allegiances. They would return, I suspect, with their appreciation of Anglicanism greatly enhanced by a fresh awareness of where it has a contribution to offer, and much less certain about some of its vaunted excellences. They would also return humbly aware that the values of other Churches are not just 'uncovenanted mercies' but rather glorious manifestations of that grace of God which must always transcend in glory the encompassing capacity of little human minds, cast in their insular moulds. My fancy leads me to add that a similar prescription in reverse would do no serious harm to prospective leaders in other Churches.

I end with a cautionary tale, uncomfortably reminiscent of the closing sentence of the quotation from Kitson Clark which prefaces this chapter. At the Toronto Anglican Congress in 1963 I was having dinner one evening with my much beloved friend, Richard Roseveare, then Bishop of Accra. In my diary for that evening I have recorded what he told me of an encounter which he had had that afternoon. He arrived, so he told me, towards the end of a conversation between a certain English Diocesan Bishop and another man. As he joined the group the Diocesan Bishop was remarking that, as far as he could see, when all the verbiage in the document about 'mutuality' had been eliminated, all it added up to was just one more appeal for money. At that Richard weighed in about the meaning of 'mutuality', of a new attitude of respect and concern between the different Provinces of the Anglican Communion. The English Bishop, in reply to this, said 'But, what can they offer, these Africans, surely they are only savages.' Richard, so I gathered, recovered, after swallowing hard, and gasped out, 'Savages—what on earth do you mean?' 'Well,' said the English Bishop, 'are many of them literate?' While Richard was digesting this one, and trying to conjure up an appropriate reply, the Bishop drifted amiably away, still convinced that all Africans are savages.

That was as late as 1963. Hopefully, it was an extreme case. But it indicates what we are up against. As long as the Church of England contains that kind of illiteracy at any level, there will not be much mutuality about our relationships with the Provinces overseas. We have seen what political *hubris* did with a number of European empires. Ecclesiastical *hubris* could do the same with a Communion. There are more forms of idolatry than one.

II

1942 - 1963

Journeyings Oft

Much have I seen and known; cities of men
And manners, climates, councils, governments . . .
I am a part of all that I have met.

TENNYSON

Ulysses

A traveller's joy lies precisely in being part of all that he has met. Tennyson's Ulysses speaks for all of us. Part of the 'all' is people, and part is places. And it is the commingling of the two which provides the accumulated wealth of memory.

Never will I forget that moment when, high up in the Japanese Alps, I saw, of a sudden, the lifting of the mist and there, unveiled, floating between heaven and earth, was Mount Fuji, its great cone surely one of the loveliest shapes in all creation. I gazed and gazed. Every minute it changed, now riding clear above the clouds, swimming in the air, now as clearly earthbound, a sigh of aspiration, all its lines as eloquent of the ambition to reach beyond the earth as any Gothic cathedral. Yet how different are the ways in which that common aspiration is expressed! What does it mean to the Japanese soul that *there* is this marvellous symbol of the ascent of the spirit?

In complete contrast, but equally unforgettable with a beauty all its own, was that night in the rain-forest of Nigeria with a full moon shining. A river, flowing across the road, had brought us to a halt. While reserve transport was being arranged Mary and I were able to hear how alive a forest is at night. It wasn't only the astonishing chorus of frogs, a chorus which would have delighted Aristophanes: it was all the other myriad sounds of insect and animal life: and, sheltering them and us, the vast forest trees, their blackness dappled by the moonlight. I can hear that forest still. Our companion was an African, Alfred Bovi. His entirely improbable bowler hat and Chaplinesque antics had enlivened an uncomfortable journey. Actually, he was a very competent schoolmaster, and his thoughtfulness for our comfort measured up to the highest standards of African courtesy. Rain forest, the *brekeke.kex ko.ax ko.ax* of the frogs' symphony, and Alfred, have a frame all to themselves.

Then there was the road from Delhi to Bareilly, eleven hours of very slow travel. It could have been tedious. In fact it had the fascination of a panorama. There was the bewildering variety of India's people; here, one blanketed against the morning chill; there, one stripped to the waist; here a sadhu in his saffron robes, there a student in immaculate white trousers; and the whole crowd splashed with colour by the saris of the women—and always a bullock cart, always moving slowly, always in the way. How often I had read the story of *Kim*! Here I was, on part of the very same road, and seeing it all in the company of Murray Rogers, a friend of long standing, than whom I know few who, being foreigners, have yet gone so deep into India, entering with love, with a real desire to understand and to interpret.

Back to Africa—I am standing at night high up on the Mau plateau in Kenya. I only have to lift a hand to pluck a hundred diamonds from the velvet blackness of the sky. Sir Philip Mitchell, Governor of Kenya, was our host for the night at the house in Subukia which he had built for his retirement. Always I shall be glad and proud that, in the closing decade of colonial rule in Africa I was fortunate to be the guest of so many of the last pro-consuls of our race, without exception men of a temper well chosen for the delicate task of 'running down' an empire. Kenya, Uganda, Tanganyika, Nigeria, Ghana, Sierra Leone and the Sudan. It is a memorable portrait gallery.

Such are four vignettes picked from the hundreds in my collection. They may serve as an introduction to some longer descriptions of 'cities of men and manners, climates ...' which I have met and of which, because memory holds the door, I am for ever a part.

I might have been desk-bound, a chair-borne executive. The air-age and an imaginative Executive Committee combined to keep me moving. Masefield's poem *Roadways* speaks to my experience:

> My road calls me, lures me
> West, east, south, and north;
> Most roads lead men homewards,
> My road leads me forth.
>
> To add more miles to the tally
> Of grey miles left behind,
> In quest of that one beauty
> God put me here to find.

The quest has been a thrilling one, each 'finding' a lure to fresh discoveries. I have found beauty in so many people, beauty born out of the murmuring sound of the life around them, sealed and accepted as their own. The round human peg in the round human hole, the perfect fit fulfilling the purpose of the Master Carpenter, is a beauty God sent me out to find. I have seen his craftsmanship in every country in which I have travelled, as the following pages will show.

Beauty in the natural world of sky and sea, of great mountains and wide prairies, of forests and rivers, of the good earth, yes and even of the wilderness without the rose, is all there for the finding. I have found much of it and, revelling in colour as I do, I have come much nearer to spiritual ecstasy in such findings than I have ever experienced in a church. This does not make me a 'blue-domer', but I must write of what I am. Nor will I sentimentalise about nature. In her beauty nature can sometimes be terrifying. I discovered this beyond any sort of doubt during an electric storm over Queensland, with the lightning apparently flashing inside the plane. I have known it, as must so many have done, who have felt the 'hiddenness', the shivering hostility of the mountains that frame the frontier from the Hindu Kush to the sea.

Coleridge has a passage, in *The Theory of Life*, whose truth I have proved in the practice of living. He wrote 'As light to the eye, even such is beauty to the mind ... Hence the Greeks called a beautiful object ... a *calling on* the soul.' I like that, Beauty is a visitation. You can endure quite a lot of committees and survive a fair number of conferences and retain your reason, as long as, in the intervals, however brief, you can allow some beautiful object to call on your soul.

I am more than glad that my roads so often led me forth, and no less glad that, in due course, they also led me homewards. To understand these years upon which I have been reflecting, account must be taken of all this travelling, of all the encounters which are part of me.

An invitation to preach the sermon at the opening service of the Synod of the Cheng Hua Sheng Kung Hui, the Anglican Church in China, at Shanghai in August 1947, took me, first, across Canada by train. Watching the sunrise over the prairies, twisting my neck for hours on end trying to see the tops of the Rockies, enjoying the magic where the mountains met the sea, these were the prelude to my first plane journey from Vancouver to San Francisco, and then over the North Pacific. Between Vancouver and Seattle an Irishman, who 'had drink taken', started an argument with me about the Anglican Communion, the British Empire and George VI, including all in a blanket of disapproval. As he was not 'beastly drunk', I entered into the spirit of the thing, if that is not an unhappy expression, and came back at him with some enthusiasm. He started to apologise, but I stopped that and told him to cheer up, as I was born in Dun Laoghaire myself and was never so happy as when in an argument. Deeply moved, he tried to share a bottle of Irish whiskey with me. We parted in the end with expressions of mutual esteem.

This island-hopping trip, Hawaii, Midway, Wake, Guam and Okinawa, brought us to the Yang-tse-Kiang delta. Here we were flying low, not, I imagine, much over two thousand feet, and I had a wonderful view of that great alluvial plain, laid out from horizon to horizon in what appeared to be multiple prototypes of China's willow-pattern porcelain. There were the little houses dotted across the plain, the intersecting rivulets, the bridges and temples, a pastiche in vivid greens, browns and silver, an exquisite introduction to China.

My excuse for being in China was the preaching of the Synod sermon. This experience I did not enjoy. It had to be done by interpretation. The pulpit was actually above the great revolving fans and offered no relief in what, it was generally agreed, was the hottest summer in Shanghai for fifty years. I fortunately had been presented

with a fan, and it was fun learning quickly to work this into the rhythm
of my speech. In China you have to learn quickly, as I later discovered
at my first Chinese feast, where it was assumed I had used chopsticks
from infancy.

More pleasant, because more relaxed, was a later session at Synod
where I presented greetings from the five Provinces of the British
Isles, and a gift from the Dean and Chapter of St. Paul's of an enlarged
and finely-framed photograph of St. Paul's Cathedral standing triumphantly amid the ruins after the blitz of 1941.

I treasure a note scribbled on half a sheet of notepaper from Bishop
R. O. Hall:

> Dear Max, that was terrific. Its simplicity was exactly right for
> China and the inspiration of St. Paul's among the ruins will be
> repeated again and again in every church in China. Your restraint
> too, in not saying more yourself and leaving it to the picture was
> exactly right. Don't be disappointed at apparently slight response.
> That's only surface. Sunday and Friday have gone deep down. R.H.

I was still very much of a tyro at this sort of occasion, and that kind
note from R.O. meant a lot.

How very glad I am that, however, briefly, I saw something of the
old China before Chairman Mao's reformation. Will his reformation
endure? Or will the essential China remain, its bamboo resilience having bent to the winds of Mao, but remained unbroken? Our great-
grandchildren may have the answer. This reflection was prompted by
a visit to Hangchow, called in China 'The City of Heaven below'. For
its setting and charm it is well-named. I had for host that notable
sinologue and C.M.S. missionary, Doctor Sturton, who took me
round the city and over to the islands on the lake. It is a remarkable
fact that, in all essentials, Hangchow, when I saw it, could be recognised as the Hangchow which Marco Polo saw in the fourteenth
century. His description of the streets and their specialised merchandise,
the famous restaurants on the islands, all tallied with what I saw.

Circled by its hills, reflected in its quiet lake, linked with the sea by
its river, rich in centuries of tradition and beautiful in its outward
display and in the skill of its merchants, Hangchow is as exciting as
Marco Polo found it. Hard by the lake are two Pagodas dating from
the eleventh century, so Marco Polo must have seen them too, and
wrote of them, Christian-tourist like, as 'temples of their idols'. On
the hill nearby is the monastery which housed the monk from India
who first brought the tenets of the Buddha to China. Chairman Mao
has formidable competition when it comes to survival value.

A quite unforgettable visit to Nanking to stay with Bishop Y. Y. Tsu; our pilgrimage to the Purple Mountain to see the great memorial to Sun Yat Sen; lunch at the American Embassy where the principal guest was General Wedemeyer of the U.S.A. on a Mission of enquiry into what use was being made of American aid; our meeting with the ambassador from India; and visits to various Chinese government departments — all culminated in an exasperating, potentially embarrassing, but in retrospect, very amusing incident. Harry Wittenbach and I arrived at the station in good time for the night express to Shanghai. At the ticket barrier we were told that our tickets were wrongly dated. Back to the ticket office we went for a prolonged farce. Harry, a fluent Cantonese speaker, only had a few words of Mandarin. The ticket-office staff presented a united front of inflexible obstinacy in refusing to provide us with other tickets. Time was passing. An attempt to ring Bishop Tsu failed. We were in near despair when a clerk from the back of the office slipped out by a side door came up behind us and told us to follow him. The train was whistling for the start as we ran a hurdle-race over countless sleeping bodies, dashed through the barrier, raced down the platform and just managed to jump into a carriage as the train began to gather speed. As we ran we had been conscious of a great deal of whistling but paid no attention. Once on the train we turned round to see half-a-dozen soldiers waving at us and asking for our passports. But by now the train was going far too fast for any such diplomatic niceties. Reflecting on the experience, Harry said that a few judiciously placed bank notes at the ticket office would have saved all the trouble, but he wasn't going to waste them on men who couldn't speak Cantonese!

We didn't sleep much on the journey. I was nicely sandwiched between two men, one of them asleep, the other active throughout the night in clearing his throat and spitting across me out of the window. I hope Chairman Mao has done something about this habit, in what is, after all, the oldest and, in some important respects, the most sophisticated civilisation in the world.

Harry Wittenbach, my companion during this visit to China, deserves far more than a passing reference. A C.M.S. missionary in that country since 1925, he had spent four years in internment in Stanley Camp in Hong Kong, becoming the civilian prisoners' elected representative in all dealings with the Japanese. Physically wiry, he was, spiritually, one of the imperturbables. If ever I were to be in a tight spot, whether of physical danger or of some embarrassing difficulty, I would rather have Harry as a companion than anyone else I know. He still wears better than any other of my contemporaries. In addition to all his other qualities of mind and spirit, he possesses the skill of a cartoonist. How often was there an occasion at our Thursday Secretaries' Meeting in Salisbury Square, when feelings were getting overwarm and tempers were rising. So easily, something could have been said which would have taken a lot of un-saying. At the critical moment a sheet of foolscap would be passed from Harry to his neighbour, and on it a superb cartoon illustrating the contention of the moment. A roar of laughter as it passed round the table saved the situation. In my possession is a remarkable collection of these gentle dissuasives. They may not qualify as major works of art. But to defuse disagreement of bitterness is a great art in itself.

The journey home from China was broken by a brief visit to Hong Kong which contributed one of those encounters that make travel so entertaining. I was staying at the Church Guest House. Coming down rather late for breakfast one morning I found there was only one vacant seat. After introductions to my immediate neighbours, we discovered to our mutual surprise that we were all three related, one of them sharing with me a great-grandfather, the other only a little less closely connected.

Hong Kong held much of absorbing interest but here I must confine myself to the journey back to England. This, by flying-boat, took four days and was as politically illuminating as it was spiritually exciting. Among other experiences it gave me a view, not counting the Yangtse-Kiang, of eight others of the world's great rivers—the Mekong, the Irrawaddy, the Brahmaputra, the Ganges, the Indus, the Euphrates, the Tigris and the Nile—not a bad collection for one trip by one whose earliest enthusiasm had been geography.

At Rangoon we came down on the Irrawaddy. Civil war was in progress and the night was made lively by small-arms fire. This was the first illustration of an empire in dissolution. The next was when we came down on the Hooghly, one of the channels of the Ganges. The good Bishop Tarafdar, assistant Bishop of Calcutta, had come to greet me. We had two hours together and he told me how his particular area of responsibility, the Nadia district of Bengal, was now divided by the international frontier between India and Pakistan. That same evening, after flying over the India of Kipling's Jungle Books, we came down on the water near Karachi. There I was hoping to meet Archdeacon Spence, the Secretary of the New Zealand C.M.S. Sind Mission. But he had to ring me to say there was a curfew in Karachi and he was unable to come. One final evidence of the end of the Pax Britannica came twenty-four hours later when the captain of the flying-boat announced over the inter-com that plans for us to sleep at Shepheard's Hotel in Cairo had been cancelled, and we were to sleep on a house-boat. The explanation was that the Prime Minister of Egypt was due back that day from Lake Success after an abortive attempt to hasten British withdrawal from Egypt. The temper of the population of Cairo, so we were told, was uncertain as regards British citizens. The precautions were exaggerated and I spent two pleasant hours with members of the Egyptian Church and our missionaries in the very heart of Cairo. But that any precaution was necessary was evidence that a power vacuum was waiting to be filled and that, meanwhile, chaos had come again.

Among my travelling companions was a one-time President of Rangoon University, and another was a doctor, the P.M.O. in Burma, with whom I had much talk. Burma, I would judge from what they told me, had never been valued as one of the brightest jewels in Britain's crown. I rather gathered that here, more than elsewhere, we left 'unwept, unhonoured and unsung'. Altogether, viewed politically, this was a journey which haunted me during the coming years when so few, even in well-informed government circles, seemed willing to see the signs of the times. The debacle of Suez was less than ten years away.

But if the journey was disturbing to my politically-conscious self, it contained by contrast a spell of unbroken excitement for a student of the Bible. After leaving Karachi we had come down for lunch on the Shatt-al-Arab at Basra. While idly speculating about the Garden of Eden and looking at a forest of date-palms, it seemed obvious what was the fruit that made Eve's mouth water. Where did Thomas Hood, Mark Twain and the English-speaking world generally get the idea that it was an apple that caused the trouble? But putting vain imaginings aside, it suddenly dawned on me that we might see the ruins of Ur of the Chaldees. I had a rough picture in my mind of Woolley's excavations. So, directly we were air-borne I went, armed with my Bible, to the observation platform, that remarkable provision on flying-boats which provided about three hundred degrees of vision. Presently I was joined by the captain. I asked him if we would be anywhere near the site of Ur. He said, 'Yes, we'll be there in a matter of minutes.' Sure enough, I was soon looking down on the ground plan I had vaguely memorised. Imaginatively, the captain circled the site at not much more than fifteen hundred feet. Then we struck due north-west, with the Euphrates away to starboard. This seemed an odd manoeuvre, but the captain explained that the Saudi Arabian authorities were unwilling to permit flights over this northern triangle. So we flew steadily towards Haran. By now I reckoned I was going to be on Abraham's trail for the rest of the day. Sure enough, about where Haran must have been, we banked steeply and were soon flying south-west. Presently, the mountains of Lebanon came into view and, somewhere in the haze below, must be Damascus, the home of Abraham's faithful steward, Eliezer. We flew on due south until, over the mountains of Moab, we swung due west till we came to the oasis of Beersheba, and from there on followed the ancient trade route to the banks of the Nile.

It had been a long day. We had taken off from Karachi at 3.0 a.m. By the time I had spent two hours with friends in Old Cairo it was 11.0 p.m. and I was ready for bed. But what a day! What an experience to follow, albeit very comfortably, that old wanderer's way, to salute that great nomad of faith, venerated alike by Christian and Muslim as well as Jew! Comparatively few people can have followed that precise route the way I did. Very few of them are likely to have given a thought to Abraham. Flying-boats were soon taken out of service. I think I can safely risk claiming a unique opportunity, uniquely taken, to provide a unique experience. Its spiritual impact has gripped my imagination ever since.

One sequel to the I.M.C. Conference at Whitby in 1947 was an invitation to the first post-war meeting of the German Conference of Missionary Societies to be held at Herborn in 1948. At Whitby there had been three remarkable Germans, Pralat von Hartenstein from Wurtemburg, Dr. Walter Freytag from Hamburg, and Dr. Ihmels from Leipzig. With Dr. Freytag, in particular, I struck up a deep friendship which was to endure until his death in 1959. I was to be honoured with an invitation to contribute to a *Festschrift* celebrating his sixtieth birthday, which happily was available for him to read shortly before his death.

Dr. Freytag and I were first drawn to one another at Whitby, when we found that we took the same serious view of the world scene. He, of course, had been through the apocalyptic experience of a Christian living in the Third Reich and hating it. He had endured the terrible ordeal of the allied bombing of Hamburg when, on three successive nights, three-quarters of the city were systematically reduced to rubble, as I was to see for myself. For my part I had experienced no comparable suffering. From fifty miles away I had watched the night sky alight with London's burning. I had fire-watched there during part of the war when the V.1s and V.2s were not exactly sedatives. But all this was trifling beside Walter Freytag's experience. Yet I had travelled through the twilight of a great empire. I knew enough history to know what happens when an empire passes.

Walter Freytag and I read the same riddle and arrived at the same answer. We were both in our several ways horrified by the very superficial interpretation put upon events by so many of the North Americans present at the Whitby Conference. We were equally nervous about what appeared to be the eloquence and undue influence of the American dollar. This conjunction of thought, together with a common interest in, if not identical views upon, eschatology, did, I believe, lie behind the invitation to Herborn for I was the only foreigner present otherwise than three members of the I.M.C. staff.

One of the I.M.C. staff was Betty Gibson. She was one of that brilliant group of women who were early captured for the Ecumenical Movement and who, in particular, contributed so largely to the work both of the I.M.C. and the C.B.M.S. by the thoroughness of their research. Betty Gibson was a most gracious personality whose extensive knowledge and wide and long experience were carried with charm and gentleness.

What I had not bargained for on setting out for Herborn was that I was to arrive at Frankfurt airport in the middle of the Berlin air-lift. In that tense period no one there was particularly welcoming to a British civilian. Fortunately the British consul was brother of one of our C.M.S. missionaries, and I finally reached his office. I was then faced with the problem of how to reach Herborn which was some sixty kilometres away. A strict regulation demanded that if I was to travel anywhere in the American zone I must have a military title. I was taken along to the office of the British Army liaison officer, who proved remarkably amenable, said he would gladly give me a temporary commission, and politely asked what I thought would be suitable. Not to be outdone in courtesy, I asked for guidance. 'Well,' he said, 'we give Bishops the rank of Brigadier-General.' With proper modesty I demurred at this implied compliment and settled for being a full colonel. Never having reached higher rank than a corporal in the Marlborough O.T.C. I thought the rank of colonel was a sufficiently dramatic promotion.

That conference was a valuable experience and the start of more friendships. It was a sobering experience to see what Germans were living on at that time, a monotonous diet of gruel and potatoes and very *ersatz* coffee. When, later, I saw what the R.A.F. had done to Hamburg, Dusseldorf, Essen and Cologne I realised how lightly we in Britain had escaped both as to bombing and food shortages.

Walter Freytag, the conference ended, drove me first to Kaiserswerth, the famous mother-house of the Lutheran deaconess order. Then we drove to Hermannsburg, passing on the way the monument to that first German blitzkrieg which in A.D. 9 destroyed Varus and his legions. At Hermannsburg we found ourselves staying in what has been a great centre of spiritual revival and the centre of a vigorous missionary society.

Bishop Stephenson of Nelson, Mrs. Stephenson, Canon R. J. Hewett, Federal Secretary of C.M.S. of Australia, and Mrs. Hewett being presented to Her Majesty the Queen during the C.M.S. Third Jubilee at C.M.S. House, 1948

Present and past — with Canon J. V. Taylor

The author's portrait by Brenda Bury unveiled by the Archbishop of Canterbury

The Chapter of Westminster Abbey in session, 1972. *From the left:* Canon Ronald Jasper; the author; the Dean, Dr. Eric Abbott; Canon Edward Carpenter; Canon David Edwards; the Receiver-General, Reg Pullen

Driving across the North German plain, Freytag and I gave ourselves to a long unhurried discussion of various passages in the New Testament. He allowed me to enter into the secret place where his real life was lived. It is always a wonderful experience when another human being allows you over the threshold into the very temple of his spirit. And in this way I came to know this German friend at a new level.

In Hamburg he drove me round the city. It was an appalling sight of desolation. But from him came no hint of bitterness. He reckoned that somewhere in all this was the judgment of God, and as a Christian accepted for himself that judgment.

In the evening we attended a play written by one of Freytag's sons and performed in a little church on the outskirts of the city. It was an interpretation of the book of Job conceived as an evangelistic exercise. So vividly was it presented and so contemporaneously interpreted that it could be readily understood by someone as innocent of the German language as myself.

This first visit to Germany gave me a feeling for that country and for her people which, being built upon my earlier contact with many German-Jewish refugees, helped me to a new understanding of the enormous seriousness of the German mind, a seriousness which is as important for understanding German history as it is for understanding German theology. I think the Germans view us as an essentially frivolous people. Perhaps we are. Yet, muddle-headed though we may often appear to be, it is possible for a nation to take itself too seriously. I have on record an intriguing testimony to this from an unexpected source. I remember M. M. Thomas of India addressing an American audience and, in the course of a very witty speech, saying how dangerous it was to paint issues in blacks and whites. 'In India,' he said, 'we have come to have a profound veneration for the British way of doing things and not least for "muddling through".' That remark produced a great laugh. He held to his position and added, 'You see, the merit of "muddling through" is that you do not worship logical consistency. You do not define issues in ideological terms. You insist on a pragmatic approach. There is a profound theological truth behind the philosophy of "muddling through".' Admittedly that was a 'throw-away' remark and I must not bind 'M.M.' to a position about which, by now, he may have reservations.

But none of these observations leads me to underrate the importance of German thoroughness, or my gratitude for all that I owe to so many of their great theological teachers.

I am unlikely ever to land on the moon. But I did once fly direct from London into the late Stone Age. It happened like this.

A pressing invitation came from the C.M.S. of Australia that I should visit them for consultation about our common interests. Their Federal Secretary, Canon John Hewett, with great imagination decided that, before I met the more recent immigrant population, I should have a chance of seeing something of the original Australians. John met me at Darwin in North Western Australia. There we transferred to a small seven-seater Avro-Austin plane and spent the next week flying about Arnhem land, the largest area in which Australian Aborigines still, at that time, followed much of their traditional life. In this way I had an experience very few Australians had enjoyed other than a handful of administrators, cattle-men and missionaries. This was in 1949. Since then there has been much development, a great deal of prospecting and mining, and a radical change in the Australian Government's attitude to the Aborigines and their welfare. At that date all welfare was in the hands of the missionaries, Methodists, Anglicans and others.

This was the real 'out-back', the furthest 'out' from the main centres of population. We visited Katherine and the Roper River Settlement, Oenpelli, and Groote Eylandt. It was at Groote Eylandt that I really felt myself transported to the 'olden time'. One evening it was suggested that we joined a party of Aborigines for a fishing expedition out in the waters of the Gulf of Carpentaria. While we were waiting for the canoes we hunted about for coral, one beautiful little piece of which I have before me as I write.

As, later, we were to eat some of our catch, the first thing was to get a fire going. This our Aborigine companions proceeded to do with delicate skill, first fashioning two sticks so that a quick rotating action of the one in a small hollow carved in the other quickly produced two little glowing embers. Kindling was added, blown into a flame, and we had our fire.

There we were, a group of Aborigines absorbed in the oldest act known to mankind, watched by an equally absorbed group from a sophisticated culture whose whole technology has been built upon what the earliest men discovered about fire.

Then, leaving one or two men to keep the fire burning strongly, the rest of us made for the canoes, roughly hollowed tree trunks, into which we scrambled. John and I, neither of us a light-weight, nearly swamped our canoe. No sooner in, than we had to get out, to push the canoe into deeper water. Getting into the canoe was now even more precarious but we managed it thanks to the boatmanship of our Aborigine partners. The fishing was as dramatic as anything I have ever watched. Up in the bow, feet planted on the extremely narrow sides of the canoe, stood the fisherman, a flaming torch in his left hand, a spear in his right, and a supply of spears at his feet. The sheer acrobatics of his feat were astonishing, for, whether it was flinging a spear, or stooping to pick a fresh one up, he never shook the canoe. But if the acrobatics were amazing, his eye-sight and skill left one awe-struck. Remembering the refractions of light on water and its distorting effect on objects moving below the surface it was little short of miraculous to see how he would spear a moving fish perhaps a dozen or more feet away and never miss. I can swear to this for I hauled in the spears with the fish attached.

After we had made a sufficient catch we paddled back to the shore, glad to get in, as a swell had got up and we were shipping water. Then came our reward as, after watching the fish being cooked in the ashes of the fire, we each were given our share on a shell for a plate: and firm delicious eating it was.

For some hours, men of the twentieth century had lived in the Stone Age way with men who were native to it. There was ample evidence of our common humanity. Elsewhere, these primitive skills had been developed to serve wider purposes. But the life behind the skills and their development had been continuous. This sense of continuity and oneness I brought away from Arnhem land, the oneness made holy when, on a Sunday morning, I assisted John at the Holy Communion where, except for a few missionaries, the whole congregation consisted of Aborigines.

John was a grand companion to have on a trip like this. He was enjoying himself as much as I was, and always good for a laugh, though he had much on his mind. The Federal Secretary of the C.M.S. in Australia has a difficult task. The distances separating the units are enormous. The mentality, which, at that date, still arranged that the gauge on the railway lines varied so that at the border of each state you had to change trains, spilt over into the mentality of the Society's branches in each state. Apart from their sharing in a dominant missionary concern, each State Branch appeared to have a common suspicion of the Federal organisation, and argued, vigorously and endlessly, their local independence. I suppose this is the sort of thing that happens in continents. What I saw in Australia in the way of confusion and waste of effort and nervous exhaustion reconciled me to life in a small island!

But side-by-side with administrative individualism went an enormous zest. The enthusiasm of the C.M.S. League of Youth, for instance, both in Australia and New Zealand, from which has come a stream of recruits for missionary service, has no parallel in the Church life either of Australia or New Zealand. Conservative in their theological views, and sometimes apt to be intolerant of those who do not share them, these young enthusiasts have an indisputable depth in their devotion to Christ. As such they are a spiritual force that the missionary movement can ill afford to lack.

Anxiety arises chiefly as to what may happen when men and women with such 'ironside' dispositions meet with men and women deeply rooted in ancient religious cultures; or with those who have revolted against former orthodoxies and found their home in Independent Churches; or, again, with those whose nerve ends are acutely sensitive to any hint of superiority from a foreigner. Anxiety about this is proper, but also is the hope, fully justified by experience, that enthusiasm can be tempered without losing its drive, and zeal be aligned with discretion without forfeiting its warmth. The Church in Australia and New Zealand, as well as nearer home, needs to be much less stuffily suspicious of what is over-easily dismissed as 'conservative Evangelicalism'.

Australia and New Zealand, of course, spelt infinitely more than Aborigines and the C.M.S. League of Youth. It spelt most gracious welcomes from Archbishops and Bishops, some of whom found C.M.S. difficult to fit into their frames of reference. Australia also meant frequent adventures with the Australian Broadcasting Corporation. They are delightfully casual in comparison with my experience of Broadcasting House in London. I have found myself in a Perth studio chatting with a producer and then being told, without time for rehearsal, that I would be on the air in half a minute for a ten-minute broadcast. In Brisbane I was intercepted outside the Cathedral and was given a minute to collect myself before being asked to speak into a microphone and give a two-minute interpretation of the World Church as I saw it. There was just time to ask that best of friends Jack Dain for one thought. He told me of the diocese of Central Tanganyika with its thousand churches, over six hundred founded in the last ten years: and the Government's request for more graduate teachers for Christian education for girls. I got that in with three seconds to spare!

Yes, Australia was not dull, least of all when staying with Archbishop Mowll for a week in 1949 when Dr. Martin Niemöller was a fellow-guest. We each had out own heavy programme during the day. But we relaxed together of an evening. I was entranced by this man whose faith and courage had been proved to be of such heroic proportions. Later, Mary and I were privileged to have him as our guest when he spoke to a crowded congregation in St. John's Church, Blackheath.

There was one delightful incident at Melbourne when, outside the Stadium where a big C.M.S. rally was to be held, I met Mr. and Mrs. Sandford. In a small hair-dressing establishment off Fleet Street, Mr. Sandford had for some years been cutting my hair. On one occasion he told me he was emigrating to Australia. I gave him the address of the C.M.S. office in Melbourne. And here he was to greet me, happily settled with a house and a job. To cap it all, Mrs. Sandford recognised Mary, having heard her speak at a Mothers' Union meeting in their London parish. This was a very happy encounter.

Many of my journeys have been in Africa. It was, I believe, Heraclitus who said, 'He who does not hope for the unexpected, will not find it.' In Africa I did not have to do any hoping. The unexpected was always just round the next corner. One morning in 1950 Mary and I were being driven along the road from Yei to Meridi in the Southern Sudan. Rounding a corner we were intrigued by what was obviously a roughly constructed open-air church. We stopped and got out. A glade of trees provided the frame, six of them on one side I recognised as mango trees; on the other, unrecognised by name, were five with fine white bark. At the east end there stood a fine tree in solitary grandeur, nicely balanced by one at the west end. Immediately in front of the tree at the east end was a lectern, the reading desk of which was formed out of an old army camp cooker, hammered flat. Flanking it was a chair covered by a mat. The pews were rough planks balanced on small cross-pieces.

A passer-by told us that the man responsible was a Christian living in a hut which we could see in the distance. Presently he arrived with others from the hamlet. His name was Petro, we discovered, given him in baptism when, during his army service in North Africa, he had been converted. A keen Christian, he had started this little church on his own initiative. There he gathered all the folk he could and taught them what he knew. On a Sunday he would get as many as seventy in his congregation. He was not a pastor, nor a teacher, and he was not paid. What he did he did out of love for Christ, one of Africa's many throw-backs to the first centuries of the Christian Church.

A November day in 1949 found me travelling from Dar-es-Salaam to Dodoma with Bill Wynn-Jones, Bishop of the diocese of Central Tanganyika. It was the first time I had been on this kind of journey in Africa since I left Nigeria, twenty-one years before. The very countryside itself, its colours, its smells, the trees, the outcrops of rock, the sun beating down, all reminded me that I had 'been here before'. The years fell away and, as we halted for a rest in the shade of a tree, I remembered just such a halt when on trek with Guy Bullen in Northern Nigeria. And there was also a remarkable resemblance between Bill and Guy. Each journey had been continually interrupted as we stopped off to greet an African farmer here; an African pastor there; to look in on an isolated European trader; to take lunch with a friend in government service; and so on, every few miles. Bill and Guy were men made in the same mould with the same outgoing friendliness which sheds a light on life which, once seen, is never forgotten. St. Augustine in his 'Confessions' speaks to God of his friend, Simplicianus, 'whom I knew to be your good servant, for your grace shone in him'. So, in a remarkable degree, was it with Guy and Bill. Grace shone in them. It was incandescent and entirely unconscious. What I was not expecting when we set out that morning was this quite extraordinary recapitulation of an experience enjoyed more than twenty years before.

But the day still held another surprise, an unexpected beauty of another kind. When we started on the road again the sun was sinking fast and there were still thirty miles to go. We were travelling through bush which was fairly thickly treed though very dry. And then I saw a transfiguration scene beautiful beyond adequate description and as unexpected as I found it unexplained. Away on our left running from north-east to south-west was a line of hills, about fifteen miles away. Just beyond them the sun was dipping out of sight, the sky was a vivid lemon yellow, the colour of lemon-rind where white and yellow mix. It was glistening bright. Below, the hills were a sharp purple, deepening to indigo. Suddenly, the lower slopes of the hills were transformed into a blue that made me gasp. Perhaps it was a mist caught by some trick of light, but however caused it was beautiful. And by way of sharing our excitement a mass of cumulus away to the north suddenly blushed pink. There is a hymn which I have heard sung in many different parts of America, a vesper hymn, beginning 'Day is dying in the west'. Each verse has the refrain,

Holy, Holy, Holy, Lord God of Hosts! Heaven and earth
   are full of thee,
Heaven and earth are praising thee,
   O Lord most high.

I felt like that on that road in Tanganyika, though I actually used the first verse of Psalm 103. People and places met are part of me.

In the same year a two-hundred-mile drive in Uganda had its quota of the unexpected, shared with George Grimshaw, the C.M.S. Regional Secretary for East Africa. Through his binoculars I had the great good fortune to see the mighty mountain range of Ruwenzori, its snow-covered peaks clear of cloud, a sight you are only likely to see perhaps once in a hundred times on the road we were travelling.

Then there were the beauties of lake Bunyoni, lovely with its water-lilies, the whole enfolded by hills, cultivated to their very summits; while, brooding in the distance, was the crest of one of the great string of volcanoes which run down into Rwanda. Our destination was the leper island of Bwama to be reached by a two-mile trip in a canoe. Part of my duty that day was to take a share in a service at which twenty-six lepers, now symptom-free, were to be given their discharge certificates, a very happy occasion. The unexpected came to me in the hospital. There I found a man suffering from a severe rheumatic condition which sometimes attacks the victims of leprosy. He was running a daily temperature of between 105 and 106 degrees, and was in terrible pain. I knew him to be a very keen Christian so felt bold enough to say that I hoped the Lord was helping him in his sickness. I can see that man still as he looked up at me, gave me a radiant smile and said, 'My body is full of pain but my heart is full of peace. Praise the Lord.' Pain is an inscrutable mystery. The great Healer of lepers had not touched this child of his in the place of his physical need. But he had done something else. He had showed this African how to triumph *through* suffering. He was being allowed to witness through his pain. His radiant, patient faith was a benediction to everyone in that hospital.

On that same journey I had met a group of African clergy. I asked them, among other things, what they looked for in missionaries. I did not know what to expect by way of an answer. I give it as it was translated to me by one of their number, Erica Sabiti, one day to be the first African Archbishop of the Province of Uganda-Rwanda-Burundi. 'We want missionaries who have God's vision; God's insight; able to preach the Gospel; fearless to rebuke sin; who have wisdom; who have an experience in their own lives.' Artlessly spoken, it was no bad definition of what ought to be expected of every member of the Ordained Ministry.

Straight from meeting those clergy I was taken off to a very simple lunch party where we all sat on the ground and ate mashed banana and corn-off-the-cob. The others present were all members of the Revival Fellowship, known in Uganda as the Abalokole. Lunch over, six of them, three girls and three men, told me very simply of their experience of Jesus Christ. They wanted me to know who and what they were, and thought this was the best way of introducing themselves. Were they so very wrong? It was quite unexpected and most convincing, especially that of a young girl who had been a Muslim and had found a transforming experience in Christ. The force of her testimony was tremendous. It had to be translated, but the flash of her eyes and the vigour of her speech showed that she had paid a price for her freedom. Each testimony was followed by the Abalokole chorus 'Tukutendereza'. I can well imagine that constant repetition of the chorus could be somewhat tedious. But it is worth noting that the purpose of the singing is to take the focus off the individual and on to the dying love of Jesus. That would seem to be good psychology and good theology rolled into one.

Throughout this journey of 1949–1950 in Tanganyika, Kenya, and Uganda, the Revival Movement was the main talking point wherever one stopped and with almost everyone I spoke; this included the Governor of Uganda who was particularly incensed because, during the war, many of the Revival brethren had taken a pacifist line and refused to co-operate with the Government. The main talking point, however, was on the potential divisiveness of the movement. Perhaps the sharpest tension was found between the missionaries, who completely identified themselves with the Revival, and those who, no less conscientiously, found themselves unable to do so. Most difficult of all was the role of those who stood in the middle, saw the point of view of both sides, and were appreciated by neither! That the Church in Uganda avoided anything like a schism was due, under God, so I believe, to the wisdom, patience and statesmanship of two men—Bishop Simon Stuart on the one hand and, on the other, an African layman, William Nagenda, perhaps the most outstanding leader of the Revival Movement.

Meanwhile, it had spread to Kenya where, when the Church had to experience the testing fires of the Mau Mau, it was supremely the members of the Revival Movement who proved to be the 'Confessing Church', and may be said to have saved its soul.

Following this journey, I did a great deal of research and, in 1954, produced a small book with the title *Revival-an Enquiry*. For my considered judgment as it was at that date I must refer the reader to the book itself. But something of what I myself felt about the Revival can be gleaned from my dedication of the book and a footnote of explanation. The dedication read:

In gratitude
for the living and dying of
many Christians of Africa
and
in particular for
GANTHON and REBEKAH,
man and wife
two Kikuyu Christians,
whose faith in Christ and very practical

Christianity were sealed by death
on January 18th, 1953

The footnote ran as follows:

> Ganthon was a school-teacher, and he and his wife Rebekah were
> leaders of the Church in the village of Mioro in the Kikuyu reserve.
> One day some tired and thirsty British police officers stopped to
> rest in their village. The ever-hospitable Rebekah made tea for them.
> For that kindness the Mau-Mau exacted the penalty of death. They
> were murdered on Sunday night, 18th January, 1953. These two
> Christians had just returned from a convention meeting of the
> Revival at which Ganthon had been one of the speakers. He and
> his hearers were all marked men and women. Ganthon's last words
> at the meeting were his testimony to his stand as a Christian—'I can
> never go back, whatever happens.'

Lovely and pleasant in their lives, in death they were not divided. I
never had the privilege of meeting Ganthon and Rebekah. But I
salute them in the Spirit. Had I met them I would have been proud
to be part of them.

Of the thousand of miles travelled in West Africa, and of innumerable experiences grave and gay, I limit myself to one. And here my
naval grandfather enters the story again. It was 1957 and the Church
on the Niger was celebrating its centenary. The day came when, at
Onitsha, a party of us were to meet the leading chiefs of the town and
then we were to pay a ceremonial visit to the Obi in his palace.

Protocol demanded that we go first of all to the old centre of the
town where, in 1857, the then Obi had his palace, as had his successors
down to this century. This part of Onitsha was, in 1957, virtually
bush. The old palace no longer existed but they had put up a rough
imitation of it on the actual site. There we were met by the councillors
and elders and Chiefs. Each was wearing his traditional red cap of
office, a conical-shaped headgear with varied ornamentation of feathers.
These worthies were all densely packed in and sitting in their traditional
order. The whole proceeding followed exactly the pattern described
by my grandfather in his diary when he came to salute the Obi of
Onitsha on 1st August, 1869. The drums which were in action, muted
or loud, throughout the proceedings could well have been some of
those he heard.

The Odu of Onitsha indicated to us who all the notabilities were.
Then came a special welcome for Archbishop Horstead and the other

visitors. My moment came when I had to make a speech on behalf of all the visitors. After an appropriate reference to the centenary and an expression of thanks for the welcome we had all received, I went on to say that I had a special reason for being proud to be here. I then told them that on 1st August, 1869, two British ships had anchored off Onitsha, and that from them had come my grandfather, the officer in command, with a message from Queen Victoria to the then Obi. I then told of the description in grandfather's diary of his march from the river to the then palace, and of how he had been received by all the councillors and Chiefs, and how then the Obi came and they exchanged compliments. I did not think the occasion demanded that I should develop the warnings my grandfather had given in 1869 against any possible misdemeanours!

When my recital had been fully translated there was a tremendous excitement and in a few minutes a little old lady came forward to whom I was presented. She was the grand-daughter of the Obi to whom my grandfather had presented the compliments of Queen Victoria. It really was rather exciting. In a life which has been filled with remarkable coincidences this is one of the most remarkable.

For me it was a moving moment with all its contrasts and similarities. What a contrast between the deadly climatic perils faced by grandfather and his crews, and the ease with which we were able to face the same perils! What a contrast between a naval expedition forshadowing the establishment of British rule in Nigeria, and our visit at the imminent end of that rule. And yet what similarities! Grandfather, for all his profession as a naval officer, was a man of peace, and his diary records his pleasure that he was not involved in a punitive expedition but a 'peace' expedition. What a coincidence that he travelled on from Onitsha to Bida with Bishop Crowther as his passenger, while now we were celebrating the centenary of the Mission which Bishop Crowther had started!

Sometimes coincidences happen and for a moment history is telescoped, time stands still and we know a oneness between past and present, and, surely, with the future too. I have in these pages recorded some rich experiences and a few unique ones, but in its own way this meeting with the old traditional Chiefs of Onitsha at precisely the spot on which my own grandfather met their predecessors eighty-eight years before was an experience in a class by itself.

A few days later the 'old lady' came up to the Bishop's house to be photographed. She had asked permission to bring with her 'the mothers of Onitsha', twelve old darlings representing the grandmothers of the town. We were all photographed together. Then my 'old lady', Mrs. Okala, was photographed with Mary and me. We were then presented to her uncles and brothers and sons and daughters. Speeches were made. We were given gifts, and the happy occasion was concluded with one of Mary's inspired spontaneities. She embraced Mrs. Okala. This proved to be the completely appropriate action, unexpected though it was. Mrs. Okala was hugely delighted and we were given the Ibo greetings of 'those who belong to the family'. That was as nice as anything that happened to us in Nigeria.

Memories can be nostalgic, enfeebling, a croaking 'never more'. But just as journey's end is a place of meeting, so to remember ought to have a sacramental value, a counting as present that which memory holds. So it has been for me, and that is my excuse for this chapter, if excuse is needed. For if the truth be told, journeying was for me a spiritual necessity. I am not by nature, gifts or temperament an administrator, though I have had to do a lot of administering. I dislike administration because it takes up so much time, often, it seems, to so little purpose. So my travels did something for me, without which I could hardly have survived so many years at Salisbury Square. As it was, the journeys enabled me to see what my administration was in fact about, to observe what I had to interpret, to check what I had to write. Because I had seen and known I could speak with confidence *yes.* and write with conviction.

In these days of air-travel at thirty-five thousand feet above a sea of clouds, possibly the dullest form of travel ever invented by human ingenuity, there is only the quick way of getting from A to B. There is none of the richness of human encounter where place and people meet and where, because you have belonged for a moment, your belonging is for ever.

Such moments have been multitudinous. A few must represent the many. I begin with a conversation overheard in the office of a Mission Board executive. Eugene Smith, the General Secretary of the American Methodist Mission Board, had taken me to see the new offices high up on 475 Riverside, New York. They were designed 'open office' pattern and I was out of sight, but unavoidably within hearing of one conversation. Eugene was talking over the phone with a young missionary who had obviously overstepped the mark in a flagrant disobedience to regulations, and had caused a lot of people a great deal of trouble in consequence. I can imagine how many a business executive would have handled the affair. It was a revelation to overhear Eugene at work. Here was a combination of firmness and gentleness, of insistence on obedience together with forgiveness. It was a model of how a Christian should help a fellow-Christian, 'overtaken in a fault'. It was Galatians 6:1 coming to life. I have much for which to be grateful to Eugene, but for nothing more than that conversation he did not know I had overheard.

Remembering assumes its sacramental character most immediately when, at the Holy Communion, the Christ and the whole company of redeemed mankind, are known to be 'present'.

Three such moments, in circumstances as different as can be well imagined, live as though they happened yesterday. A teacher-training college in Nigeria gives one setting. The Principal, Seth Kale, later to be Bishop of Lagos, a friend now for well over thirty years, was celebrating the Holy Communion on the last morning of term. The prayers were said with a meaningfulness all too rarely heard, perhaps because the one who said them breathed through his whole life a reverence for God and man and all life. We are apt to think of the Indian as a man with a peculiar genius for worship and adoration, and we may be right. But Africa has also something to teach us. That morning in the chapel at Oyo there was this added, a deep sense of wonder, of astonishment before the goodness of God. That early morning in Africa is unforgettable.

And so is a late evening service in the city of Yezd. A tiny Christian community welcomed a passing visit from their Bishop, Hassan Dehqani-Tafti, with whom Mary and I were travelling. He celebrated and I assisted with the chalice. It might have been any time in the first three centuries. Here was a little group of some twenty Christians, a barely tolerated minority in a very hostile environment. What a mixed bunch we were. One or two old men were obviously very poor. There was one very old woman. And there was a group of young men and young women. What I found especially interesting was that there were several friendly Muslims present and a Zoroastrian woman doctor. Here was no 'veiling of the mysteries'. Rather here was the Royal Table set for all who wished to see. It was an implicit invitation. 'We Christians have nothing to hide. To sit down and feast in the Kingdom is for all men from East and West.' Of course the Muslims and the Zoroastrian were present only as reverent and interested visitors, that was all. But the invitation in the Holy Communion Office and the service itself were a setting forth of the Gospel.

Far removed from that dark little room in a Persian city was the beautiful light-filled cathedral in Kobe. And what a happy laughter-filled memory that cathedral holds. Here was a Holy Communion services instinct with gaiety. The procession of clergy was led in by nine minute acolytes in tiny cassocks and surplices. At the beginning of the Offertory hymn they were led out by the celebrant, Bishop Yashiro, and then returned with him carrying, one a ciborium, one a cruet of wine, one of water, each with something. In happy disarray they crowded round the Bishop, each handing up his burden. One by one, their duty over, each scampered off. The youngest, three years old, stood at two feet nothing. What a splendid way of bringing children straight into the heart of the Eucharist! But I think only in a Japanese cathedral could this have been done successfully. It demands both a Japanese attitude to children and also the Japanese capacity for reverent irreverence.

But communion bespeaks community. What of the isolated? On the road from Isfahan to Shiraz we stopped to call on two Christians, a man and his wife. In an area totally destitute of medical services they were a medical team. The wife was a fully qualified nurse. The man, with much medical experience, was unlicensed and was technically unqualified, but worked under cover of his wife's qualifications. They were meeting a great human need and providing a magnificent Christian witness. The nearest fellow-Christian was eighty miles away.

There are many such isolated Christians, and not only in Iran. A parable of their importance is the Persian garden. We travelled for hundreds of miles over what the Persian poet Hafiz feelingly describes — 'Dark is the stony desert, trackless and vast and dim.' But ever and anon we came to a walled enclosure and through the gateway saw what a little water could do by way of bringing enchantment to a desert. We saw what it meant to speak of the desert blossoming as the rose. Those two Christians were a 'Persian garden' as fragrant a memory as any rose.

Peshawur presented a sharp contrast. The Pakistani parish priest took us one afternoon to visit a *basti*, the quarters in which the servants and sweepers of the big houses live. In one of these *bastis* there lived a group of eighty-five Christians. We found a courtyard about eighteen yards wide. Round it on four sides were low buildings not more than seven feet high. In these mud structures were seventeen openings, leading into rooms eight feet by eight. In these dark caves the people lived, approximately five to a room. The cooking was being done outside as it was fine. Conditions when it is wet beggar description.

We were entertained by a dozen of the girls, all in their late teens. They sang us songs and hymns accompanied on a *tabla*. The devastating poverty of the scene; the pathos of the singing with the word *Masih*— Saviour—coming regularly; the knowledge that everyone there was illiterate, and that humanly speaking there was no prospect of any betterment in their condition, saving a revolution, all this was quite overwhelming.

Before we left, the pastor of that flock said a prayer and then asked me to give the blessing. I have often felt inadequate, but never more hopelessly inadequate than then. Who was I to bless this little company of Christ's neglected poor? I hope I will never lose the pain of that moment. I know that the memory helps to keep me in a state of sizzling anger at the ghastly complacency of our Western Christianity. Yet, how hard it is to make anger effective, to help to build above the intent the deed. Much of the spiritual apathy of our day surely derives directly from our powerlessness to match the needs we see. The Gospel answer to the riddle is very difficult to discern. Pressed by this dilemma, we are forced to accept the fact that the whole missionary enterprise is one great act of faith: that somehow, in ways beyond our seeing, our obedience to the divine commission plays into the hands of God, for the working out of his purpose. That is not defeatism. At the back of every act of Christian pioneering down through history has been just such a faith, for human resources have never yet matched human need. To arrive at the end of ourselves is to find that we are, in Oswald Chambers' fine phrase, 'on the margins of God'.

For me, a glimpse of this answer came in unusual fashion on a very cold early winter day nearly four thousand feet up on the high central plateau of Tasmania. A heavy snow storm had driven all the colour out of the world. Presently our road ran beside a lake whose levels, raised for purposes of electric power, had killed the surrounding timber. Gaunt trees, their trunks submerged, strained tortured branches to the sky. Steel grey and icy blue all flecked with white it was like a vision of a dead world in which spirits, suddenly embodied, had been frozen into statues. It was an eerie sight. I could well believe that seen by moonlight it would condition one to see ghosts.

On this roof of the world, as it seemed, austere in its cold beauty, man was dwarfed. Here was solitariness, the kind of lonely place John Buchan described in *Sick Heart River*, where one finds God or goes mad. That afternoon we met two people who had found God. We came to a little log cabin in a clearing in the bush. It was the post office of a place with the cold, grey, appropriate name of Steppes. Somewhere in the neighbourhood trails may have led to other steddings, but this was the only house I can remember seeing. Here we were made welcome by two remarkable people, both in their seventies. Their father had come to Tasmania and built this log cabin in 1858 and here both the man and his sister had been born.

Right 'off the map', you might say: yet they were most wonderfully in the world. They had made their clearing a bird and animal sanctuary. The place was alive with the sound of birds. Opossums and other wild things came to be fed. The sister was a bird-watcher and was in touch with a research station in Northumberland. This visit was certainly a benediction to my spirit. Here were two people who had taken the wilderness to their heart and blessed it. Here was part of God's purpose being fulfilled. For surely, in creating man to crown the natural order, God intended that, with understanding, man could co-operate with God, and so make of all creation a response of worship and praise by the creature to the Creator. That cold world of icy blue water and bare mountainside had become something different because two people had made it home, consciously part of the Father's house. This was, as I have said, a parable of the meaning of the Gospel, for creation out of chaos, redemption out of sin, and the sanctification of all life, what is that but the meaning of Mission?

Such then were a few of the 'moments' which for me have given time the dimension of eternity, moments that will always be part of me.

By 1949 our two girls, Rosemary and Pat, had reached years of sufficient discretion to look after Granny and be looked after by her. Mary now felt free to join me on many of the journeys. This was wonderful, for every surprise of joy was doubled, each day's experiences were shared, and strains and stresses inescapable, if one was to enter into other people's problems and anxieties, could be faced together. There were not a few occasions where the strains and stresses among missionaries were such that I think sheer despair would have broken me, if Mary had not been there to help me recapture the perspectives of God's grace. More often, to our mutual gladness, were the many opportunities when a woman, a wife, and a mother could bring a touch of healing beyond the wit of a mere man. This is no perfunctory acknowledgement. Mary and I have always done everything *together*, but there is an extra degree of satisfaction when the harness is visible!

The long dull journeys by air and the hours spent in airport lounges held one great advantage. They provided the opportunity for long uninterrupted spells of reading. In this way, among other things, I made up for my previous ignorance of the Greek classics, though I had to do this in their English translations for my slender New Testament Greek was quite insufficient. At least I learnt something of what Plato thought, got somewhere near the spirit of the great dramatists, and followed the vicissitudes of the Peloponnesian war with Thucydides. All this was a great refreshment, having a minimal direct relationship with anything I was about to do, and yet, because great writing is always related to life, was an immediate stimulus. But I did also take with me on many a journey some book which might prepare me for future encounters. In preparation for India I took with me on one trip the latest translation of the Bhagavad-Gita. Within a few days

of arrival I met a group of teachers in Krishnagar in Bengal, among
them a Brahmin who was as surprised as he was delighted to discover
how I had prepared for that meeting. I also took the precaution of
having with me Professor Arberry's translation of the poems of
Hafiz before arriving in Iran. This was just as well because I found that
the Bishop had arranged for me to address the local notables in places
like Isfahan, Kerman and Shiraz. In Kerman there was a very big
turn-out of everybody who was anybody, due, the Bishop was sure,
because they were all convinced I was a British spy! Kerman was a
key centre in the 'great game' under the Raj, the nearest significant
centre to India. The British Consul there used to have a special guard
of Indian cavalry. All these notables remembered those days. But my
quotations from Hafiz disarmed them. You can get away with a lot in
Iran if you can quote from Hafiz.

Inevitably, on many of these travels I had to meet the Press. One
such occasion stands out as unique. I was on a lecture tour in Scandi-
navia. In Helsinki the conference began with five men photographing
me from half-a-dozen angles, each taking about five pictures with
flash bulbs — the heaviest photographic assault I have ever experienced.
Then came one whole hour with seven journalists, who grilled me on
every conceivable aspect of the Christian Mission. I have never met
a group of journalists who asked such uniformly intelligent and
penetrating questions. Where else, I wonder, would you get a journalist
quoting Toynbee and the whole group entering into a discussion of
the ideas of Radhakrishnan and Koestler and Aldous Huxley? That
was the level of this press conference and it was the journalists who
started it at that level. What emerged in the Finnish Press I do not
know. What I do know is that the conversation would have done
credit to a senior combination room in any English university.

Some of these journeys came near to resolving themselves into
talking marathons. This was true in particular of Australia and the
U.S.A. In neither of these countries is allowance made for a visiting
speaker to have time for rest between engagements. Rarely does it
occur to one's embarrassingly generous hosts and hostesses that one
needs time to prepare if one is to give a serious talk to serious people
on a serious subject. Again and again I have had to go quite unprepared
and almost 'blindfold' into a meeting, with only the sketchiest idea as
to what the audience was expecting. On such occasions one has simply
to throw oneself upon the grace of God, shooting an 'arrow prayer'
for guidance. And the guidance has come. That is my testimony out
of innumerable such experiences, some of them so dramatic that I
felt myself standing and watching and wondering, a third party in
which I was the listener not the speaker. I have found myself getting

on to my feet, mentally exhausted, and without an idea as to what to say. And suddenly the shape of a talk has been given me, some half-forgotten incident has flashed into my mind and I was away. Sometimes I had an overwhelming sense that God had some special word for someone present and was using me as his mouthpiece. Later I have found it was so—a thrilling experience, yes, and also awe-inspiring, and in retrospect rather terrifying.

I am not at all interested in psychological explanations, valid as they may be. I have a theological explanation which I find quite sufficient. People were praying for me, in the meeting perhaps, or on the other side of the world, but certainly praying. An old African pastor in Tanganyika welcomed me at the end of one long journey with the words, 'We have been praying for you.' That I am sure was the secret not only of what I myself was enabled to learn but also of any value I may have been to those I met. *Amen!*

10/22/77
Over the Atlantic

12

1942 - 1963

Home-base

The home is the abiding place; in the home is reality;
the home helps to attain Him Who is real. So stay
where you are, and all things shall come to you in
time.

KABIR

Poems

KABIR was right. And Hoyland was saying the same thing in his *Sacrament of the Common Life* when he wrote:

> A home is a treasury of God
> Where purity, beauty and joy
> Are stored, for his purposes, inviolate.
> For a home is in itself the triumph of God
> Banishing Night, and Chaos and Necessity,
> Indwelling this lifeless clay
> With the spirit divine of freedom and joy.

Recently, a friend of long standing and I were reminiscing. She remembered, very well, one time of considerable stress. I was feeling completely exhausted by a long-drawn-out battle for what I thought to be matters of principle. And I had complained to her that I did not see how I could go on very much longer. To this complaint she responded with one simple question, 'Where are you happy?' 'At home,' was my instant reply. At that she was reassured that I would not give in. She knew my home. By the word 'happy' she and I meant all that Hoyland describes, all that Kabir means by that experience of reality which helps one to attain to 'Him Who is real'.

For eighteen years, when I was not travelling abroad, I often had to travel from Blackheath to Blackfriars during the rush hour, sometimes five days a week. And, on days when Leslie Fisher and his car were not available, I also came home in the rush hour. This was an education in itself. I learnt why men and women with a day in the office behind them and two such journeys each day rarely turned out for evening meetings laid on by the Vicar!

But what bliss it was to get home, to learn of the day's events; for there was always much to be told of neighbours and newly-made friends, and to hear about school and its doings from Rosemary and Pat. Home was the beginning and the end, and how true it is that in the end was the strength for a new beginning.

Before looking at what home meant to us as a family, I would make a confession of faith. In the home-base I found the real sacrament of the Christian life, the outward and visible and most enjoyable proof of the grace of God. Evangelical religion has been aptly described as being in its essential genius the religion of the home. It is no mere play of words if, in reply to the question 'What do I mean by Evangelical religion?', I reply that I mean a deeply-felt and lived-with assurance that I am at home with God. For me that is one way of trying to put into words just a small fraction of the infinite mystery of at-one-ment which is the heart of the Christian Faith.

There are, I know, many good Christians who recoil from this Evangelical emphasis on 'assurance'. To them it seems dangerously presumptuous, is calculated to lead to spiritual pride, and so to intolerance. This recoil is very understandable. Assurance of being at home with God can lead to a familiarity which wholly lacks reverence and awe. All too easily, it can breed the outlook of a pharisee. It can become a cosy religion, far removed from the fiery outpouring of the love of God. All these dangers are certainly there. But the road to the City of God is always full of dangers. The way is straight. There are deep falls on either side. To this there can be no gainsaying. In the Christian life there is a choice of dangers, and they are real dangers. The Christian has no choice but to choose.

This assurance of which I write is, to put it quite simply, a day-by-day, deliberate reliance on the promises of God. And these promises become personal in the person of Jesus, the Lord. In him we know the reliability of God. And at the very centre of this life-under-promise is the assurance of forgiveness, daily rediscovered in the experience of being forgiven. And home is above all a place of forgiveness. Marriage, parenthood, childhood, life together — the seal on all these is that mutuality whose bond is forgiveness, and whose characteristic fruit is patience. In the home is the place where we first learn what it means to 'take up the Cross'. 'Daily' or 'day-by-day' is a word most redolent of the home-base. While our Lord meant much more by his challenge, at least he meant this, that we are to take our own share of the forgiveness of which his Cross was the symbol. By that Cross we know that God has made us at home with himself and that he wills us to be at home for others.

No doubt all this is assured for us, if we will, in the great Sacraments of the Christian Faith. Equally beyond doubt, this is part of the common faith of all Christians. All I am suggesting here is that Evangelicals, by and large, find themselves experiencing this assurance most profoundly at the domestic level. Certainly for me, and I know I can speak for Mary in this also, the assurance of which I am writing has become most vividly a living exeprience in the life of our home, shared together with Rosemary and Pat, and later with the enlarged family which Rosemary and Pat have provided, and with a multitude of friends.

Evangelical religion is, of course, much more than this. It is the whole Christian Faith held in a particular balance. There is no question of claiming a monopoly. The Evangelical is no more Christian than others who, in understanding and practice have worked out a different balance, another proportion of Faith.

This insistence upon the diversity of balance in which the Faith is held is, so I judge, a matter of very great importance indeed. To ignore the equal validity of different understandings of the mystery of our religion, or the equal authenticity of the experiences which result from such different understandings, is a disastrous obstacle to true Christian unity. Failure frankly to thrash out the theological significance of our differences is one reason for the paralysis which today threatens the whole movement towards Christian unity. An equal threat to any discovery of true unity is to pretend that differences do not matter, whereas the spiritual challenge is positively to enjoy them.

The wholeness of the Christian experience in this life can be, for any of us, only partial. God has made us so different that he must desire that we should seek wholeness in different ways. In my prayers, among those whom I remember before God every day, is a Roman Catholic friend. My prayers for him are entirely concerned with gratitude for him, and an entering through intercession into his fulfilling of the immensely important and responsible ministry to which God has called him. It never occurs to me that he ought to change his allegiance and become an Evangelical Anglican. I know him and love him and enjoy him as a brother in Christ. And the same applies to many another of my friends who find some of my most cherished convictions spiritually unpalatable. I hope that in their prayers for me they are concerned only that I may be found faithful.

So, for me, Evangelical religion is first and foremost the religion of the hearth. That it must from there go out to explore the ends of the earth is only the obverse of Kabir's insight that if you 'stay where you are all things shall come to you in time'. The encounter with all things comes from always being at home wherever you are, which, in turn, has something to say about the Atonement and its precise and immediate relevance to life. But you are only likely to be at home wherever you are if you know the two fixed points of heaven and home. Like a snail I have always taken my home with me —and heaven.

I would not have my confession of faith, thus expressed in simple terms of experience, suggest that I am indifferent to theology, to the need to bring to the understanding of the Faith the powers of the mind. Twice, during my time as a Secretary of the C.M.S., I was asked to produce a theological interpretation of how it is I understand the meaning of the term 'Evangelical', within an Anglican setting. The first occasion was in 1944 when the then Bishop of Rochester (C. M. Chavasse) invited me to address the Diocesan Evangelical Fellowship. What I said there was published in the same year by the Church Book Room Press under the title, *What is an Evangelical?* The second occasion was in 1962, when I was invited to write for the S.P.C.K. series of 'Simeon Booklets' on what I believed to be the Evangelical contribution to a world of change. This pamphlet had for its title *The Sevenfold Secret*. Much of the material is common to both. But in the latter I quote at length from what is the finest description of the doctrine of Assurance that I know. It comes in a paper read by Gerald Scott at a conference in London in 1948. It appeared in a volume entitled *Evangelicals Affirm in the year of the Lambeth Conference*. Published by the Church Book Room Press in that year, this article appeared with the simple title 'Assurance'. It could with great advantage be reprinted, both as teaching Evangelicals something about their own heritage, and explaining to others what this doctrine is and why it is so important.

I have chosen to make this confession of faith here because I think it properly belongs at this point. It might have come in any one of a number of chapters, but nowhere more naturally. I would, however, be extremely sorry if the reader should picture 15, Eliot Vale, Blackheath, as over-heated by a self-conscious Evangelical piety. In point of fact, it was an uproariously happy place in which we all knew freedom and joy.

Our home in Mortimer Road, Cambridge, after we had left Holy Trinity Vicarage in 1942, was useful as a place where some members of the C.M.S. House staff could spend a few days away from air-raids on London. But it was obviously not a place from which I could go to work, once the war was over.

We had never had any contact with Blackheath before. But during the autumn of 1942 I was sent on a C.M.S. deputation weekend to St. Margaret's Church, Lee. The Vicar, Norman Bradyll-Johnson, took me for a walk on the Heath, and I told him of our need of a home in the London area when peace came. A few weeks later he rang up to say that a member of his congregation wanted to sell her house and he thought it might suit. Mary went down to see it. When she discovered that the owner was prepared to remain as a 'tenant-at-will' and give us vacant possession whenever we wanted it, we decided to purchase 15, Eliot Vale. We moved to Blackheath in the summer of 1945.

This was to be our home for eighteen years. Here, Mary, Rosemary and Pat, my Mother and I had a base in which to experience together growing up, growing old, and from which we all, in one fashion or another, learnt the art of going out. It was a valuable experience having three generations under one roof. This is not always a success. Grandparents can find grandchildren a little taxing. I know, being now a grandfather! And grandchildren can sometimes find grandparents a disappointment and very perplexing. This too I have observed.

Nevertheless, when the living together works out well, it provides a sense of continuity which can be an important element in spiritual, as well as social, stability. What is more, family portraits on the walls demonstrate that Granny herself was once a grandchild. So history is unconsciously absorbed.

This particular granny was astonishingly active. Even after she was over eighty she thought nothing of going up to C.M.S. House to address envelopes for three or four hours, at least once a week, and sometimes more. For her, Salisbury Square meant something very personal. Here, Father had worked from 1914–1920. Here, I was working. But this represented only a fraction of her energies. She was a beautiful needlewoman, and all through the year she worked at this skill to provide the bulk of the things for the annual sale for C.M.S. which we held in our home. This annual event which sometimes raised seventy pounds for the Society was a remarkable occasion in every respect. To it came an unlikely company of supporters of C.M.S., Roman Catholics and humanists, people of every kind, vying with a polychromatic crowd of Anglicans, to enjoy meeting each other and Granny, as well as spending money usefully.

Granny remained interested in everything until the last year of her life, when the sheer physical weariness of age made her increasingly listless. She died in 1958 three weeks after her ninetieth birthday. Our dear friend Evered Lunt, Bishop of Stepney, used the following prayer at the funeral:

> We worship God for the life and example of Mary Kathleen Warren, through ninety years. We offer our thanks to Him for her endurance, as a good soldier of Jesus Christ —for her indomitable spirit of self-discipline—for her exalted conception of public service and for her dauntless devotion to private duty —for the unquenchable fire of her missionary zeal and for the selfless offering of time and talents to Christ, His Church and His children —for a life which, in every part, proclaimed the blessedness of those who have not seen and yet have believed.

The last thing that Mary did, when saying 'good night' on 3rd July, was to sing to her a greatly loved hymn. Early in the morning of 4th July she saw him in whom she had believed 'face to face'.

The time of our coming to Blackheath was fortunate in more ways than one. Rosemary was eleven and Pat nine. We were able without difficulty to get them accepted at the Blackheath High School. During the war the school had been evacuated. Now the headmistress, Miss

Janet Macaulay, was having to make a fresh start and there were plenty of vacant places.

Apart from Miss Macaulay's own fine leadership and the inspired Scripture teaching of Miss Mary Child, it was an immense source of strength to us that there was never any kind of clash between what the children learnt at home and what they learnt at school. Both places shared the same values.

Rosemary was the more reserved of the two during school days, Pat the more gregarious. But I have a vivid memory of countless parties of schoolgirls taking place at 15, Eliot Vale. And in the process of growing up there came the memorable day when, in preparing for one such party, Pat, with a happy directness, said, 'We don't want you to arrange the party, Mum, just the eats.' Pat, even then, could shrewdly assess the 'main chance'. It is only a matter of time now before that age of gold comes round full circle.

As in everything else we were very fortunate in finding a church, St. John's, where we at once felt at home. Our first Vicar was the Rev. J. L. ('Tony') Waite, who had a magnificent record of heroic ministry, particularly during the 'Doodle-bug' phase of the air-war, when Blackheath was on one of the main routes into London and was often the terminal point. After he left to go to Leeds, as Vicar of St. George's, we were again most fortunate in having as his successor the Rev. Martin Parsons. A one-time missionary of the Church Mission to Jews in Warsaw, he had subsequently been the General Secretary of the Hibernian C.M.S. So we had much in common from the outset. It was, for Mary and myself, a very real joy that he was the one to prepare Rosemary and Pat for Confirmation, for we could trust his spiritual sanity. He was a magnificent expository preacher. His 'sheep' looked up and were always fed.

During these years I had been giving detailed study to St. Paul's letter to the Galatians. From this study came the material for four Pastoralia Lectures, which the Divinity Faculty of Durham University invited me to give. They were published in 1955 by the S.C.M. Press, with the title, *The Gospel of Victory—A Study in the relevance of the Epistle to the Galatians for the Christian Mission today*.

I have only referred to this study of my favourite Pauline epistle because of the dedication which ran:

In Gratitude to
MARTIN PARSONS
a Minister of the Word
who 'minds his business'.

Every Sunday, on our way to St. John's, we passed the Church of All Saints', so superbly situated on the Heath. The Vicar, during much of our time, was the Rev. H. C. Green, beloved by so many under the designation 'Parsie'. With Bee, his wife, Mary struck up a close friendship. In the years to come when we were at Westminster they came, year after year, to occupy our house when we were away on holiday. This was and is a very rich friendship indeed. Had Blackheath been a genuine village, with only one church and that All Saints', I have no doubt of how greatly we would have benefited from 'Parsie's' ministry. But St. John's proved to be our spiritual home.

The change-over from Cambridge to Blackheath was far more difficult for Mary than for me. In Cambridge she had had a leading place in the life of the congregation, and a wide circle of friends and acquaintances in town and University. When we arrived in Blackheath she knew no one and had to begin from scratch. I had my work at Salisbury Square.

Mary had a three-pronged attack on this problem. Being resourceful and without shyness she occupied as much time as possible in our small front garden. There, without difficulty, she broke the local reserve by talking over the garden fence to every passer-by. Eliot Vale was something of a 'pocket', with about twenty houses, and very soon she was on friendly terms with almost all their inmates. Being also a determined woman, she joined a 'Health and Beauty' class in order to get to know another group. The pursuit of health and beauty, as it was explained to me, consisted mostly of rolling about on the floor, amid gales of laughter, in order to work the fat off the hips: not that Mary ever needed that particular therapy. Then, as she explained, the members of the class invited each other home to cream teas to put it all back again! But the important thing for Mary was the enlarged circle of acquaintances. The third prong of the attack came from her talent for 'buying up opportunities in the market place'. The late forties were years of severe rationing and queuing was a necessary part of a housewife's existence. Queues can be long. But there was always the person in front and the person immediately behind. Conversations with these soon revealed the fact that Blackheath was full of young wives and young mothers, whose husbands were at work all day, and for whom time lay heavy on their hands—and, also, not a little loneliness. So Mary started a coffee party on Monday mornings. They came first in twos and threes, a little shy but greatly relieved to find that their babies were as welcome as themselves. These coffee parties were essentially informal opportunities for chat. But, in the way things have, one and another would inject some question of graver import such as 'How do you teach a child to pray?' and Mary was well away. Over the years a great many folk came to these coffee parties, and some went to the ends of the earth and we still hear from them. For a home which is an acknowledged 'treasury of God' does things to people. Some, we know, found a living faith from this encounter. In one case a marriage was saved from wreck.

A great part of my own enjoyment of Blackheath came from getting home on Monday evening to learn of how the 'party' had gone that morning. Dealing with the frontiers of the Kingdom in Asia and Africa was exciting enough. To know we lived on one in Blackheath had a tonic quality of its own. The frontier trails did not run out and stop, as in Kipling's poem *The Explorer*. With us they merged, and ran on.

Among the 'all things' that come if 'you stay where you are' was a great host of visitors. We married on the basis of running a hotel, and what enormous fun we have had, and what privilege!

There were those Christmasses when almost always we had some men and women from overseas. They always made a delightful contribution to the gaiety of the Christmas Eve carol party, to which our neighbours came, and some thirty or more would cram themselves into our sitting room. Children and all, we sang ourselves hoarse, and ended up with the Christmas Collect and a simple prayer. For some people there it 'made' their Christmas.

But all through the year friends were coming from overseas, from Canada and Australia, from New Zealand and the U.S.A., from West Africa and East Africa, from India and Iran, from Jordan and Japan. Not a few of these were later to occupy positions of high responsibility, as Ministers in newly independent countries, or as Bishops of the Church. It was to mean much in my own work in C.M.S. that, in corresponding with Church leaders overseas, we had 'eaten salt' together. We already knew each other in a relationship which was unofficial.

In particular, in the years 1947–1949, we made the most of our opportunity to welcome Chinese friends. Three times, Bishop Michael Chang of Fukien came to stay with us, and others included Bishop T. K. Shen, Dr. Francis Wei, Dr. M. K. Yue and his wife, and James Pong, later to be Bishop in Taiwan. It meant a great deal to us, when the 'Bamboo Curtain' came down, that China was not a faceless multitude, but some very faithful and devoted members of the Body of Christ. Guessing what he was almost certainly going back to face, I sent Bishop Michael Chang a copy of Dr. Selwyn's magnificent commentary on 1 Peter. I hope perhaps it was of some help to him in those grim brain-washing experiences which he had to endure.

Our Visitors' Book for these years, 1942–1963, is a 'roll of honour' to us, for it includes the names of so many who have had to prove their faithfulness, sometimes under actual persecution, but more often still in the carrying the heavy responsibilities of high position, or in the humdrum. Who is to define where the battle is fiercest, when we pray for the Church Militant here on earth? But there is hardly a corner of the earth where we do not know someone so embattled.

In a particular degree it was our good fortune to have a home to which we could invite missionaries on furlough, recruits during their training, and some who, doing practical work in a Blackheath parish, made our home their own base. During these years in Blackheath we had many hundreds of visits from these welcome guests who came to stay a night, many of them more than once.

Mary's activities were by no means limited to keeping 'open house'. She was frequently out exploring the Southwark diocese as one of the speakers on the Overseas panel of the Mothers' Union. And she was very much at the disposal of the C.M.S. Deputations Department. Less demanding as to travel was the Committee of the Clergy Orphan Corporation on which she served for more than thirty years. Having been at school at St. Margaret's, Bushey, this was an engagement she rarely missed, feeling an intense loyalty to what that school, and its great headmistress, Miss Boys, had given her.

For over twenty years she was also on the governing body of the two Haberdashers' Aske's schools in Hatcham. For five of these years she was chairman. They happened to be more than usually difficult years, preparatory as they were to the reconstitution of school governing bodies within the Inner London Education Authority. For her service to the schools the Haberdashers' Company made her a Freeman of the Company, which carried with it being a Freeman of the City of London. This was a great source of pride and delight to the family.

There came the time when growing up led on to the going out. Family holidays, for many years, were great fun and we explored many parts of the country. Then Rosemary found her way to Switzerland, and Pat to Sweden and Germany. With schooldays behind them, their paths separated. Rosemary had a yen to teach small children and went for her training to the Maria Grey Teacher Training College. She then taught in a variety of schools, specialising in the under-sevens, thereby acquiring no small skill for the bringing up of her own children, and an ability to offer sage advice to her sister, when similarly occupied.

Pat got a place at Girton where she read Geography, producing for the second part of the Tripos a thesis on 'Land Tenure in County Cork', which held promise of future authorship. She also proved to be the family athlete, getting her 'full blue' for lacrosse and her 'half blue' for cricket. The latter provided occasion for an unusual 'double'.

During the three years she played for Cambridge they always beat Oxford. On migration to Oxford to take her Diploma in Education, she found herself co-opted to play for Oxford, when, on the eve of the University match, one of the Oxford team fell ill. That year Oxford beat Cambridge! For teaching practice she went to St. Swithin's, Winchester, and then taught for three years at the Sherborne School for Girls, before, in 1963, offering to C.M.S. for missionary service.

Meanwhile our niece, Sheelagh, seven years older than her cousins, had tasted a variety of educational institutions, first in Kenya, then in Cambridge, and at St. Margaret's, Bushey, from which she went up to Girton. There she read English with distinction, and went on to take a Diploma in Education at Birmingham. After teaching experience she offered to C.M.S. and went back to Uganda, the land of her birth. Here, her very great teaching ability and all-round talent for drama proved itself at the Gayaza High School for Girls: and here, in 1972, one of the most critical years in Uganda's history, she became the acting-Principal, no sinecure of a post in a time of unsettlement and acute staff shortage. The courage, nicely laced with humour, with which she handled the situation won the admiration of everyone.

Sheelagh's mother, after Jack's death in 1929, went back to Uganda and served with great devotion at the C.M.S. hospital at 'Ngora in the Upper Nile diocese. Retiring in 1957, she worked in general practice for a number of years. She died on 10th September, 1963, since when Sheelagh has made her furlough home with us.

Two family events during these years stand out. The first, in point of time, was the celebration of our Silver Wedding in 1957. We had a joyful lunch party at the Royal Commonwealth Society, a reunion of many friends from different periods of our lives.

A meeting at the C.M.S. Summer School in 1959 was the prelude to a more important event. For it was there that a friendship began between Rosemary and Gregory Warner which brought us all to St. John's Church, Blackheath, for their wedding on 11th August, 1962. A happy family link was provided by Cecil Bewes, a first cousin of Mary's, who gave the address. Greg is Nottinghamshire born and bred, his father, who was to live to the age of eighty, was a parish priest whose whole ministry was spent in the Southwell diocese. What with one thing and another, we find it difficult in our family to avoid a clerical colouring, though Greg has brought in a refreshing contrast by way of his work in the Inner London Education Authority, first as a Youth Employment Officer, and more recently at County Hall with a special responsibility for handicapped children. In addition to all his other qualities, Greg more than compensates for my own ten-thumbness, to which I made early reference, by being an artist with his fingers. Whenever we have needed some domestic amenity for which the skills of a handyman were needed, Greg has been on call.

Life for Mary and myself, as these pages will have revealed, was reasonably full. We had our own methods of relaxation, but one key to our survival was a regular withdrawal to St. Julian's, a place and an experience to which a number of references have already been made. I have had to talk about St. Julian's in many places, not least in the United States. I became a member of the governing body in 1950 and from 1954 to 1974 I have been chairman, an office from which I have only just resigned. But when asked to explain what St. Julian's is I am always baffled. Those who would discover its secret must visit it themselves. But some clues will be found in that brilliantly sensitive book by J. H. Oldham, *Florence Allshorn and the Story of St. Julian's,** in which he not only gives the reader a glimpse into the life of one of this century's most remarkable women, but also shows how St. Julian's is the outcome of her vision.

For us, St. Julian's was an unfailing resort for the much-needed re-charging of our spiritual, mental and physical batteries. The beauty of the place, whether at Barns Green or afterwards, when the Community moved to Coolham, breathed an immediate benediction to a tired spirit. To walk through the front door was to know you were come to a Palace Beautiful. To enjoy the family who made it beautiful, was to enter into the further stimulus of Bunyan's other inspiration, the Inn of Gaius, where people were encouraged to think. Out of this world, in the best sense, 'yes'—in and of the world also, in the best sense, 'yes'—such is St. Julian's. Here was a place where you could let quietness and peace do its healing work. No one would ever intrude upon your stillness. But always available was the little 'Society', part of whose serious responsibility it was to keep mentally alert, widely read, in touch with the wider world, and so be ready to meet the troubled and the perplexed should they ask for guidance. No—it cannot be described. It is an experiment in Christian living to which I know of no precise parallel, though the daughter-house at Limuru in Kenya is exploring a similar pattern in the setting of a nation and a continent on the move. Something of the rigorous discipline which lies behind what St. Julian's has achieved and is achieving can be gleaned from *The Note-books of Florence Allshorn*, carefully reproduced for publication by Margaret Potts, who succeeded her as the Leader of this *Society*, this 'union for a common purpose'.

*First published by the S.C.M. Press in 1951, it has recently been published as a paperback by Hodder and Stoughton (1974).

I trace back to St. Julian's, in large measure, the fact that while heavily involved in administration and much travelling, it proved possible to write quite a number of books. St. Julian's with its peace, and with its splendid library, provided the opportunities for sitting back and thinking. But I had one particular stimulus. There had been formed in 1942 an Evangelical Fellowship for Theological Literature. This had a strictly limited theological purpose, that of producing articles and books which represented an Evangelical contribution to the contemporary debate. It was in no sense a 'pressure group'. It was not interested in Church politics. Anyone who was interested in this kind of writing and was willing to accept the name 'Evangelical', with or without a prefix, was welcome. In its early years it owed everything to Gordon Hewitt and Michael Hennell, its first two Secretaries, whose wisdom and efficiency gave the Fellowship its stability.

At the time of its formation, serious theological writing in Britain was largely confined to Free Church scholars such as C. H. Dodd, and Vincent Taylor; the distinguished members of the Westminster College Staff in Cambridge; and Scottish divines like John and Donald Baillie, to mention only a few; *or* to Anglo-Catholic scholars, as represented by men like Sir Edwyn Hoskyns, A. G. Hebert, and Kenneth Kirk, again to mention only a few. There was place for a school of thinking which could be a complement to these others. E.F.T.L. provided this.

Over a generation it did something to encourage serious scholarship. Without making undue claims as to its usefulness, it is interesting to note that, whereas in 1942, Evangelicals were making little contribution in this field, by 1972, when its work was done, it could number among its members the Regius Professors of Divinity at Oxford and Cambridge, the Regius Professor of Ecclesiastical History at Oxford, the Lady Margaret Professor at Cambridge, and the Lightfoot Professor and the Van Mildert Professor at Durham. In addition there was a considerable number of men actively engaged in serious writing, men like Dr. Henry Chadwick and Dr. F. W. Dillistone, to give but two examples. The membership, at its peak, was in the neighbourhood of two hundred.

I mention this bit of history because I was a founder member and played some part as a goad to better men and as an encourager of younger members who were apt to be overawed by the giants. The Fellowship held an annual conference which was an intellectual fiesta, greatly stimulating to those of us who, whether in parishes, in administration, or in teaching, needed the inspiration of first-class minds.

One by-product of the Fellowship was an annual register which recorded the names and addresses of members, their subject of research, and such publications as they had produced in the previous year. This register was, as I happen to know, consulted by Archbishop Fisher while he was looking for Evangelical scholars to serve on commissions or in negotiations with other Churches.

Another invaluable by-product was that, from the Fellowship, came the writers of *The Fulness of Christ*, noted in an earlier chapter: a volume of essays celebrating the bi-centenary of Charles Simeon's birth: and a series published by the Canterbury Press to which the present Archbishop of York (F. D. Coggan), D. E. W. Harrison, the present Bishop of Barking (F. W. P. Chadwick), F. W. Dillistone, F. J. Taylor, later Bishop of Sheffield, E. C. Dewick, and I contributed. From the Fellowship there also came members who had most fruitful conversations with members of the Community of the Resurrection at Mirfield. In this brief summary of a theological venture one figure deserves particular mention—the Rev. W. A. Kelk. At the time of the founding of E.F.T.L. he was the far-sighted editor of the *Record*. For many years a 'reader' for Longmans, he was an enthusiastic promoter of theological writing. And he was an invaluable and highly competent critic. It was through his good offices that Longmans published *The Triumph of God* in 1948, a book of essays on the Christian Mission by a number of writers. As Editor of this volume, I received, and still possess, one of his letters with his trenchant criticisms, particularly, of my own essays. To those of us who were privileged to know him he was a real 'father figure' in the first ten years of E.F.T.L.

This Fellowship was a continuing inspiration to myself, not only because of my own interest in scholarship, but because I was deeply convinced that the work of C.M.S. needed to be undergirded with a strong theological foundation. Only so would it make the kind of contribution so urgently required in the Churches overseas in which it served, at a time of such dynamic change. Through the E.F.T.L. I was able to play some part in recruiting a number of very able younger theologians to join the staffs of theological colleges overseas.

From what I have written in this chapter it will be clear that life in Blackheath was no 'suburban captivity'. But Blackheath was a suburb, a very delightful one which still retained some of the qualities of a village, the Heath being the village common, surrounded on three sides by houses, and on the fourth by one of the most beautiful of the royal parks. Here neighbours were neighbours, people one could know, people whose joys and sorrows we could share. Now we were to move in to the centre.

10/24/77

13

1963 - 1973

Westminster

... You are not here to verify,
Instruct yourself, or inform curiosity
Or carry report. You are here to kneel
Where prayer has been valid. And prayer is more
Than an order of words, the conscious occupation
Of the praying mind, or the sound of the voice praying.
And what the dead had no speech for, when living,
They can tell you, being dead: the communication
Of the dead is tongued with fire beyond the language
   of the living.
Here, the intersection of the timeless moment
Is England and nowhere. Never and always.

T. S. ELIOT

Little Gidding

ARLY in 1961 I had told Sir Kenneth Grubb and my colleagues, that I was clear that my time as General Secretary of the Society should end in two years' time. In January of 1963, as planned, I submitted my resignation to the Committee. We had no idea at all as to what might come next. What came, almost immediately, was an invitation to join the staff of an American Theological Seminary as Professor of Missions. I asked for a little time in which to make up our minds.

Events then developed with a rush. On 19th March I received a letter from the Prime Minister, the Rt. Hon. Harold Macmillan, to say that two Crown appointments were about to fall vacant, one of them a canonry at Westminster. He took the unusual course of inviting me to choose, but asking that, before I made up my mind, I should consult with the Archbishop of Canterbury and the Dean of Westminster, Dr. E. S. Abbott. Some further perplexity was added by my receiving, a few days later, an offer from a diocesan bishop of a position in his diocese carrying with it a residentiary canonry.

Having known both the Archbishop and the Dean from undergraduate days, I knew I could rely on sympathetic and wise advice in what was a difficult decision. After taking their counsel I decided to accept the canonry at Westminster. What determined me was the assurance by the Dean that a canonry at Westminster carried with it a large measure of freedom to be at the wider service of the Church as a whole. I saw this as meaning that I could still be of some service to the Church overseas, and so it proved.

The summer of 1963 was a strenuous one. I had to get ready for the Anglican Congress in Toronto in August, which meant preparing a number of addresses and writing interpretative articles. I also had responsibilities in connection with the meeting of the missionary executives of the Anglican Communion, followed by the Anglican Council on Missionary Strategy, both to be held in Canada immediately before the Congress.

It was a great joy to have John Taylor at the meetings at Huron College in Canada preliminary to the Toronto Congress. His appointment as General Secretary of C.M.S. was the one for which I had hoped. I was sure that the Society needed a new style of leadership. And John, with the sensitiveness of a rare imagination, provided it. The moment of euphoria in Africa and Asia, where so many countries had obtained political independence, was bound to pass. The tumults which follow upon the disillusioning discovery that true freedom is a spiritual, and not a political, reality, was to test the statesmanship of rulers everywhere. As a servant Society this was bound to be the new context for C.M.S. in both Church and State overseas. John had the gifts for this new phase. In addition he already had a profound know-ledge of Africa and a deep insight into what constitutes 'Africanness'.

The University of Glasgow took this summer as the occasion for conferring on me an Honorary D.D., the citation of which, explicitly referring as it did to matters missionary, was very gratifying.

In the middle of all this, on 15th July, I was duly installed at West-minster Abbey. The occasion was inscribed in my memory because on that day the psalm for Evensong was Psalm 78, and it was sung in full. Supported by the Precentor, the Receiver-General and the Abbey's Legal Secretary, I waited in the Jerusalem Chamber for what seemed hours. By curious coincidence the recitation of this Psalm was annexed to the Honorary Canonry of St. Petroc, in Truro Cathedral, which I had held since 1945.

In view of what was now to be so close an association with the Dean, Eric Abbott, it was another happy coincidence that, during that sum-mer, a book of essays appeared in which we had both collaborated with other members of Jesus College, under the editorship of P. Gardner-Smith, who had been Dean of the College when we were undergraduates. The book, *The Roads Converge*, aimed at being a contribution to the question of Christian reunion. Under Eric Abbott as Dean, Westminster Abbey has made no small contribution to ecumenicity, interpreting the *oikumene* in the broadest terms possible.

As token of our long acquaintance, I have in my possession some snaps which are evidence that we shared together in the undergraduate escapade during the General Strike in 1926. With his tin hat, elegantly askew, a special constable's armlet on his sleeve, and armed with a truncheon, Eric was obviously ready for anything. With the years, a profounder level of acquaintance led on to friendship, and I greatly looked forward to being with him at the Abbey.

As already recorded, my travels have taken me to many parts of the world. Very rarely have I been anywhere in the last ten years without being greeted with the question 'How's Eric?' The world over, as well as throughout this country, he is known and loved as a spiritual coun-sellor. The central position of the Abbey served him well in this ministry.

Severely handicapped as he has been following several strokes, the courage with which he has nevertheless nerved himself not only to be regularly in his place in the Abbey, but also to preside on innumerable important occasions, has been the admiration of us all. Many honours have come to him. The honour which means most to him has been life-long office as a true *servus servorum Dei*.

When I joined the Chapter the Sub-Dean was Dr. Adam Fox. His gentle courtesy and quizzical sense of humour, combined with very pronounced views on the privileges of canons and the general decay of manners, gave him something of the quality of a period-piece. He had one quite remarkable characteristic, an almost complete indifference to cold. I remember meeting him one bitter winter day, with the wind howling round the cloisters. We met near 'kill-canon-corner', aptly named. I was wrapped up in everything I could put on. He was not even wearing an overcoat or gloves. Asked if he never got chilblains, he paused, thought for a moment, and replied that he had never had chilblains since 1892! To be able to say that was almost as good as hearing it said. He resigned in the autumn of 1963, but continued to live at 4, Little Cloister.

Edward Carpenter, after Adam Fox's retirement, became our senior canon. Incredibly erudite, with an apt historical or literary quotation to inject at almost any point in a Chapter meeting, he was one of the most generous-hearted men I have ever met. He appeared to be constitutionally incapable of saying 'no' to any request, and was widely in demand. He could speak on any subject. And, if occasion called, he could rise to heights of great eloquence, as he did, when, at very short notice, he gave the address at a spontaneous Memorial Service following the assassination of President Kennedy. He was the member of the Chapter with a special pastoral responsibility for the entire Abbey Community. He fulfilled this duty superbly.*

Michael Stancliffe was Rector of St. Margaret's and Steward of the Abbey until, in 1969, he became Dean of Winchester. He was no stranger to us. When, from time to time, we felt a need for a certain kind of intellectual stimulus, we would come up from Blackheath to sit at his feet. He had a preaching style all his own, being a master of original illustrative material. This he would work out with considerable elaboration, ending up with an entirely unexpected, but very powerful 'punch' line. Often I found myself sitting on the edge of my seat in St. Margaret's or the Abbey, waiting for the denouement. It was always a spiritual challenge.

The vacancy caused by the resignation of Adam Fox was filled by Bishop Joost de Blank who, after a courageous tenure of office as Archbishop of Cape Town, had, on health grounds, to return to this country. He was the most colourful personality among us. Colourful is the right word in more sense than one. Joost in full episcopal evening dress was dazzling. A 'bon viveur' by temperament, hospitable to the core, he combined this with a deep-rooted piety, and at heart a

---

*Dr Abbott retired in February 1974. Edward Carpenter was appointed Dean in the following April.

very simple religion. I found myself very close to him. We all loved
Joost and it was a sore blow to us all when he died on 1st January, 1968.

Joost's successor was Ronald Jasper. Already well known for his
biographies of Bishop Headlam and Bishop Bell, he came to us with
an established reputation as a Liturgical Reformer. There was never
any risk of being dull in his company. Naturally conservative as I am
in matters liturgical, and more than content with '1662', I can yet be
very happy with Series II or III in a parish church. I am not myself
satisfied that an Order of Service calling for a great deal of audible and
intelligent participation by the congregation suits the physical structure of the Abbey. But that is a matter of private judgment. Ronald,
I know, would disagree. We saw more of him and his family than of
any others in the Abbey circle, and we greatly enjoyed all that we saw.

The last to join the Chapter while I was a member was David
Edwards, again no stranger. I had seen a lot of him when he was
Director of the S.C.M. Press and I was a member of the Board. He
very generously continued the honourable practice of the Press of
publishing my books, with little prospect of their ever making any
money, and a large probability of their making a loss, and he gave
unstinted support to the *Christian Presence* series, of which I was
Editor. How can one speak otherwise than well of such a man? As I
make it a practice to read right through any book I review I charitably
assume that David does the same. In view, however, of his productivity
with his pen in the pages of the *Church Times*, not to mention many
other writings, my charity covers a multitude of doubts! Meanwhile,
he remains one of the most provocative writers of this generation.
You can never be complacently certain that there will not be a very
uncomfortable and therapeutic sting in the tail of anything he writes.

If I had one regret on leaving the Abbey it was that, as a body of
canons, we never combined to produce something in the way of corporate thinking. During the last few years it so happened that all four
of us had this in common, that we knew something of the discipline
involved in writing history. We could, I believe, have produced
something of value for our fellow-Christians, and even reached
some who would not wish to be so considered. But it did happen.

Work of considerable value was, indeed, produced by individuals
during these years. Edward Carpenter's *Cantuar* is a magnificent
achievement, which may yet be surpassed by his forthcoming life of
Geoffrey Fisher. Ronald Jasper brought his own historical expertise
to the long-drawn-out labours of the Liturgical Commission. David
Edwards produced his eminently readable *Leaders of the Church of
England*. Beside this record my achievement was minuscule. But in
one respect I had my hour. Professor A. J. Arberry was invited by the

Cambridge University Press to produce a large two-volume book, *Religion in the Middle East.* He had three Sub-Editors —Dr. E. I. J. Rosenthal of Pembroke College, Cambridge, who was responsible for *Judaism*; Professor C. F. Beckingham of London University who had the huge task of assembling writers on *Islam*; and myself with the assignment of *Christianity.* I had to persuade a Roman Catholic, an Orthodox, a Syrian Orthodox, an Armenian, a Lutheran, a Calvinist, and several Anglicans to produce something which was recognisably Christian. To all but the Anglicans I was a complete stranger. As Christians, they all responded nobly. But they were also authors and, as such, had no idea whatever how to restrict the flow of ink off their pens. In some cases I had to insist on 'cuts' running into thousands of words, in one case to more than ten thousand. That to a measurable degree I succeeded, and retained the friendship of all concerned, was in a modest way a diplomatic triumph. After all it was the Middle East.

I only wish I had had the chance of playing editor to Edward Carpenter, Ronald Jasper and David Edwards. That would have been an heroic enterprise, but might have been my Waterloo.

Of the musical life of the Abbey, a large and important part of its life, I am incompetent to speak. I only enjoy music with a swing to it, and swing is a characteristic absent from most of the work of the great masters of English Church music, whose memory it is the pride of the Abbey to keep fresh. I must accept banishment to the outer dark where barbarians are.

I can, however, pay tribute to those who maintained the complex organisation which lay behind the musical life of the Abbey—to Douglas Guest the Organist and Master of the Choristers, to the assistant organists, the Lay Vicars and the Choristers, and to Francis and Betty Tullo who presided over the carefully planned life of the Choir School. These combined to provide the musical context within which the services were conducted and sung by clergymen chosen for their musical ability.

During my time the Abbey was served by four men of great distinction in this field. Our immediate neighbour when we first arrived was Gordon Dunstan, who later went on to be Professor of Moral and Social Theology at King's College, London. Apart from his theological and musical ability, he proved a good neighbour, more particularly in the skill with which he could coax our temperamental Aga cooker into some kind of co-operation.

Our Precentor was Rennie Simpson. His zest for living, wonderfully demonstrated in his triumphant survival of a desperate illness in 1967, was a tonic to us all. Our paths frequently met at the entrance to Little

Cloister. Did any of his medieval or modern predecessors ever combine seriousness and gaiety so successfully? Only one thing ever dimmed Rennie's sense of the providential ordering of life, and that was his responsibility for proof-reading the endless stream of service papers. It is difficult to believe that a 'time and motion' expert would justify the use of so much energy. There are many kinds of martyrdom. Rennie had his. I salute him with gratitude.

Our Sacrist was Chris Hildyard. The veteran of the community, he had come to the Abbey when the world was young. In addition to his part in singing the services he was responsible for the complicated arrangements for great occasions, the ordering of which was a peculiar distinction of the Abbey. Chris, to my private delight, shared one or two of my musical prejudices, though not, I hasten to add, my musical ignorance. Among his other gifts was a considerable artistic talent. One of our treasured possessions is a beautifully drawn sketch of the head of the 'boy' Jesus, which Chris gave us on our first Christmas at the Abbey. His little 'monastery garden' was one of the loveliest corners of Westminster.

After Gordon Dunstan had moved to King's College, his place was taken by William Leah, a Cornishman. We differed in our ecclesiastical preferences, but he was indulgent because of my long association with the Cornish Saint Petroc. Memory recalls with especial gratitude the sensitive imagination with which he chose the special prayers at Matins, when this Service was said in St. Faith's Chapel. William, too, had an unsuspected athletic potential. A stimulating sight was to see him being raced round Westminster by his two dogs, a spaniel and a whippet, both built for speed. There are more ways than one of contributing to the happiness of a 'cloistered' community.

The Abbey was well served by its laity who, of course, were the overwhelming majority of those who composed the Dean's *familia*, as surely all of us should properly be known. Mary and I had most happy relationships with them all. In a genuine sense the Abbey was the parish church of a small 'village' community. Perhaps only so could it, with integrity, be the church of a nation, and a focus of interest to visitors from all over the world.

I do not think it would be an exaggeration to say that this 'integrity' of the Abbey owed as much to Reg Pullen, our Receiver-General, as to anyone. As Clerk to the Chapter he was the silent listener to many an odd discussion, yet always the meticulous, though carefully tactful, recorder of the resulting minutes. Above all, he was the administrator of the Abbey's affairs which are multifarious beyond description. Viscount Samuel discovered this when he tried to describe them in a volume dealing with the administration of a number of great national institutions. An administrator could very easily become so burdened by detail as to cease to be humane. Reg had the pastoral sense and ability of a devoted parish priest, with the added expertise of a business executive, together with wide experience in public service in Westminster. In addition he could fairly be described as our 'continuity man'.

There came an unforgettable day when lightning struck one of the towers of the Abbey, and a huge block of masonry crashed on to the roof of the Jerusalem Chamber when the Chapter was in session. The Dean, being the lightest in weight, levitated about three inches, the rest of us about an inch and a half. One alone remained anchored to his chair—Reg. This immobility holds a parable. Had the masonry come through the roof it would have landed on the table at a point which would have obliterated the Dean and canons. I have little doubt that, after shaking himself, Reg would have quietly and punctiliously reported the event to No. 10 Downing Street. Then the affairs of the Abbey would have continued to be carried on with competence pending the appointment of a fresh supply of transient clergy. That is what I mean by describing Reg as our continuity man.

The lay element had other notable 'pillars'. Our High Steward was Lord Clitheroe, and the High Bailiff was Lord Redcliffe-Maud. Also closely linked with the Abbey, by interest as well as by history, were the two headmasters of Westminster School—John Carleton and John Rae, who, with their wives, were good friends of ours. With them were successive Masters of the Queen's Scholars. But all of these were personal friendships. In other respects my contact with the School was slight, though Mary had many friends among the masters' wives.

The ladies of the Abbey were so numerous, so talented, and so gracious, that only a Paris with a death-wish would risk offering an apple to one rather than another, let alone expressing a preference for any one of them other than 'as in private duty bound'. May this brief tribute to the better half of our 'collective' be accepted.

The Abbey is a magnet. Anyone who doubts it has only to go in between 10.0 a.m. and 4.0 p.m. any weekday, at almost any time in the year. There he will discover what G. K. Chesterton meant in his poem *Gold Leaves*:

> Where shift in strange democracy
> The million masks of God.

Eric Abbott, among his many inspirations, instituted a minute of prayer to be said from the pulpit on weekdays at each hour between

10.0 a.m. and Evensong. This minute of prayer brought the noise and bustle of the crowds to a halt. Rarely during this minute was the hush broken. Many a visitor found it an unexpected reminder that the Abbey is a place 'Where prayer has been valid', and where it still is. I believe that that minute of silence is of immense importance as witnessing to the presence of God and his grace. Also it exercises some kind of restraint on the almost terrifying pressure of the crowds.

Here I would pay tribute to the men who bear the real heat and burden of the day in dealing with the crowds—the Abbey Vergers. Their steadiness under the most trying circumstances; their patience with endless enquiries; their consideration for the multitude of foreigners mostly innocent of English; and their taking of the rough end of the tongue from many disgracefully behaved tourists; in all these ways they are, and I say it with conviction, illustrations of the fact that 'prayer is more than an order of words, the conscious occupation of the praying mind.' In their work is their prayer.

Yet, one must still ask what is the role of the Abbey in a world like this? Is it more than a great tourist attraction, a splendid museum of history? Can it be more than a place in which some of its visitors, looking up into its 'distances', have a momentary awareness of some transcendent meaning to life, to which it bears witness? These are serious questions. Paradoxically, one answer can be discovered in the notices frequently posted at the doors, 'Closed to visitors'. This curt refusal of entry does not signify some esoteric rite in progress. It means that from being a tourist attraction, proper as that is, the Abbey is either being prepared or is in use for some great act of worship. For essentially, the Abbey is not designed 'to inform curiosity', or provide material for a snappy 'report'. 'Closed to visitors' means that some very representative company of men and women—it may be nurses, or students, judges and barristers, Scouts and Guides, some professional organisations celebrating a centenary, any one of fifty groups—is meeting quite deliberately in the nation's principal shrine for an act of worship. That this corporate act shall be worthily rendered is the peculiar responsibility of the Dean. For each such service the Dean composes a special preface which gives the keynote to the common action. Here, the Abbey, in a peculiar sense, comes into its own as reaching out to the wider world of mankind's manifold activity. Somewhere here, as well as its providing a superb setting for sacred music, can be seen a continuing role for the Abbey to which no limit can easily be applied.

No one who serves Westminster Abbey, particularly on royal occasions, can easily forget that 'here, the intersection of the timeless moment' really 'is England'. In another sense it is 'nowhere' because everywhere, especially when there is some great ecumenical service with Roman Catholic prelates, Orthodox patriarchs, leaders from every Christian communion, joining in the sound of voices praying.

For ten years we were part of all this, but it remains very difficult to define what it meant in my own experience. There were moments of great exaltation. There were also moments of near despair. But it is the more ordinary emotions upon which I am happiest to dwell. During the last five months of my time at the Abbey I made the practice of recording each day in my diary as an object of gratitude, some person or thing associated with the Abbey. When I came to count these up I found there were one hundred and forty-one people or things for which I had thanked God. There were so many individuals whose friendliness, devotion to duty, and loyalty, were an inspiration. There were the varied, uncountable, beauties of the building and its surroundings. There was the 'timelessness' of the regular activity of corporate worship. This might not always, or often, give wings to faith, but by its regularity, it gave order to one's living. Without this discipline and order there is no ultimate freedom for faith to work itself out by love. And, of course, for anyone with a sense of history the Abbey was timeless. Here 'what the dead had no speech for, when living, they can tell you, being dead.'

I have a vivid memory of one winter day early in 1973 when I was walking down Whitehall from Trafalgar Square. At a certain point the Abbey comes fully into view. It was late afternoon, that day, and a mist was rising. There stood that great grey mass of stone, dwarfing everything within sight, even the Houses of Parliament, seen from that angle. The Abbey seemed to speak of the indestructibility of spiritual values. If it is dangerous to confuse the material with the spiritual, it is fatal to divorce them. The Abbey stands as an historic experiment in holding the balance. That was what that vision said to me that afternoon. That, in some deep sense, is what the Abbey meant to me during those privileged years under its shadow.

The Dean's assurance that canons of Westminster were reckoned to be at the wider disposal of the Church soon proved correct for me in my turn. First, if I remember right, came an invitation from Michael Ramsey to be a member of a small group to consider a 'Revision of the Anglican Calendar of Saints'. We submitted a drastic rearrangement of the Calendar, aiming to present it in global terms, emphasising, not so much individuals, as the saints, martyrs, and confessors of the Church in different parts of the world. In an age of personality cults this was an attempt at a healthy corrective.

I was also asked to chair a small commission of three on the future of St. Augustine's College at Canterbury. Our final report had to state a number of unpalatable facts. I doubt if it was approved by anybody. In the end, financial stringency resolved all the arguments.

A more perplexing assignment was to be one of a group of six under the chairmanship of Bishop Launcelot Fleming to advise the two Archbishops on Church finance. My sole qualification for this assignment was presumably my interest in trying to ensure that, in considering the needs of the Church of England, we did not ignore the needs of the Church overseas. Our annual report to the Archbishops always contained a pious paragraph on this subject, for the inclusion of which I can, I suppose, claim part responsibility. I gained much from these meetings, among other things, an awareness of the immensely complicated nature of the financial infra-structure of the Church of England.

In 1966 I received a frightening invitation to be chairman of yet another commission on the relations of Church and State. Deeply interested in the subject, I rashly accepted, and settled down to read the reports of the previous nine commissions. Further reflection convinced me that if I was to discharge the role of chairman, as I understood it, I would have to travel widely over the country in order to get at 'grass-roots' opinion. A commission sitting in London and calling for evidence is no substitute for meeting people in local situations and discovering where the shoe pinches, if it pinches at all. I soon realised that the physical demands of what I believed to be necessary were more than I could sustain, and I had to beg leave to resign. As it turned out it was a right decision for, within a few weeks, I was incapacitated by a serious thrombosis.

On other grounds, I reckon, I was wrong to accept in the first place. On this whole subject I am frankly an empiricist. I am quite unconvinced by the theological arguments against an Establishment of the Church, *in the particular circumstances of England*. I would not argue against some modifications in practice. But I believe that the State connection is important. Break that connection, and an invaluable opportunity for witness to spiritual values in the nation's life would be lost. I do not believe that such a break would be in the interests of true religion.

Over the years I have had ample opportunity, for instance, to discover how Bishops are chosen in other parts of the Anglican Communion. I am not at all impressed. It appears to me to be quite unproven that any of the other methods are more likely to be honouring to the Holy Spirit than are the procedures now operative in the Church of England. This is a pragmatic attitude. But I also have a theology on the subject. This I tried to set out in three lectures which I gave in the Abbey in 1963. These were published by the Epworth Press with the title— _The Functions of a National Church_. From what I read of the report of the commission, when finally published, I am sure that my views would almost certainly have caused at least one of the commission to have a thrombosis, which in that case might have been fatal!

yes!

On the whole I think I served the wider Church better by some other activities than in the grave matters which I have listed.

In 1964 Mary and I received an invitation from Archbishop Patterson and the other Bishops of the Province of West Africa to visit them. This was a most happy renewal of many friendships made in 1957. Perhaps we justified the expense they sustained when, several years later, the then Bishop of Guildford (Dr. G. Reindorp) consulted me with regard to which part of the world the diocese of Guildford might best be linked. I suggested West Africa.

In the same year I was invited to attend and address the Triennial Convention of the Episcopal Church of the U.S.A., meeting in St. Louis. Early in the following year, I was in Winnipeg to give five weekday lunch hour addresses during Lent on the general subject, 'Springs in the desert'.

Later in 1965 the Archbishop of Cape Town and the Bishops of Grahamstown and Pretoria invited me to give a series of lectures to their clergy. Mary was able to accompany me. I took as my subject 'Interpreting the Cross',* and that for two reasons. I was to address men who were, in various ways, experiencing the crucified life, doing so in circumstances I could only dimly understand. To talk to such men was a properly humbling experience, and one cannot have too many of these, especially when one is comfortably situated in Westminster. More important as a reason was that it is possible to view the Cross of our Lord Jesus Christ as an objective reality, which can be interpreted as such, leaving to the hearers to judge the relevance of this objective view to their own subjective experience.

In 1969 an invitation to lecture in the Free University of Amsterdam and in the University of Utrecht took us to Holland to stay with our friends Professor and Mrs. Van den Berg and their family. This visit coincided with the wonderful Rembrandt Exhibition in the Rijksmuseum in Amsterdam, and with the Erasmus Exposition in Rotterdam, two unforgettable experiences.

The year 1970 saw two journeys. In August I went to Uganda at the invitation of Archbishop Sabiti to attend a conference of Church leaders. They were having to face some urgent problems of Provincial

*The addresses were later published by the S.C.M. Press with the same title.

organisation about which differences of opinion were running very deep indeed. My part was to take the daily Bible-readings. While in no way personally involved in the problems, long acquaintance with Uganda, knowledge of many of the personalities, and some good briefing, ensured that I was aware of what was agitating the minds of those listening to the Bible-readings. That they listened so quietly and so appreciatively suggests that I was enabled to point to a place from which some new perspectives might be seen.

The visit to Israel two months later was to attend a 'Colloquium' on 'Religion, Peoplehood, Nation and Land' sponsored by the Harry Truman Research Institute of the Hebrew University of Jerusalem and several other bodies. Here were gathered very distinguished scholars of international reputation. The presence of this ugly duckling among all these splendid swans was really due to a near confidence-trick perpetrated by my good friend, Peter Schneider. Asked to advise on some possible theologians to be invited from England, he provided a list of ten, among whom he improperly included me. The other nine all excused themselves. So I found myself, at somewhat short notice, asked to read a paper on 'The Concept and Historic Experience with Land in major Western Religious Traditions'. I had thirty minutes in which to convey a summary of Roman Catholic, Lutheran, Calvinist and Anglican thinking on the subject. As might be expected it was at this point that the Colloquium touched rock-bottom. Otherwise it was a most exciting and stimulating experience in which to share.

As memorable as anything in this visit was a trip to Masada. I had hoped to climb to the top. But half way up the historic Roman ramp I realised that my heart could not manage it. Fortunately a small cave offered shelter from the midday sun. There I sat and meditated on the prophet Elijah, for the landscape I looked out upon must have been very similar to what he saw after his escape from the vengeance of Jezebel.

Before going to Israel I had suggested to our Chapter that it might be a useful ecumenical link if the Archbishop in Jerusalem, George Appleton, could persuade the Greek Orthodox Patriarch to present the Abbey with a hanging lamp. The Patriarch, His Beatitude Benedictos, was graciously amenable, and I had the privilege of receiving a beautiful lamp at his hands. It hangs outside St. Faith's Chapel in the Abbey, its light beckoning to a place set apart for private prayer.

There were many other outside activities besides travel. In the summer of 1969 there appeared the monumental Report on British Race Relations, with the title *Colour and Citizenship*, edited by E. J. B.

Rose. Reading it, I was dismayed to note the strictures on the general failure of the Church of England to take any significant steps towards promoting a Christian conscience on the subject. So urgent did I feel the issue to be, that I sent a memorandum to the Archbishops of Canterbury and York. In this I urged the need for a long-term programme of education which would bring things home at the parochial level. In addition I suggested that the man to initiate the programme was available in the person of the Right Rev. C. J. Patterson, recently retired from being Archbishop of the Province of West Africa. I knew that he possessed the indispensable endowments of gentleness and tact, which would be needed. A barnstorming agitator would have been a disaster. The parochial clergy of the Church of England are allergic to barnstorming. They do, sometimes, respond to sweet reasonableness. In the sequel, after much negotiation, and thanks to the financial support of C.M.S., Bishop Patterson was appointed the Representative for the Archbishops of Canterbury and York for Community Relations.

Over the next three years valuable work was done by Bishop Patterson, as I can testify, for I was on the small advisory group which met regularly with him to discuss his programme. But the steadily deteriorating race situation in this country provides a grim commentary on the years of indifference. It is much to be hoped that the increasing vigour with which the British Council of Churches is tackling the subject will be successful in rallying all the Churches to see the race issue as a spiritual challenge for the soul of our nation.

Another preoccupation was the civil war which had, for seventeen years, been desolating the Southern Sudan. The Anglican Bishop there, Oliver Allison, and I had been friends ever since he succeeded me as curate at St. John's, Boscombe. This close friendship meant that I had been in intimate touch with the Sudan situation during these years. When in 1971 the C.B.M.S. and the B.C.C. decided to set up a joint-group on the Sudan I was happy to accept the chairmanship. The Rev. R. Elliott Kendall of the C.B.M.S. was the convenor. This group was able to take a number of small initiatives which, when negotiations for peace came to a successful outcome in 1972, proved to have laid some part of the foundation for a big relief programme.

No. 3, Little Cloister, from the very centrality of Westminster, provided an ideal meeting place for a variety of groups, with many ramifications. It was the obvious venue for the regular London meeting of the governing body of St. Julian's, as for the Council of Ridley Hall. Here, three or four times a year, the Research Group of the College of Preachers would meet from mid-morning until after tea. The object of the group was to wrestle with the content of preaching in the intellectual and social context of the day. The 'College', founded in 1960 to promote more effective preaching, had, under the inspired leadership of Prebendary Douglas Cleverley Ford, drawn more than fifteen hundred clergy to its courses on preaching, as well as two hundred and fifty Readers and Local Preachers. The Research Group was designed to give depth to the programme. Its members were drawn from other Churches, besides our own, and included a Roman Catholic, a Methodist and a Baptist. We drew, from a wider circle still, the paper-readers, who introduced each session of the group.

Our house, for several years, was also the meeting place of a group convened by David Paton to discuss how best to use the balance of money left over after the winding-up of the World Dominion Trust. David, a former missionary in China, and a long-time friend, was the author of *Christian Missions and the Judgment of God*, which, published in 1953, was the first serious attempt to discuss the significance for Christian Missions of their debacle in China. I greatly valued this chance of seeing something of him while the group continued its independent existence.

One more group, which we called the 'Cloister Group', consisted of a number of those who, being deeply committed to the missionary enterprise, saw the need for serious theological thinking about methods and message. This group, for all its useful discussions, never realised its potential, for the members were so often away from this country on official duties. I remain convinced, nevertheless, that without some such small intimate group of the kind which J. H. Oldham so success-fully pioneered in earlier days to do serious corporate thinking, the Missionary Movement from this country could all too easily become little more than a conveyor belt for material aid for the Church overseas.

There is much need for serious theological thinking about Mission, and much is being done, though all too little of it in little groups where mind can sharpen mind. Individual thinking is no substitute for the thinking of a group. I have been lucky in one respect in having as a son-in-law a missionary in North India, who engages with me in a continuous correspondence on the subject of the Christian in his relation with men of other Faiths, both of us being deeply in debt to the imaginative pioneering in this field of Bishop Kenneth Cragg.

Ever since, at an E.F.T.L. Conference in 1959, I had read a paper on the Renaissance of the great world religions, I had been increasingly preoccupied with this as a subject calling for Biblical and theological study. To be able to engage in mutual dialogue with Roger has been a tremendous stimulus. His intimate contacts at first-hand with Hindus, Muslims, Jains and others in Varanasi, and his work as a student in the Sanskrit University, have enabled him to challenge and correct my own thinking. I hope my own purely academic studies have been of some service to him.

The Abbey has made its own distinctive contribution to thought on this subject ever since, towards the end of the celebrations of the nine hundredth anniversary year, 1965, a first experiment was made in an inter-Faith activity. This took the form, repeated with variations in subsequent years, of bringing into the Abbey representatives of other Faiths, so that we might share together our common insights as to the spiritual nature of man. In so far as all concerned are equally sincere, one cannot deny to such a sharing something of the character of worship. But the moment you speak of worship in such a context you provoke the anguished concern of some Christians lest in some way there is a subtle denial of the uniqueness of Jesus Christ as the world's Saviour.

Deeply and unreservedly committed as I am to belief in this uniqueness, while ever concerned to know how best to define it, I have a lively sympathy with the reaction of those who have protested against anything like 'Inter-Faith Services' in Christian Churches. Yet, the Abbey is 'England and nowhere'. England today is a religiously plural society: it is not, in any meaning of the word, homogeneously Christian. What does this new situation say to us? There are issues here of profound theological and sociological importance which must be wrestled with. I believe that under the wise and restraining leadership of Eric Abbott as Dean, the Abbey has been making a serious contribution to creating the atmosphere in which the theological and sociological debate can take place.

Three activities during these years proved a real relaxation from the routines and responsibilities of the Abbey. One was being invited in 1964 and 1965 by the Divinity Faculty of Cambridge University to give a series of lectures related to Part III of the Theological Tripos. In addition, in subsequent years, I led a seminar which dealt with 'Missions and Governments' and 'The Relation of Christians with men of other Faiths'. All this, in addition to the setting of the papers and examining on them, was an intellectual tonic, for it compelled me to serious reading and careful preparation.

In the second place, and indirectly related to the above activity, was my own research which took the form of listing, annotating and indexing a large part of the correspondence of Henry Venn, the missionary statesman of the nineteenth century. There is here indispensable source material for the study, not only of Missions, but of British imperial policy in the three middle decades of the nineteenth century. In connection with research I had the stimulating experience of being consulted by a number of research students from different parts of the world, who were specialising in the history of Missions. One of them, a pastor from Finland, spent the month of August in 1971 wading through my papers. Wondering, as I often did, if I was doing anything useful at all at the Abbey, it was no small joy to have eager young men and women coming along to discuss their theses, and to be able to encourage them.

A third source of relaxation, though of a very different kind, was my membership of the Council of the Minority Rights Group. Our chairman was Jo Grimond, M.P., and Professor Roland Oliver was vice-chairman. Among others on the Council we had some leading personalities from the field of journalism. Laurence Gandar of the *Rand Dail Mail* was our first Director, to be succeeded by Ben Whitaker. M.R.G. conducts a vigorous educational campaign on behalf of ethnic and religious minorities. Its activities have covered countries as varied as Ulster and Japan, the Soviet Union and Brasil, Rhodesia and the Sudan, and many others. The practice of M.R.G. is to produce reports by persons intimately acquainted with the areas and the minorities concerned. These reports are carefully checked by independent authorities. So far, the findings of these reports have not been challenged by any government. Eschewing the role of a political pressure group, M.R.G. aims to serve minorities by keeping its concerns before a responsible section of the reading public. While the Council itself is London-based, its sponsors are international. In common with many other voluntary enterprises, it operates on a shoe-string budget, works by faith, lives in hope, and is a registered charity!

I have always found its bi-monthly meetings a great refreshment, taking me, as they have done, into the world of journalism and providing a glimpse into those places where the shapers of opinion foregather. One sees ecclesiastical affairs in better perspective when one can move from time to time in a circle where such affairs rarely surface in any serious conversation.

No. 3, Little Cloister, which was our home, was a modern house built to replace one destroyed in the blitz in May 1941. The house was ideal for hospitality. But its unique position was that it alone of the Abbey houses not only looked across to Henry VII Chapel, but also to the Houses of Parliament. And we derived some special satisfaction from being the only private house which the Queen passes between leaving Buckingham Palace and arriving at the House of Lords for the State Opening of Parliament. This was always an opportunity for getting a party of friends to join us. On a number of occasions we received an unmistakable wave of the hand from the Queen. An American friend staying with us on the last occasion was so exhilarated by this unusual opportunity of paying tribute to a descendant of George III that he took over eighty photographs.

Part of the delight of living where we did lay in the pleasure it gave to so many, particularly visitors from abroad, to stay in such historic surroundings. Our front garden consisted of the grass-covered nave of the medieval chapel of Saint Catherine, in which the long-disputed precedence of Canterbury over York was determined in an historic and disreputable episode. In the same chapel, Henry III, having nearly bankrupted England with the cost of rebuilding the Abbey, had to pledge his re-acceptance of Magna Carta before an enraged baronage. Part of the medieval wall of the Abbey was outside our front door, and over the wall was Edward III's Jewel Tower. We lived in history.

But we also lived in the contemporary world. When the door-bell rang, we never knew who of our contemporaries we would find on the other side, or from what remote corner of the earth they had come. Notable among such visitors were the Bishops attending the Lambeth Conference in 1968, one hundred and three of whom came to lunch on one day or another, some even coming to lie down and recover from the contest of eloquence. To entertain so many of them in that year was one of the happy possibilities of living at No. 3. Here also we were able to have parties for the Abbey community; and also small parties of friends who might later go on into the Abbey with Mary for some concert, while I was more congenially occupied in washing up.

Two friends, out of the multitude who gave us the joy of entertaining them, I must mention, however invidiously, because of a particular significance. One was Dame Diana Reader Harris. She was chairman of the C.M.S. Executive Committee at the time of my resignation, and later succeeded Sir Kenneth Grubb as President of the Society. She was able to visit us quite often, and sometimes to stay the night, when in London for an Executive Committee. In addition to herself as a friend, she signified for me, what I had always so highly valued, the pre-eminent role played in the life of the Society by its women members. Her appointment as President was a striking witness to the Society's view of the role of women in the Church.

The other friend who visited us frequently in Westminster was F. W. Dillistone, 'Dilly' to all his friends. Our friendship began at Toronto in 1943. Among much else that he gave me was an insight into the world of symbols, and the importance of symbols if there is to be any successful interpretation of the Gospel to minds trained in modern technology. I was to spend much of my life in very prosaic activities. To have a friend whose approach to knowledge was that of a poet was another of the good gifts of God.

But despite all the activities with which No. 3 was associated, it was primarily a family home. Here in 1972 Mary and I celebrated our Ruby Wedding with representatives from all the main chapters of our life together. It was from here that Timothy and Colin were taken in to Henry VII Chapel for their Christening. It was here that we were informed one day that a young historian called Roger Hooker, as yet unknown to us, was coming on a visit. It was from this house that on 24th October, 1964, I escorted Pat into the Abbey to be married to the said Roger. Here was the home to which Rosemary and Greg and Timothy and Colin came up for lunch and tea on many a weekend and for many a Christmas. It was good to have them so accessible, and to enter into their deep commitment to the work of the National Society for Mentally Handicapped Children, their Timothy being a mongol. With this experience as part of their own lives, they are able to help many others – a frontier of Mission as important as North India.

And it was here, immediately on return from an exciting evening with a group of overseas students at C.M.S. House, on 16th February, 1967, that I came back to collapse with a thrombosis, to be watched over for more than three hours that night by our most generous friend and doctor, Basil Wilson-Kay, who certainly pulled me through that valley of the shadow of death. Here Mary's sister Evy, a trained nurse, came to look after me for a month. This gave the chance for growing into a deeper friendship than ever with a very beloved person whom distance, through her work in Edinburgh, had necessarily made, at best, an occasional visitor to our home. As in so much else, the 'rule' of this illness proved, what Sir Thomas Browne so wisely saw, 'under the *Providence* effects of chance . . . the mere hand of God'.

In the sequel to this thrombosis I was several times an in-patient as well as a regular out-patient at St. Thomas's Hospital, first under the care of Professor Semple, and later of Professor Cranston, and in one particular under our old friend, from his undergraduate days, Professor Ilsley Ingram. By all of these I was kept in working order, at least up to a point. An undeserved bonus was the friendship which we have ever since enjoyed with Christine Metcalfe, the then Sister of the Medical Out-patients' Department.

Thanks to the skill of all concerned it proved possible for Mary and me to fly out to India at the end of that year to stay with Pat and

Roger in Agra, and make our first acquaintance with Richard, their firstborn.

No one can experience a serious illness of the kind which had come so unexpectedly without becoming in a new way conscious of the precariousness of life. Seeing that we were living in a 'tied' house I was clear that, for Mary's sake, we must try to find a place which could be a home for our retirement, and in the event of my death, provide a roof over her head.

We began looking about. Then in 1969 a friend and former colleague in C.M.S., Wilfred Brown, at the time a Vicar in Putney, died. His widow told us that she had to sell her house in East Dean, near Eastbourne. We asked for 'first refusal', which she gladly gave us. The house proved to be just what we needed and so we acquired this priceless possession. From the first it became a place of 'retreat' when some escape from London was indicated. It provided an ideal family base for Pat and Roger and Richard and Mary when on furlough from India in 1970, the more so in that Friston, part of the same parish, was the home of Roger's father and his step-mother and his sister Pat.

Roger's father died very suddenly in December 1972. We felt this greatly for we had become real friends and were looking forward to seeing much more of him when we moved to East Dean. It had meant much to Roger and Pat that he had been able to visit India and get some flavour of the world in which they were working.

Here then, to a place full of friends and good neighbours, we retired in June 1973.

This book is a record of 'journeyings oft'; of rich friendships innumerable made, and continuing, through the years; of problems faced and decisions taken; of cut and thrust in debate; of beauty enjoyed; of hope and of despair. And through it all the experience of the never-failing forgiveness of God.

We have named our house 'Waymarks'. We have taken it from the Revised Standard Version of Jeremiah 31:21—'Set up waymarks for yourself, make yourself guideposts; consider well the highway, the road by which you went.'

An epilogue is unnecessary. While our house is smaller than some others in which we have lived, it is still a 'Welcome Inn'.

10/12/99
Beautiful.
A crowded canvas,
indeed.

Fix your gaze where truth is whitening toward the dawn.

ST. AUGUSTINE

Confessions

Index